Teaching Albert Einstein
to Fly

Peggy C. Siegel

Published by Seeking the Essential Press

www.seekingtheessential.com

ISBN: 0615672299

ISBN 13: 9780615672298

Printed in the United States of America

Cover photo by Dan Siegel.

To Dan,
For your unwavering love and support—
which has given me freedom of flight.
I love you.

Prologue

I'm in Washington, D.C., to see a client when I get a message. It doesn't come in the usual way by email, cell phone, or text. Instead it appears on the top of my mental "to do" list; only I didn't put it there.

Sometimes I argue with my intuition, but like an invisible navigation system which knows my higher good, I almost always benefit from its silent suggestions. For ten years now this inner sense of direction has guided my life.

Today I'm being directed to visit the Albert Einstein Memorial in front of the National Academy of Science building. I walk a mile through busy city streets to finally enter this secluded circular space surrounded by elms and hollies. There before me with rumpled clothes and a casual glance sits the bronze Albert Einstein, larger than life. He seems ready to teach me something.

Children are crawling all over his twenty-foot frame, sitting in his lap. I stand there for some time, trying to take in all the symbology represented by the mathematical equations on the paper he holds and the images of stars and planets I am standing on. An entire night sky is mapped in a circular granite base.

Before long, the teachers call the children over to the near-by sidewalk and the group moves on. Left behind in the quiet, I ask silently: What brings me here today? Could there be a message? I wait. Nothing. So I wait quietly a bit longer. Just as

I am about to give up, I feel a nudge. *Walk behind the monument.* I take a few steps behind the low wall where he sits and I'm surprised to see a quote engraved in the stone.

> "The right to search for truth implies a duty.
> One must not conceal any part
> of what one has recognized to be true."

His words bring tears to my eyes and I feel a strange but very real connection to Albert Einstein. I have been on a search for truth these ten years. I am deeply grateful for my encounters with intuition, dreams, and healing. In each, I have found parts of myself I'd never known. Some were broken, howling in pain, or silently numb; others radiated joy and possibility. The search went beyond healing; it called me home to myself.

I walk back around the wall and stand before the statue. Einstein never knew how his theories would be received, or even whether he would be believed. He put them out there anyway, sharing everything he discovered. His generous heart matched his genius.

Looking down at the celestial bodies at my feet I am reminded of my own nighttime encounter with Albert Einstein. The dream had become a guidepost leading me to my own latent talent. Like Einstein, I was unraveling universal mysteries, making my own small contribution. But the engraved quote is calling my bluff; I have concealed what I've found.

I wander back to stare at the quote again. This chiseled message is for me. Through it, I can feel his message, the words forming deep inside me:

> "Write about *your* search for truth.
> Write what *you've* recognized to be true."

Well Albert, I've given it my best shot.

—m—

Part I

1993-1994

—m—

"When you come to the edge
of all the light that you know,
and are about to step off into
the darkness of the unknown,
Faith is knowing
one of two things will happen:
Either there will be something solid
on which to stand
Or you will be taught to fly."

Barbara J. Winter

CHAPTER 1

—◆—

Saving

Ossining, New York – 1960

I grew up among Catholics who knew the Truth. And I was a born believer.

"Baltimore Catechism question #10—How shall we know the things which we are to believe? Repeat together," said Sister Annunciata.

"We shall know the things which we are to believe from the Catholic Church, through which God speaks to us."

God had a lot to tell us in second grade. I was seven and I was listening.

"Question #1—Who made you?" Sister Annunciata asked waving her ruler in the air and pointing when it was our turn to recite the answer.

"God made me," we said.

"Question #6—*Why* did God make you?"

"God made me," we slowly chanted in unison, "to know, love, and serve Him in this world and to be happy with Him forever in the next."

With that, I knew my purpose in life—to be good now so I could go to heaven for eternity, which was a very long time. Apparently, this had a lot to do with something called a soul. My teacher, Sister Annunciata, was in the business of saving them.

At ninety, she stood four feet nine inches tall, but she carried herself through the halls of St. Augustine's Elementary School in Ossining, New York, with a quiet authority; as she had surely done every year for the past seventy.

"The soul resides in the body," she explained one day. "You can't touch it and doctors can't see it, not even during surgery." She looked around at the forty-five of us, sitting with hands folded on our desks, making sure we knew this was serious business. Sister Annunciata continued, "The soul of a saint is pure white. God wants *your* soul to be this way too."

For weeks during religion class she told us about something terrible called *sins* which tinted the soul. Sins came in two categories: *Mortal* sins colored your soul black; *venial* sins were a little less serious and covered it with black dots or shades of gray. The soul of a Catholic who missed Mass one Sunday or, say, an axe-murderer was completely black. A girl who disobeyed her parents or told a lie had a grey or speckled soul. Although I couldn't even take a peek at my soul, I imagined it looked like a peeled Idaho potato—one that might suddenly get a bad spot or rot completely if I wasn't looking after it.

Luckily, all the Catholics around me seemed to be taking care of their souls during their everyday life. My family said grace before meals, prayers before bedtime, and attended Mass every Sunday. At St. Augustine's the fathers worked blue-collar jobs in town or rode the commuter train into New York City wearing suits, ties and hats. Each morning my father would yell, "Heading out!" to let us know that he had his briefcase and hat and was ready for our quick goodbye hugs and kisses. My mother, baby on hip, would be racing around making sure that all of us school kids had our shoes on and had packed our lunches in our book bags before we headed out to the bus stop. In 1960, mothers stayed at home and had children. Many children.

"How many brothers and sisters do you have?" and "What number are you?" Our birth order became our identity, our family-size our status. By the time I was in second grade, our family had five—ages eight, seven, six, four, and one. I was number two in a headcount that would eventually top off at seven. Still, I thought of myself as number one, since my brother Kevin, only eleven months older than me, didn't count in my opinion. Kevin didn't help out at home or take charge of the little ones like I did.

At school, Catholicism was woven throughout our day. We recited morning prayers led by Sister Mary Joseph over the school's loudspeaker system. In front of every classroom was a crucifix, and several statues or paintings of Mary, Jesus and various saints. On the top center of each assignment we wrote "JMJ," which meant "Jesus, Mary and Joseph, help me." During recess, when the church bells rang at noon, we had to freeze in the midst of our playground games and silently pray the Angelus—one Our Father, three Hail Mary's, and one Glory Be. When the nuns rang their big hand bells, we were allowed to play again.

Between the Holy Days of Obligation, First Fridays, Lent and Advent services, we spent many school hours in church. St. Augustine's, built with huge cold stones in 1856, was lit inside by candles and the sunlight streaming through the Bible-story windows made of vibrant colorful stained glass.

Back in second grade religion class, Sister Annunciata explained that all babies were born with souls tainted black by something called "Original Sin." Adam and Eve had caused this problem, apparently, by eating an apple. I thought Adam and Eve were really dumb for making so much trouble for everybody over an apple. Fortunately, once babies were baptized, their souls turned pure white. Since babies and little children didn't really know better, their mistakes didn't count as sins until they reached "The Age of Reason" which, Sister Annunciata explained, the Church had determined was seven. With this news, I took my seventh birthday very seriously.

To me, getting into heaven was a bit like playing musical chairs. It all depended on where you were standing when the music stopped. Since you never knew when that would happen, the goal in life was to stay close to a chair, which in this case, was a white soul. If your soul was pure white at the time of death, you went straight to heaven. If your soul was gray or speckled with black dots, you had to go to a really boring place called purgatory.

Sister Annunciata made it clear that only baptized Catholics could go to heaven. The Pope said so. This explained why she worked tirelessly to save the souls of babies not fortunate enough to be born into the Catholic faith. She called them pagan babies and she pointed out Peru on our classroom globe, situated way below the equator. Babies in Peru often didn't live long because their parents were poor, so it was important to save them before their blackened souls sent them to burn in hell. For every ten dollars we collected, she told us, the Maryknoll Missionaries in Peru would baptize a cute pagan baby, so he could join God and the angels in heaven. I loved babies more than anything, so when she enlisted our full support, I gave it.

My class worked diligently, and each time we collected ten dollars, we received an eight by ten photo of the baby we had saved. We posted each photo on the classroom wall, and by the end of the year, the faces of beautiful pagan babies encircled the perimeter of the classroom. We saved more babies than any other class that year and I was proud.

I was not only learning to keep my soul white and heaven bound, but I had helped some babies reach this same "state of grace." A few months later, my parents gave me a nun doll for my birthday. A new doll named Barbie had sashayed into toy stores the year before. Blissfully unaware, I played missionary with my nun doll, saving the souls of beautiful pagan babies in far-off lands.

Like Sister Annunciata, I accepted the Church's exclusive claim on heaven as fact. But every afternoon when I stepped off the school bus, I thought about each of my neighborhood friends as I walked past their houses on my way home. There was Diane Silberstein, Donna Cohen, Madelyn Melnik, and Roberta Goodman. They were all *Jewish*. These girls were no more likely to get into heaven than a pagan baby in Peru.

I thought about this as my best friend, Diane, and I played with my tea set one day. Diane was good at making up songs; she always took turns and shared, and she made up the best pretend games. In that moment, I knew I loved Diane. I really loved her. A lot. And I decided that if I were God, she would definitely be allowed to go to heaven. My stomach tightened and I broke into a sweat.

Did I think I was more loving than God? I gasped. What if some angel overheard my thoughts and reported me? God is everywhere. We all knew it. It was the answer we recited to Baltimore Catechism question #15, Where is God? Had God heard me thinking about Diane just then? But I loved Diane and I knew God loved her, too. I had to save her.

Then I remembered a mention of "special situations," like if you came upon a car wreck and there was a station wagon full of dying Methodists or Peruvian pagans that's when Sister Annunciata said, "The Sacrament of Baptism is usually performed by a priest." She paused and then added, "But, in an emergency, any Catholic can baptize another person." This was definitely an emergency.

That day, while Diane was sitting on the floor dressing her doll, I walked behind her and spilled a little water from my doll-sized teacup on her. "Woopsies," I said aloud as I mumbled under my breath, "I baptize you in the name of the Father, the Son, and the Holy Ghost. Amen." Diane continued dressing her baby doll, unsuspecting, and I finished setting up our tea party, relieved that my best friend's soul was saved.

When summer rolled around, I secretly baptized each of the Jewish children in the neighborhood while we played under the sprinkler.

CHAPTER 2

—᳙᳙—

Waking

Richmond, Virginia – 1993

I leaned on the pedestal sink, cold tile under bare feet, and spoke to my reflection in the bathroom mirror: "I'm fine."

I looked fine. I wanted to be fine. But every night in my dreams, I was stabbed, mugged, or shot. I'd sit up in bed just before I "died," heart racing, lungs gasping for air. I was terrified.

In a few hours, I'd fix breakfast for my kids, then see my husband off to work and drive carpool. By day, I trained teachers who were implementing the statewide sex-education program I'd developed for special-needs students. By night, I made dinner, helped Julia and Tommy with homework, caught up with Dan. Why was I having life-threatening nightmares?

I stared down at the orderly designs of the black and white one-inch tiles, memorizing their pattern. The clock had read 3:13 when I woke up, gasping. Now I was wide-awake and afraid of getting "killed" again if I went back to sleep. The nighttime terrors had persisted for over a month. What crazy kind of insomnia was this anyway? I was becoming sleep deprived.

I used to love my dreams. In school, my friend Dorothy and I would trade nocturnal adventures at the bus stop. Later, I often asked my children about their dreams while we ate breakfast. Now my dream world was at war with me.

Okay, so maybe my waking life wasn't fine either. A malaise had settled over me, like a heavy, slow-moving, gray fog. With it came an unsettling feeling.

I no longer wished to live.

No amount of trying could make me care about my life. The vitality and energy that once fueled my active life had left me—just in time for my fortieth birthday.

In the mirror, I saw the dark circles under my eyes and the sadness in my face. I was not fine. I walked into the dining room, turned on the light, stared at all my piles of work, found my "to-do" list and at the top wrote in bold letters, "Get referral - call therapist." I went back to bed, snuggled up beside my husband, and finally fell into dreamless sleep.

CHAPTER 3

—⁂—

Believing

Ossining, New York – 1960

Whether it happened under a sprinkler or with drops of holy water, Baptism was one of the seven sacraments. In second grade, every Catholic child got to receive *two* of the seven sacraments. These ceremonies, First Confession and First Holy Communion, earned us God's grace. In my family they also earned a celebration, bigger than any birthday party, with religious gifts, Godparents visiting, and photo portraits to mark the occasion.

That spring, my First Confession went off without a hitch. Sister Annunciata had asked us to think back over our lives in the months since our seventh birthday.

"Notice what sins you may have committed since then," she instructed. "Have you disobeyed your parents or told a lie? Have you eaten meat on a Friday? Missed Mass on Sunday?"

My parents ran a tight ship. At home, we followed all the Church laws. Rules were clear and expectations for good behavior were high. I hated being punished and preferred getting my share of attention by helping out. At school I liked to please my teachers. I never talked during class or tried to make my friends laugh unless the teacher left the room. Luckily, I was an expert at predicting when she would return, so I rarely got caught. I was having trouble coming up with the sins I needed for my First Confession.

Finally, I remembered that wasting food was a sin. I counted up the number of days since my seventh birthday and multiplied it times three. On the day of my First Confession, I was nervous. As a class we walked in line over to the church and stood in the center aisle awaiting our turn. When Sister Annunciata pointed to me, I went into the confessional, a pitch-black closet at the rear of the church, and I waited to hear the priest's small opaque window slide open.

"Bless me Father for I have sinned. This is my First Confession. I wasted food 237 times and told one lie." I added the one lie in case I had counted incorrectly or had forgotten to mention some other sin. The priest cleared his throat and I awaited my penance.

"Say three Hail Mary's. May God forgive you your sins. Amen," he said.

I walked up to the front of the church, knelt in front of the altar and quickly said my penance.

Two days later I received my First Communion with all the other second graders. The boys wore blue suits and ties and the girls dressed up in puffy white dresses with big petty coats. We were beautiful. The life-size statue of Mary smiled down upon us.

In that moment my soul was pure white. I was soul full.

CHAPTER 4

—⚬—

Meeting

Richmond, Virginia – 1993

I was biting my nails as I sat in the waiting room looking at my day-timer. A tall woman in a flowy skirt opened the door, introduced herself, and ushered me in. This time, my confessional was a light-filled office facing Main Street, but still I didn't know what to say.

I sat on the corner of the couch, legs crossed twice so I wouldn't swing them furiously, an old grade school habit. Anne sat in an overstuffed chair and asked about my family and work life. I folded my arms across my chest to hold myself together. "Things are actually really good." My children, Tommy and Julia, were seven and nine; they had good friends, played soccer, and did well in school. My husband, Dan, liked his attorney job with a downtown firm. We'd survived some struggles in our thirteen-year marriage, but we'd worked with a therapist and were doing well.

I told her about my work in sex education, training teachers and writing. It was controversial work, bringing sex ed into special ed classrooms statewide, but I'd held my own and received mostly positive feedback. Besides my work, I was president of two organizations and volunteered for four. As I explained all this, I thought, maybe I'm just overextended and stressed out.

Finally, I described my insomnia, lack of energy, chronic stomachaches and headaches that were becoming more and more frequent. Then I shared the latest murders I'd sustained in my sleep.

As I finished talking, she bolted upright, looking right through me and beyond me. In that moment, I was sure she knew exactly what was wrong with me. Maybe now I could get some help. She put her hand over her heart and blurted, "Oh my God, your soul is dying."

I sat silently, confused. How could she say that? I didn't even believe in the soul any more. Was she one of those New Age people? I hadn't come to discuss religion, so I didn't ask her to explain. I just stared at her as if she was crazy. After a brief pause, she continued as if nothing had happened.

When I left her office, part of me felt defensive and indignant about her comment. But another part whispered, "It's true, you know. Your soul is dying and you need to do something about it."

But what was I supposed to do? There was no over-the-counter remedy or doctor to call. I couldn't imagine any church that could help me. My soul had already been saved when I was baptized. Plus, weren't sixteen years of Catholic education enough to keep my soul healthy for a lifetime?

Apparently not. I turned this notion over and over in my mind. Maybe my dream world was saying, "Wake up! Part of you is in danger." Now I was awake and I couldn't seem to get thoughts about soul off my mind.

What is soul? I wondered.

For a moment I yearned for those explicit instructions of childhood, when everything was so definite, right, and clear. But at the age of forty, my inner world was full of doubt about myself, the meaning of my life, and whether there was a god in the world.

I was silently lost.

CHAPTER 5

—ᴍ—

Obeying

Ossining, New York – 1960's

I had received my First Communion, confessed my sins and experienced a state of grace. My soul was pure white. Now, I wondered, how do I keep it that way? If the music stopped, I wanted to be ready.

I was determined to observe all of the Church laws and commandments so that God would love me and take me to heaven. I imagined terrible things happening in purgatory or hell. Maybe you got shots and slept on a bed of nails? I wanted to avoid pain at all costs, so I apologized to God constantly.

I went to Confession every chance I got because the priest, as God's representative, had the power to forgive my sins and make my soul white. I ended each Confession with, "and one lie" to cover me in case I miscounted or had forgotten to name one of my sins. I loved knowing just how to keep my soul ready for eternal life. Most of the time, I felt secure knowing I had some control over my fate. Other times, I'd find myself getting anxious over every little mistake.

When I wasn't apologizing to God, I was concentrating on earning indulgences—the equivalent of merit points in the Catholic Church. Indulgences earned you time *out* of purgatory. Since the afterlife was eternal, the number of years one could earn was substantial. The nuns told us that pretty much everyone had to "do time" in purgatory for any sins they hadn't confessed to a priest. Each sin was assigned a corresponding number of purgatory years. Each indulgence, on the other hand, earned a certain number of years of forgiveness. Saying a rosary, for instance, might shave fifty years off your sentence in purgatory.

I intended to bypass purgatory and go straight to heaven when I died, so my indulgences provided an afterlife insurance policy. You could earn them by saying rosaries, keeping relics from saints, wearing a scapular, collecting holy cards, fasting, doing good deeds, and bearing all suffering quietly and with dignity. I loved counting up the indulgences in my invisible, but very real, stash. My friends and I would point out good deeds—like sharing cookies or being nice to a boy with cooties—toward our store of indulgences.

When we learned about monks and priests wearing horsehair shirts or sleeping on the bare floor to earn points, my best friend, also named Peggy, helped me cut burlap squares out of a potato sack, which we safety-pinned inside our undershirts. The idea was to duplicate their "quiet suffering" that had earned them lots of indulgences. But the ensuing rash forced us to give up and concede the holy superiority of monks and priests. We went back to saying rosaries and doing good deeds.

CHAPTER 6

—※—

Denying

Ossining, New York – 1960's

At school, the unspoken rules about the human body held as much power over us as any Church law. We just never mentioned them.

The body was a source of shame. We were never to talk about it, ask questions about it, or pay attention to it. In soft tones of disgust, the nuns often implied that the body itself was base; its physical desires and urges were evil. Everything we needed to know about the body was summed up in three facts, which Sister Dominic presented in religion class in fourth grade.

1. The soul is separate from the body.
2. The soul is more important than the body.
3. One of the best ways to get close to God is to deny the body.

These attitudes were also reflected in my home life. At home, I'd been taught to keep the body covered. I wouldn't even change clothes in front of my sister or mother, much less a girlfriend. If a boy saw my underwear, God forbid, I would be ashamed for days.

Vanity, too, was a terrible sin. We wore school uniforms, which kept us from paying too much attention to how we looked. Plus, there were no mirrors in the bathrooms at school. At home, the medicine cabinets over the bathroom sinks housed our only mirrors. If I gave myself much more than a quick glance, I felt guilty.

Fasting provided another way to deny the body. Before Mass, nothing but water passed our lips for three hours or overnight and through breakfast the next morning. I was especially good at denying the body when it came to food. By fifth grade, I weighed fifty pounds and looked like a third grader. My parents expressed concern, bought vitamins, and encouraged me to eat more but they never broached the subject of nutrition. I was pleased, instead, that I could subsist on small amounts of food.

Words like digestion, circulation, or respiration were unknown to me. I had no idea how the body worked and no one was going to teach me. When I had sharp pains in my stomach or chest pains that took my breath away, I imagined offering myself up to God as I quietly died of a heart attack.

At eleven, I saw a television advertisement for an antacid. I told my parents I felt exactly like those people on TV.

"Could that medicine help me too?" I asked.

My father laughed and said, "Only adults have heartburn, not children."

I believed him. My body feelings weren't real, he was telling me. But I still didn't know what to do with them.

In school there were no physical education classes until President Kennedy was elected. He was revered as a saint, being the first Catholic to become president. When he instituted the President's Physical Fitness Test, teachers began taking us to the auditorium for a new class they called gym. Gym involved doing repetitions of chin-ups, push-ups, sit-ups, and races, all meant to prepare us for the exam. I loved it though because it gave us a chance to run and jump instead of sitting at our desks all day long.

Sex education on the other hand was completely unthinkable. Sexuality was considered so evil that it could not be spoken about. At all. Ever.

I got the message in third grade, loud and clear.

My friend Patty and I discovered a mysterious "napkin machine" in the small bathroom near the cafeteria. It was the only napkin machine in the whole school. We asked around, but none of the girls knew why anyone would pay ten cents for a napkin when the cafeteria gave them away for free.

During our Brownie meeting, Patty and I pooled our nickel Brownie dues and snuck into the bathroom. We dropped the coins in the metal slot, turned the knob, and out came a blue wax paper ball. Slowly and carefully we unwrapped it to find a long flat cotton thing and two safety pins. We stared at the napkin; then at each other.

"What in the world is this for?" I said.

"I don't know. Let's ask the other kids," Patty said as she quickly wrapped it back up and put it in her pocket.

When our Brownie troop leader took us to the playground,
Patty and I hid behind a pillar along the auditorium entryway
and secretly invited other girls to come over and take a look.
No one had ever seen a napkin like this one. Before we knew
it, the entire Brownie troop was now circled around Patty, me,
and our mysterious napkin. A shadow suddenly fell over the
group. We looked up to see our Brownie leader, hands on her
hips. Everyone ran. Patty and I froze.

"Where did you get this?" she put out her hand, disgusted
and angry. "Is this where your Brownie dues went?"

We nodded our heads yes.

"I'll be calling your mothers," she said as she stomped away.

This is a powerful and evil napkin, we decided. Wow.

Patty and I were reprimanded that night for "stealing" our
brownie dues. The napkin remained a mystery.

In fifth grade, the Girl Scouts sponsored a mother-daugh-
ter film on menstruation. The whole time we were watching I
wondered how come my mother had never told me about all
this. My mother taught me everything about cooking, cleaning, and taking care of babies. Why not menstruation? Why
wouldn't anyone tell Patty and me about the napkin? We'd felt
so evil and ashamed. The rule was clear: "You don't talk about
this stuff."

At home, the subject of sex came up only once. I was in
eighth grade, alone in the kitchen with my mother, helping her
fix dinner. She asked if I knew how babies were born.

A girlfriend told me about sexual intercourse in sixth grade,
after some boys used gross hand gestures and slang words on
the playground. I said, "yes."

That was the end of the discussion.

By that time, the Church had me confused. Sexual body parts, sexual feelings, and sexual intercourse were considered evil and base. Yet, the more children you had, the more grace God granted you. But it took *sex* to conceive children. How could something gross and evil be part of God's glorious plan? I imagined mothers and fathers holding their noses and squeezing their eyes shut to endure the disgusting act necessary to bring another baby in the world. Had my parents really done this seven times?

—⚏—

CHAPTER 7

Caring

Richmond, Virginia – 1993

I entered my sex ed career through the side door. While working on my master's degree in special education taking night classes, I was a full-time teacher with a class of nine-to twelve-year-olds who were mildly handicapped. One by one, my six girls were entering puberty right before my eyes, but unlike other eleven and twelve-year-olds, nobody was telling them what was coming.

I thought about the mysterious napkin and the shame I'd felt for asking about it in third grade. The absence of sex education in Catholic school had left me woefully uninformed as a teenager. I couldn't let this happen to my six girls. All children deserved appropriate sex education, and they had every right to feel good about themselves and their bodies. If no one would teach them, I would. I approached the school administrators and my students' parents for permission to develop special lesson plans about puberty. Nothing like this had been offered before. They were thrilled.

Later in my mid-thirties, Winifred Kempton, true pioneer in the field, reported new data estimating that ninety percent of people with developmental disabilities experience sexual abuse at some time in their lives. I shifted the focus of my work to sex education and abuse prevention for students with special needs. In the five years that followed, I wrote two books on puberty, several articles, and two curricula. Age-appropriate information was crucial, and I was careful to emphasize what should be taught, at what age, and in what way. I talked openly about sexuality nearly every day. I thought that through all my research, courses I'd taken and teacher trainings I'd participated in on the topic of sexuality, that I had erased all the negative messages about the body. I had arrived in a healthier place. But had I?

This presumption had even been confirmed by a therapist. A few years back my husband and I had chosen to work through some difficulties with a brief round of marriage counseling. After Dan and I completed our work as a couple, I continued seeing our therapist individually. I suspected I might have some sexuality issues to work out. I shared a few difficult experiences from my past to illustrate my point. She listened thoughtfully, then turned serious, "Peggy, if these were really issues for you, I don't think you'd be so good at teaching sex ed. I really think you're okay." At the time, I'd felt reassured. Somewhat.

Now I suspected my nightmares were in disagreement. A part of me knew it. There had been hints. I'd lost my usual enthusiasm for my work and volunteer projects and I definitely felt like part of me was dying. Another hint came recently, while leading a workshop. Although I'd always been perfectly comfortable talking about—even joking about—sexuality, a part of me was always bothered. I'd have this sad, sinking feeling.

When I saw Anne for a second therapy session, my body was tired and my soul felt depleted. At home, the dining room table was covered with piles, each a different responsibility I had no interest in fulfilling. As president of our neighborhood babysitting co-op, which had twenty-four families, I needed to plan next month's meeting. Division II soccer needed rosters and schedules drafted. And at school, the Parents' Council wanted me to organize the next program.

To make things worse, an accounting error left the Department of Education unable to pay me for the past eight training sessions, which had required me to travel throughout the state. I needed to call and untangle the mess, but I dreaded facing further resistance. My last sex education training session had been particularly difficult, with several teachers refusing to participate. The work would always be meaningful to me, but I was drowning in the details.

Anne suggested two pieces of "homework" to help me "get better" outside of our sessions.

"First, you need to take care of yourself physically," she said. "I want you to begin doing some kind of regular exercise. It sounds to me like you are experiencing depression. This could help you get the natural flow of endorphins going which might help you feel better physically," she explained.

"Okay," I said, "I used to swim in the mornings before work. I think I'll go back to swimming."

"That's a great start. Secondly, I want you to do one thing for *yourself.*"

"Wait, isn't that swimming?" I asked.

"No, that is to help you physically. Pick something you enjoy. But remember it can't help or benefit others in any way."

My mind went blank. I had to ask her for examples.

"You could take a dance or art class, do yoga or even go to a movie. Pick one thing and then actually do it."

This felt so "selfish." Wasn't I already talking about myself in therapy every week? How much self-centeredness did one person need? I hadn't taken a fun class or done anything for my *own* enjoyment since before my children were born. Even then, I'd been devoted to teaching or volunteering. What if Dan had to take care of the kids in the evening so I could go out? Could I hire a babysitter? Could I value myself, my well being enough to do this? This was going to be hard.

That week I began swimming a few days a week. I also started looking for adult education and art classes around town. I came across a brochure for the Women's Resource Center, which I knew almost nothing about, and noticed an upcoming class on Midlife. The course description said the class would explore the relationship between psychology and spirituality during this normal stage of development identified as midlife. Between my interest in psychology, my curiosity about my soul, and having recently turned forty, this seemed like the perfect class for me at this time. The class met Thursday evenings; I signed up.

In the meantime, I was still curious about this notion of soul. Although I was no longer Catholic and had no intention of returning to the Church, I felt like I was missing something in my life. I was longing for something I used to have.

CHAPTER 8

—◆—

Praying

Ossining, New York – 1960's

Other than my worries about getting to heaven, I was happy being Catholic. I loved singing in church, the smell of the incense, the rituals. I never tired of hearing stories about Jesus or of watching the way the light filtered through the stained glass windows. My years were dominated by the Church calendar, but my favorite month was May, Mary's month.

Every class created a large May altar with a statue of the Blessed Mother, and each day one boy and girl had their May Day, the only day of the school year they didn't have to wear a uniform. These students brought flowers to adorn the altar and led prayers and hymns to Mary.

At home, before my May Day, my mother would help me cut some lilacs from our bushes for the altar. And she'd let me wear my Easter dress to school if I promised not to get it dirty on the playground.

Besides making a small May altar on my dresser, I secretly created one in the woods behind our house. At the base of an old oak tree with big roots, I dug a hole and wrapped my small statue of Mary in a red bandana and kept her hidden under some leaves. Each day, I would come out to my secret altar and set Mary on the bandana. Then I'd pick wild flowers and place rocks around her creating a small grotto. Mary, we were taught in school, was the very best intercessory. She had a direct line to both God and Jesus. I would say prayers and talk to Mary hoping she, in turn, would put in a good word for me with her son Jesus.

May was the one time of the year that I was glad to be a girl because only girls could be in the May Procession. Wearing our Easter dresses and lined up by the color of our dresses, we processed into the church singing "Ave Maria," and we got to sit right up front. Our beautiful girl voices sang songs with words like, "Hail Mother of mercy and of love, O Maria" and "Save us, save us, Queen of Heaven." We were all honoring Mary and she had been a girl like us once, too.

In fourth grade I became enamored of the angels and saints. My friends and I would playfully scoot over in our desk seats, making room for our guardian angels. For as long as I could remember, I'd prayed to my guardian angel every night.

The saints were another story. I was both awed and horrified by the gruesome deaths of those that were martyred because of their beliefs.

In third grade we had memorized the answers to one hundred questions to prepare for the sacrament of Confirmation.

We were now supposedly able to state all of our Catholic beliefs, not only for the Bishop who confirmed us, but to any nonbeliever who tried to challenge them. I worried about this grave responsibility. After all, the saints had died answering these questions, "standing up for their faith," as Sister Dominic would say. But the people who challenged these beliefs tended to be violent and unreasonable, at best. I thought about crossing my fingers and lying if I came across a particularly disagreeable non-Catholic.

In the meantime, I loved hearing about courageous saints like Joan of Arc and hearing about the visions of St. Bernadette. Our reading, history, and religion books all had stories of saints and how they were each martyred in different gory ways for their goodness and their love of God. The nuns expected nothing less from us. They especially emphasized the stories of child saints who were unable to deny their glorious visions and so, I thought, they were all martyred.

As part of Church law every child had to be named after a saint. We all had to be called by our saints' names in school. For eight years I went by the name Margaret during school hours but was called Peggy elsewhere. Although I hated the name Margaret, Saint Margaret had a vision where she had seen the sacred heart of Jesus, so I was glad to be named after her.

It was during this fixation on the saints that I began a new nightly ritual. My little sister Jeanne and I shared a small upstairs bedroom, which had our two beds side-by-side with a dresser and a rocking chair at the foot of the beds. On my half of the dresser were my statues of Mary, my nun doll, some holy cards, and my rosary beads. Some nights I would awaken with a sense that someone else was there. I feared God or an angel was sitting in that rocking chair. So I started saying this nightly prayer.

> *Dear God, Please, please do not appear to me tonight.*
> *I am not as courageous as you think I am.*

I imagined them calmly telling me that I had been chosen to perform some incredible mission. I would squeeze my eyes shut as tight as I could, huddling under my blanket, imagining that someone would find out about my vision and then in response, tie me to a rope to be dragged behind a chariot in the Ossining High School football stadium in front of the cheering crowd. I would be martyred merely for telling them about the angel in my rocking chair.

When I was in fifth grade my new baby sister Kathy, number six, was born. Although she was a bright and beautiful baby, when she was just a few months old, my younger brother Jim noticed that sometimes her eyes rolled back into her head. When my mother told the pediatrician, she referred Kathy to a neurologist in New York City who immediately diagnosed her with a very rare neurological disorder for which there was no known cure. Kathy's body would grow physically, but neurologically she'd function like a six-month-old. The neurologist suggested an experimental treatment; it was new and unproven, but it was Kathy's only chance.

We all began praying frantically for Kathy. The principal led prayers for her every morning over the loud speaker at school. We prayed for her at church. We prayed for her at home. Over the next several months, my sister had a remarkable recovery and resumed normal neurological development. She was considered to be the very first cured case of Hypsarrhythmia and was written up in a number of medical journals.

"It's a miracle," everyone said, when they heard the news. "See, God answers prayers," was the message we got at church, school, and home. I was overjoyed. Kathy was a lively normal baby again, walking now and talking, as bright as ever.

I wanted desperately to believe that our prayers had brought about this miracle. I wanted complete faith in God, who had saved my baby sister. But something was bothering me, and I couldn't ask anybody about it. During those same months, we had also prayed at school for a little six-year-old boy, Kevin, who lived down the hill from us. He'd been hit by a car as he ran into the street after his baseball. Kevin didn't get a miracle. He was permanently brain injured and he never came back to school. Why hadn't our prayers worked for him?

The nuns emphasized that through faith we would have strength. Weakness came from being a "doubting Thomas" like the apostle had been. My questions made me a doubter, so I blocked them out, worked on my faith, and focused on Kathy and how healthy and happy she was.

I was in sixth grade the first time I got mad at the Church.

Between 1963 and 1965, Cardinals and Bishops from around the world converged on the Vatican in Rome to review and modernize the Catholic church doctrine and its laws and policies.

I first learned about Vatican II when Sister Christine began our religion class with an announcement: "The Pope along with Vatican II has decided there are no more such things as indulgences."

I raised my hand. "Does this mean I can't earn any more?" I asked.

"Yes, they are no longer part of Church law," she answered.

I raised my hand.

"Yes, Margaret."

"But what about all the ones we've already earned?" I asked.

"They are of no value," she said.

My jaw dropped.

Robert, the class troublemaker, burst out laughing. I was sure he had no indulgences, so he hadn't lost a thing.

I felt like I'd been punched in the stomach. By a close friend. Betrayed.

According to my careful calculations, I had accrued thirty thousand years of indulgences and I was only twelve. Now Sister Christine was saying it didn't matter?

I had just lost my spiritual insurance policy.

I was hurt, disappointed and scared. Death suddenly became terrifying. I had lost all control over my soul's destiny, and now I might be facing those thirty thousand years in purgatory.

Vatican II made me very uneasy. I liked knowing what was right and wrong and wasn't one to tolerate change very well. In my mind it was completely unfair to change the rules we'd been suffering with. For example, I'd been fasting for three hours before Communion my whole long life, and now we only had to fast one hour. We'd lost our credits for good deeds and for suffering. I wanted to tell those Bishops and Cardinals what I thought. But there was no one to argue with because discussions were not permitted in elementary school. Plus, the nuns would probably consider my thoughts to be a form of disobedience to the Pope, sinful proof of my lack of faith. At home my parents seemed to accept the changes in the Church without any question. I couldn't tell anyone about the angry, distrustful thoughts stirring in my brain.

One part of Vatican II, however, made me glad. The Church had finally acknowledged that the "only baptized Catholics can go to heaven" rule was a Church law created to encourage people to join the Church. They admitted that Jesus had never said such a thing, which made sense since I'd learned that Jesus was *Jewish*! I felt sure that, all over the world, people of other religions were letting out a collective sigh of relief now that they could probably get into heaven when they died, even if they weren't Catholics and even without converting.

Despite my doubt and mistrust, I remained a faithful Catholic. I was drawn back into the thick of the Church when Sister Winifred invited me to become a sacristy girl in seventh grade. I accepted immediately. After all, sacristy girls were the only females allowed on or behind the altar. I had always wanted to see what was behind the altar and to touch the chalice and the tabernacle. This was my chance. When Sister Winifred took us over to the church, she demonstrated how to replace votive candles, fill up the holy water containers, dust the altar, and lay out the priest's vestments for the next Mass. We were basically very holy cleaning girls. And I felt privileged.

CHAPTER 9

—ɯ—

Thinking

Richmond, Virginia – 1993

At the age of forty I no longer believed in this very concrete notion of the soul and all the ways to save it. When I was in my mid-twenties, I had left behind all the dogma of the Church, weekly Mass, Confession, the music, and the rituals. When people asked me about my religion, I generally answered, "I was raised Catholic." That simple answer seemed to satisfy them.

Also, I had fallen in love with Dan who was Jewish. During the two years that we dated, we had many discussions on how we might raise children if we were to marry. We checked out a Unitarian Church, a Reform Jewish Congregation, and several Christian churches. Then we interviewed many of our friends who had grown up with no affiliation to an organized religion. We finally came to an agreement. Dan really wanted to raise the children in the Reform Jewish tradition, and from a belief standpoint, I didn't find anything objectionable about the faith. I knew that, no matter what, I would have a strong relationship with any children we might have because of how badly I wanted children. I figured this would be a way for Dan to connect with our children. We agreed to raise the children Jewish as long as he took full responsibility for their religious education. If he ever fell short, he also promised that I could raise them in any religion I chose.

Dan had kept his word, and so my husband and children were Jewish.

Over the fifteen years since I had left Catholicism, I had tried various organized religions and even considered converting to Judaism. Organized religion just didn't feel right for me. Instead, my personal spirituality had become more and more centered in nature. The earth itself was my religion. I sat in the woods, climbed mountains, and hiked to waterfalls when I wanted to connect with something greater than myself. At death, I believed we returned to become part of the earth. I thought that the only way one might live beyond physical death was in the spirit of another person whose life had somehow been touched by ours.

I did not believe in a God who was active and involved in the world. To me it seemed the Creator had set forth this beautiful planet and decided to let us be. Therefore, I had stopped praying. With an inactive God and a life whose only possibility for meaning was in the lives of others I had touched, I was very drawn to helping others in need, especially children.

These beliefs had worked well for fifteen years. Instead of spirituality, I had focused on psychology. Always trying to understand myself, other people, and relationships, I turned to the ever-popular self-help books of the '70s and '80s. I believed we could make ourselves who we wanted to be.

Conversely, I didn't like blaming the past. I liked to focus on the present. But there wasn't some problem to figure out with family or friends in the present. At least nothing big. And yet there was malaise.

During my next therapy session Anne asked, "Have you ever been depressed before?"

"Oh, yes, for the past eighteen years I have had bouts, but I usually know what it's about and I fend it off."

"Can you tell me about the first time you experienced depression?"

I thought about it for a bit. "Actually it was twenty-five years ago—I was in high school."

"What was going on then? Maybe tell me what high school was like and what was going on in your family." And so I did.

CHAPTER 10

—๛—

Needing

Ossining, New York – 1967-1970

Following eight years at St. Augustine's Elementary School, I entered Mary Immaculate, an all girls' high school in Ossining. The Dominican nuns at Mary Immaculate were more liberal-minded than my grade school nuns. Some of them were underground feminists, who told us that it was not only okay, but *good* for a girl to be smart, even in math—my best subject. This was revolutionary.

Once Vatican II had been implemented, the Mass was said in English instead of Latin, and the priest faced the congregation rather than turning his back to us. We even had "Folk" Masses with guitar playing instead of centuries-old hymns. As students, we were given the chance to create our own liturgies choosing more modern readings and music. The nuns began wearing short white habits and black veils instead of covering their entire bodies with long habits. I was a little startled to see that the nuns had arms, legs, and hair on their heads.

It was during high school that I was finally able to ask questions and argue about Catholic theology during religion classes. We were encouraged to discuss Christ's parables and infer their possible meaning for our own lives. Many times I experienced disbelief. Was Jesus really the only son of God? Did these miracles really happen?

We revisited Church laws, as well. Will I really go to hell if I miss Mass on Sunday? Do divorced people deserve to be excommunicated? Why can't women become priests? I argued with my religion teacher, Sister Marianne, making the point that these laws didn't fit with the loving and accepting nature of Jesus. I was often mad at the Church. But then I would feel this mysterious pull back to my love of Jesus, which always felt stronger than my concerns about Church doctrine.

Sometimes I felt certain that I knew Jesus personally and had a relationship with him. As early as nine years old, when I saw the Station of the Cross where Jesus and Mary Magdalene were gazing into each other's faces, I knew they loved one another. I wanted to be like Mary Magdalene and have that special connection with Jesus. When the nuns referred to themselves as "brides of Christ," I wondered whether I should become a nun. Would that give me the close relationship with Jesus I desired so deeply?

But, I was also really attracted to boys. Even at my all-girls school, my friends and I passed notes about every boy we knew, and outside of class, analyzed each glance or comment a boy might make in our presence. We went to all the Catholic Youth Organization dances. As Catholic girls, we were expected to follow one of two paths. We could grow up to marry and have children or become a nun. My first choice was to teach and then marry and have children. My backup plan was to become a Dominican nun and teach.

In elementary school I'd practiced ignoring body-feelings like hunger, sore throats, and stomach aches. Over time, this idea of denying the body created a split between my body and soul, and during my sophomore year in high school, I reached a silent inner turning point. My body was becoming impossible to ignore. At sixteen I still hadn't started my period, and I was certain something must be terribly wrong with me. I was too ashamed to talk to anyone about this, so I carried pads to school and pretended I had my period every month, just to keep my friends from suspecting anything.

At home, my mother never asked me about my period. My sister Jeanne was so much younger; I definitely couldn't tell her. I really needed a kind word or some reassurance. The pediatrician had told me in eighth grade that it looked like I was ready to start my period any day. It had been a very long two years. I felt alone.

Instead of ignoring my body like we'd been taught in elementary school, I now loathed it. Looking at my skinny self in the mirror, I concluded that no boy would ask me on a date in my entire life, which meant that I would never have a chance at marriage or having children. I was sure of it.

At home, I was the first of the seven kids to show signs of adolescent behavior. My older brother was attending an all-scholarship high school in New York City. He came home on the train late, having tucked his "Stop the War!" pin in his pocket and went straight to his room to study. I was learning to think for myself at school, but at home my parents didn't want to hear it. I wasn't to mention anything controversial in front of the little ones.

But in 1968, controversy was everywhere. Martin Luther King and Bobby Kennedy had been assassinated only months apart. The war in Vietnam was raging on amid bigger and louder protests, even by Jesuit priests. I was strongly opposed to the war in Vietnam but my friend Claire's brother, a platoon leader, had recently been shot and killed. We wanted to honor his courageous death. We tried to believe in a noble cause for this horrible war, but we couldn't find one. My brother would be drafted before long. Would his life be tossed aside as well?

"Who had a test today?" my father asked as the bowl of mashed potatoes made its way around the dinner table. The little ones chimed in, competing for attention. I would not be discussing these issues at home.

I was also becoming angry about the unfair treatment of girls and women, including me. My brother Kevin took the train to New York City every day for school, but I wasn't allowed to take the bus to White Plains with friends unless somebody's brother came along. Babysitting paid fifty cents an hour, even for families with four or five young children. But my brothers would mow the lawn for these same families and earn five dollars in an hour or two. "Only boys mow lawns," my father told me.

I was tired of taking care of my younger brothers and sisters and doing chores at home. I loved rock and roll music, and whenever I left the house, I rolled my uniform skirt up well above my knees. For the first time in my life, I started talking back and arguing with my parents. They were completely unprepared for this change in me. By the middle of my sophomore year in high school my mother and I were at odds.

Late one night my father came down to the basement where I was studying and said in an angry voice, "You are causing your mother to have a nervous breakdown. And if you don't change your behavior right now, we are going to send you away to a detention home. Your mother is more important to this family than you are."

Stunned, I sat there in silence, my eyes filling with tears as he turned and stomped back up the stairs. My spirit was crushed. It was as if all the grocery shopping, babysitting, cleaning, ironing that I'd done, all my good grades—none of this mattered to them. They would send me away. Just like that. In that moment I decided that I was unlovable. I knew I needed help, but I had no one to reach out to—certainly not my parents.

That weekend, I bought a bottle of aspirin and began planning my suicide. I'd read a story in Reader's Digest Magazine about a person who swallowed a whole bottle of aspirin at bedtime. And I knew that, if I did this, no one would find me until morning when it would be too late.

CHAPTER 11

—w—

Dying

Richmond and Atlanta – 1993

My nightmares had ceased, and finally I was able to sleep. I was seeing Anne for therapy every week, swimming regularly, and enjoying the Midlife class I was taking.

Still, I felt unhappy and lost and I wondered why. In class, our teacher Nancy said that during midlife we're often called to heal old hurts. Sometimes it feels like we have no choice. But if we had the courage to go back and heal old wounds, it could free us to live fully in the second half of our lives.

Now, Anne was telling me the same thing in therapy. It felt true. She encouraged me to explore, a bit more closely, the not so perfect experiences I'd had growing up. My parents and I had our differences, but I still loved them, and I was sure they'd done the best they could. The fourth commandment, "Honor thy father and thy mother," had a hold on me. I didn't want to hurt my parents by pointing out their "mistakes." I just wanted to get past this...this, whatever it was and get back to my life and my work.

Inside me, a voice was raging, "No, No, No, I don't want to go back!" But deep in my heart, I knew it was time.

In my sessions with Anne, I began looking back at the times I felt my parents hadn't been there when I needed them, and times I'd been hurt by what they'd said or done. I'd always been taught that anger was evil; that I needed to accept others and forgive them. But now, in order to heal, I needed the courage to face my experience, truthfully. This anger of mine was finally coming out of hiding.

Early one afternoon while my children were still in school, I sat down at the dining room table with my journal. For the first time in my life I put these feelings into words: "I am mad at my mother and father."

Immediately, I felt like a bad person. How could I love my parents so much, honor them and appreciate what they'd done for me—and also be mad at them? Anne had said there was absolutely no need to talk to my parents about the anger, but just let myself feel it. I sat there with the anger. I hated sitting with the anger. I sat with it some more. I wrote about it. Mostly I wished my parents had known when I'd needed help. How come they didn't know? I felt like I was sliding down into a deep, dark pit.

Just then the phone rang. It was my mother. I couldn't believe it. Did she know that I was sitting there mad at her?

"Hi Mom, how are you?" I asked.

"Not so good. It's about Dad." My father had played in a tennis tournament over the weekend; had he come down with the flu or something?

She took a sharp breath in, "I'm calling to let you know. Dad went to the doctor today. He'd had some tests done last week and, today, we got the results."

"What results?" I asked, still thinking about the flu.

"He has Merkel Cell cancer," she said, "a quick spreading form of skin cancer."

I'd never heard of Merkel Cell cancer, but he'd had skin cancers before. Would he need to have another surgical excision, like the one last year?

Now my mother way saying, "...no known cure. The doctor pulled me aside and said he probably had two to eight weeks..."

"Two to eight weeks to do what? To live?"

Just like that, I closed my journal. I put the anger away and began making arrangements to go to Atlanta to be with my father and mother whom I cared for deeply.

I planned to put my own healing process on hold. Instead I would be given the chance to look at the powerful relationship I had with my father. And I would also receive an unexpected healing for my soul.

CHAPTER 12

—※—

Quoting

Ossining, New York – 1968

I was a burden to my family. I felt a sad heaviness and I longed for someone who could help me. That's another reason to kill myself, I thought. I hated my body and I was *needy*, too. Always the helper, I couldn't stand the thought of needing help myself.

I stayed at school as much as possible, and at home I kept to myself, not speaking to my parents unless I had to. Depression and sadness were totally selfish, so I tried not to display any emotion. The bottle of aspirin was hidden under my mattress, and at night, I held it in my hands as I fell asleep. Suicide was a mortal sin, but I knew I'd be making the world a better place because I wouldn't be there to bother anybody. I wouldn't need anyone's help. I knew Jesus would take pity on me and not send me to hell; I hoped God would understand and forgive me, too.

I was feeling particularly blue one Saturday afternoon, and I decided to hang out in my bedroom. Luckily my little sister Jeanne, who shared the room with me, was at a friend's house. Alone for once, I sat on the bed passing the aspirin bottle back and forth in my hands wondering if tonight should be the night.

Then I noticed a catalogue on my desk that my religion teacher, Sister Marianne, had shared with me on Friday. I was always asking her questions, and she thought I might be interested in the books they were advertising. I became curious and began looking through it, drawn to the brightly colored posters with quotes. I was turning the pages when, all of a sudden, a quote jumped out at me. My head pulled back. I'd never felt anything like it before. It read:

> "I don't know who—or what—put the question,
>   I don't know when it was put.
>   I don't even remember answering.
>   But at some moment
>   I did answer—YES
>   To someone or something
>   And from that hour I was certain
>   That existence is meaningful
>   And that therefore my life,
>   In self-surrender had a goal."
>
> Dag Hammerskjold

I read it again. What did this poem have to do with me? Why had it jumped off the page? I wanted to go talk to Dag Hammarskjold and ask what made him so sure that "existence is meaningful." How could he be certain? What happened *after* he said "yes" to life? Was there someone out there who thought *my* existence was meaningful? Was someone asking me to say, "yes"? *Could* I say "yes" to life?

I put the aspirin bottle down and got out an old composition book. I copied down all the quotes in the catalogue using colored markers. Most of them were about love and friendship. I reserved the whole back cover of my booklet for the Dag Hammarskjold quote. By the time I finished, something in me had changed.

I was curious about saying "yes" to life. Could I trust that God had something in mind for me if I'd just say "yes"? Could I stop hating my body long enough to find out what saying "yes" to my life might mean? My heart felt surprisingly light. *Why not?* I thought.

"YES," I said out loud. It felt good. I tossed the bottle of aspirin in the trash.

In the weeks that followed, I wasn't loved any more or less. I still didn't know how to ask for help, and my parents hadn't a clue that I needed it. Somehow, my body and I reached a truce. If I was going to say yes to life, I was saying yes to this body of mine, too. I let up on hating my body and focused on staying alive in order to find out what it meant to say "yes."

I felt like I'd been saved, somehow. Saved by...a quote? How could that be? A few months later when I finally started my period, I felt more normal. By junior year I was saying "yes" to everything. I sang with the glee club, was a cheerleader, was on the newspaper and yearbook staffs, played intramural sports, and acted in the school musical. On my birthday, six of my friends each baked a cake and brought it to school. *Six* birthday cakes. That same week, I was elected Miss School Spirit at the monthly school dance. Loved by my friends, I felt alive.

Just as I was saying yes, a big NO entered my life. One evening at the dinner table, my father said he had a big surprise for us.

"I've been transferred," he announced. "We'll be moving to Atlanta, Georgia in June."

None of my friends had ever moved out of state. I'd never traveled anywhere but the Jersey shore, aside from two brief family road trips to Washington, D.C. and upstate New York. I'd had the same friends since kindergarten. I couldn't believe my parents would make me leave them right before my senior year. In school, I'd learned that Georgia was a backwards state; it was very poor and had terrible schools. "No, no, no!" my insides wailed. I couldn't bear the thought of leaving.

My friends didn't have money to travel. Neither did I. So nobody would be visiting me in Atlanta, and I wouldn't be visiting New York. Fortunately, Mrs. O'Connor, my good friend Peggy's mother, who had eight children of her own, offered to let me live with them for my senior year. I was relieved. My parents asked me to take some time making this big decision.

One night I found a letter from my father on my pillow. He admitted that, of everyone in the family, the move would be hardest for me. But he asked if I would please consider coming with the family, instead of staying with the O'Connors, because my little brothers and sisters would miss me.

He also reminded me of something I'd said when I was in fourth grade. After reading a chapter in my social studies textbook, I'd clearly informed him, "One day I will teach in

Appalachia." He thought that living in Atlanta might bring me closer to that goal. The move would expose me to new people and places. I knew how much I would miss Mary Pat and Kathy, just five and six, and younger brother Joe who was nine. I relented and moved with the family that summer.

Atlanta turned out to be a vibrant growing metropolis. I entered a co-ed Catholic high school where my classmates were friendly and welcoming. Although I was still very thin, I'd finally grown and matured. Being the new girl on the block, I was asked out on a number of dates. I learned to get along with boys and liked having them around. I even had my first boyfriend.

In one short year, I had learned that I could love a whole new set of people— people who weren't cousins or neighbors or friends since kindergarten—and these new people could love me, too.

In my college application essay, I wrote, "I have always been a basically happy person." I described my wonderful large Catholic family, my love of children, and my desire to become a teacher. I was accepted at St. Mary's College, the all girls' college across the street from Notre Dame University, which was all-male. But once again, this meant I would be leaving friends, saying good-bye to my new Atlanta friends and heading off to make new ones in South Bend, Indiana.

When I arrived on campus for my freshman year, Notre Dame and St. Mary's had merged. Although the deal ultimately fell through, I took as many courses as I could at Notre Dame and spent so much time on the Notre Dame campus that, in my college experience, the line between the two schools blurred.

I became fast friends with my three roommates and found camaraderie with the other girls in my dorm at St. Mary's.

Through engineering calculus and weekend dorm parties, I fell into easy friendships with lots of guys at Notre Dame. I never missed a pep rally or a home football game and loved college life. Although I cared about my classes and spent plenty of time studying, volunteering with children was by far my favorite part of college. I assisted in classrooms and tutored, but my best-loved activity was the Saturday Recreation Program at Logan Center. One hundred student volunteers and over one hundred children and adults with disabilities gathered at Logan Center at nine o'clock every Saturday to sing, play games, do arts and crafts, and go on field trips. Run completely by students from Notre Dame and St. Mary's, I took a leadership role almost immediately. I loved the participants and found like-minded friends in the other volunteers.

Notre Dame and St. Mary's became home to me over the next three years.

My senior year would be a different story entirely.

CHAPTER 13

Healing

Atlanta, Georgia – 1993

Each of my six brothers and sisters would have described my father differently, but we all would agree he was a force to be reckoned with. And he was about to leave us.

Tall and thin with jet-black hair, his green eyes lit up with an easy smile. He loved people and greeted everyone around him. Handsome and charming, my father had a youthful air about him. He was full of life and had lots of energy.

My father taught me lots of things—how to vacuum, dust, do dishes, take care of the yard, and grocery shop. He loved that I was competent, efficient, and "a fast learner." He and I shared a high energy level and a love of work. He taught me how to do everything quickly since faster was better in his mind. I received a lot of attention and praise for taking on responsibilities at home. He loved seeing how I'd organize the playroom or invent creative ways to entertain my two baby sisters. Whether we were organizing the garage or planning for company, my father and I worked well together.

When I was ten years old, he would drop me off to do the grocery shopping on Saturday mornings. I'd race through the grocery store filling two carts with everything on my mother's list: six loaves of bread, six boxes of cookies, ten pounds of potatoes, twenty four jars of baby food, etc. When I met him at the checkout after his weekly visit to the barber, my father beamed with pride. Our goal was to get the groceries in under thirty minutes, for under thirty dollars—and I never disappointed him.

He was proud of my schoolwork and especially my mathematical ability which was a little uncanny. I was his walking phone book in early elementary school since I could remember any phone number he gave me. He also enjoyed the fact that I was athletic and could do things like ride a unicycle and jump on a pogo stick with no hands.

When I became a teacher, he collected food and blankets and whatever else I happened to mention the children in my classroom needed. After I published my books on sex education, he'd randomly drop into bookstores and schools to ask if they would like to place an order. This embarrassed my mother to no end. I thought it was pretty funny since my parents had never talked about sex at home and my books were "clearly illustrated." He never once said it to me, but I guessed he liked my books.

As a child I was proud to be associated with this generous handsome man. I especially enjoyed doing volunteer work with him whether it was planting flowers at the community pool, stapling bulletins at church, or renovating a building to create a teen center in a rough neighborhood. Through my eyes, my father was always up to something good.

An accountant at IBM, he believed fathers should never bring their work home. To him, this meant not speaking one word about his job—ever. It wasn't until college that I found out my father held an important management position with a major division of IBM. At work he was a great organizer, planner, and leader as well as accountant. I could still hear my father's boss, Mr. Thiel, who had hired me for the summer when I was twenty to help take care of his daughter who was severely handicapped, saying, "Your dad is such a great guy. No, I mean it. He is one of the best men I've ever known. Straight and true. Honest and generous. He's one of a kind."

"What's he like at home?" he asked me once.

"Fine," I answered politely.

"Well, I can never get over how clear your dad is about what's right and what's wrong and then he lives by it. Very ethical man," he commented.

I was used to hearing people compliment my dad. Once I was hired by a young woman in his accounting department to help her pack for a transfer. "You wouldn't believe what your dad did for me," she confided. "Just when I needed it, he was there." She never explained further, and my father never mentioned it.

She wasn't the only person he'd quietly assisted. His four sisters raved about how my father had stepped in to help when my uncle was committed to a mental hospital, and again, when one of my cousins entered rehab for drug problems. He kept his good works secret. I'd only hear about his generosity later, when people would refer to his saintliness. But I really admired him for it.

The consummate extrovert, my father loved having company to the house. The more people around him the more energized he was, as if the nine of us needed more company! His philosophy was, "Work hard. Play hard." He'd have us all racing around doing chores on Saturday mornings so that we could have cousins or friends over for cookouts and wiffle ball in the summer, or ice skating and sleigh riding in the winter. When my parents occasionally had parties on weekends, he'd get everyone to dance or sing—the life of the party. He'd grown up poor, never once going on a family vacation; but he made sure we spent a week or two at the Jersey shore each summer. The beach was his favorite place.

For all his outward charm and goodness, my father had another side that only showed up at home. He could be mean and abusive. When we were little, he handed out spankings and punishments frequently and often inexplicably. Later, as teens, he used brief cruel comments to shut us up or control us.

As much as my father liked me to help him, I was also the one to incite his greatest rage. When something went wrong and he became upset, I oftentimes had what I considered to be a helpful suggestion. He would not want to hear it. Other times when he was unfair or irrational, I would tell him so. My outspokenness sparked explosive anger, and my mother, brothers, and sisters would glare at me, saying later, "If you would *just* shut up." The other kids figured out that if they stayed silent when he was flying off the handle, the punishments, the smacks, or time in our rooms were not as bad and he'd cool down faster.

But it felt, to me, like I had to speak up. And his explosive reaction led me to believe, down deep that—out of the seven of us—my father hated me the most. Sometimes, after he had completely lost his temper and stomped away, my mother would shake her head and say, "You are just like him." For years I was terrified that I was a basically mean person, and that one day, I too would fly off the handle and hurt someone. I was grown before I realized she probably meant I was out-spoken, just like him, and that explained why I irritated him so much.

But as we grew up and were too old to spank, he began using powerful one-liners to punish or control us.

Some of my father's anger arose from his rigid, black-and-white attitude. If he was present, he controlled the conversa-tion; he wouldn't allow any argument, controversy, or debate. We generally stuck to safe topics; these included: the weather, sports, and cute stories about the younger siblings. He loved babies and young children.

But one night, I was home from college and invited a boy-friend over for dinner. The little ones had left the table and the conversation turned to school. I began sharing my ideas about equal rights for women. Rather than simply disagreeing with me, my father said in a loud voice, "No one will ever marry *you*." It was a barb he unleashed when he wanted me to shut up. And it cut me to the quick.

His "random words of meanness" hurt the most because I never saw them coming. I never knew when my friendly, gener-ous, fun-to-be-with father would snap. I never knew when he'd fire off the next cruel remark. Because of this, I was never any good at protecting myself from him.

Within days of my mother's call about my father's diagnosis, four of my six brothers and sisters each called me to say the same thing: "Don't try to talk to Dad about anything serious." I thought this was an odd message to receive four times in a row. I was the only family member who lived out of town, so they'd each visited my father and concluded that he still wanted to stick to safe topics: the dog, the weather, and sports. They knew I preferred to ask people how they were feeling or what they were thinking. This was not the time, they said.

I drove to Atlanta that first weekend, so I could see my father while he still felt well. But, by the time I arrived, he'd taken a turn for the worse. My mother and I drove him to the emergency room where he was admitted. The oncologist found that the cancer was in his liver, and he recommended starting a potent form of chemotherapy right away.

I called home to rearrange my work schedule and patch together childcare so that I could stay in Atlanta for the week and help out. As the doctors worked out a treatment plan, we faced some serious medical decisions. All fifteen of us (seven kids, seven spouses, and my mother) were busy trying to digest each medical update his doctors provided, and then share it with extended family and my parent's friends. Everybody wanted news about my father and each offered to help. Family relationships were strained.

I was exhausted by the end of the week and needed to get home to my family and my job. I planned to check on him at six in the morning before I left for the long drive home. But as I walked into my father's hospital room, he started yelling and cursing at me about the "stupid driving directions" my mother and I had given to friends from Florida. I was beat and didn't like being yelled at, especially by the person I'd been caring for. I lost it. I left the room and was crying in the hallway when a male nurse I had gotten to know on the oncology unit saw me and gently steered me into the family waiting area, empty for the moment. I wasn't the first caregiver he'd seen hit the breaking point.

As we talked, he helped me realize that I didn't need to put myself into harm's way any more. I needed to take care of myself. I decided to write my father a letter and leave for home. The nurse promised he'd take good care of my father until my sister arrived at noon.

In my letter, I told my father that I was amazed how loved he was by so many people. He had thirty-two immediate family members and many close friends calling, visiting, and sending notes. The hospital had become a Joe Conboy caring zone. I told him I wondered how that outpouring of concern must feel. I couldn't fully understand his experience because, in the four times I'd been hospitalized, not even one Conboy family member had been there.

During my week in Atlanta, I'd cancelled an important full-day program I was leading in Washington, D.C. Yet my father never once acted like he was glad to see me—or thanked me for my help. My brothers and sisters got the same treatment. In the letter, I noted how gracious he was when his friends visited. I also told him I honored his decision to discontinue chemotherapy since it only made him sick and wouldn't improve his quality of life or cure the cancer. In closing the letter I wrote, "You only have a short time left. How do you wish to be remembered? These next weeks matter a lot."

I passed the letter on to the nurse I had spoken to and I left.

During the ten-hour drive home I never stopped crying...about losing my father...about having a father that didn't love or appreciate me...who didn't seem to know me, really. Aside from his random meanness, I still thought my dad was a great guy and I loved him.

Ten hours later, I arrived home totally wiped out. I was grateful to see my cute kids and fall into my husband's warm embrace. I'd been in the door only five minutes when the phone rang. "It's your dad." Dan mouthed to me, his hand covering the receiver.

"Tell him I don't want to talk."

Dan quietly spoke to him and then waved me over. "Peggy, he said he needs to speak to you."

"No." Time passed. My husband stared me down.

I kept shaking my head no. Dan didn't know what had happened that morning.

He continued to mouth to me, "You have to talk to him."

I relented.

I got on the phone, "Hello," I said flatly.

"Hi," he said, voice cracking. "I don't know what to say, you talk."

"No, dad, I don't have anything to say. I said it all in the letter." I was determined not to speak.

I heard him start to cry. "I'm so sorry I'm mean," he sobbed. "I don't know why I'm so mean. I don't *want* to be mean." His sobs turned into a heartbreaking wail. He cried for quite some time and I just allowed it. I didn't say anything to make him feel better. It broke my heart open to hear his deep sorrow. I had never heard my father cry.

"I'm so sorry for all of it," he said.

I didn't know what to say so I was quiet trying to take it in.

Then he continued, "What do I do?"

His mother had died when he was only two years old, and he and his four sisters were raised by their Aunt Tesse. My mother said she was the meanest woman she had ever met. Now it seemed like my father honestly needed very basic instructions on kindness. Information a loving mother had never been able to share.

I answered simply. "You could be nice to your family. Say 'thank you for coming to see me.' Thank them for the kindnesses they offer you. Treat them as respectfully as you do your friends. That's all."

He was quiet for a moment, then asked, "So how's the weather up there in Virginia?"

I laughed. He could always talk about the weather. I asked him how he'd known precisely when to call me; I'd just walked in the door.

"I did the math," he said. "I know you always drive the speed limit, so I counted up the miles, divided by sixty, then added time for two short stops."

He was exactly right.

My mother and brothers and sisters each called me in the days following this incident. "What did you do to Dad?" Apparently, at exactly the time he estimated I would arrive home, he'd sent everyone out of his room and down the hall to the family waiting area while he made the call.

From the other end of the corridor, they'd heard him sobbing into the phone. "What has Peggy done now, tormenting him like this?" they'd wondered. I thought the group consensus was that I'd said something that upset him. As each one called me to ask, I said, "Ask Dad. It's his to share or not to share."

"But what did you do?" Jeanne wouldn't let me off the hook.

"What do you mean?" I asked.

"We mean, ever since we heard him crying with you, he's acting all nice to us. He's saying thank you every other minute. He's not himself at all."

I just smiled. *Good for you, Dad*, I thought.

He lived his final nine weeks from a place of kindness and appreciation that was truer to his nature. He was, in fact, *more* himself than he'd ever been. And to this day, that is how he is remembered.

In the end, I'd received the only thing I really needed from my father—an apology. Although I visited three more times before he died, we never had another intimate conversation. But he was consistently kind and appreciative.

Although I had further work to do in therapy, some related to the inner tangles his meanness had created in me, I was able to resolve my relationship with my father because of his sincere apology. As he cried into the phone, I received his apology and I forgave him. And it made all the difference.

My father gave me another gift during those last weeks. Although I wouldn't understand it for another four years, I glimpsed a part of myself that was just waiting to be discovered.

My father's final wish was a family beach vacation over the 4th of July. He wanted to enjoy this lifelong family tradition one last time. We didn't know if he'd even live that long, but all thirty-two of us gathered on Amelia Island in Florida for the week. My father sat on the beach for a few hours one day, and otherwise he enjoyed the view of the marsh from his bedroom window. The seven-hour drive from Atlanta was grueling for him physically, and we all acknowledged that he might not survive the week.

One day as my mother, my sister Jeanne, and I sat with him in his room he began to complain about stomach and chest pains. We moved pillows and considered more pain medication hoping to make him comfortable, but mostly we watched helplessly as his head tipped forward and he grimaced in terrible pain. I took his hand in mine, and silently began wishing with all my heart that he would feel better. I was shocked when a bright green light suddenly flashed up from his chest, traveled down his left arm, into my hand, up my arm, and shot right out of my elbow.

He lifted his head, looked right at me and said, "I feel better now."

"Great," I said. My mother and sister saw him staring at me and looked over too.

"Hey, I think I'll go check on the kids," I said nervously. A green electric current had just flown up my arm. I didn't believe in weird things like that. Nobody else seemed to have noticed it. Exiting quickly I vowed to block the experience out. Maybe *nothing* happened, I thought. There was certainly nothing I could prove. The next day, the hospice nurse examined him with a stethoscope and said it sounded like he might have suffered a heart attack.

"Amazing that he did so well with it given his weakened state," she remarked. I nodded, saying nothing.

My father was the last person on earth who'd believe in healing touch. But during those last few weeks, although we never spoke about it, anytime I held his hand or rubbed his feet, he seemed to feel better. I never thought to wonder why.

Still, I'd never forget the look he gave me after the green flash of light moved off his chest and out of my arm. Something had clearly happened to make him feel better. The proof was in his eyes. My father saw something in me that I wouldn't know myself for another four years.

> "There is no greater agony than
> bearing an untold story inside you."

Maya Angelou

CHAPTER 14

—∽—

Grieving

Atlanta, Georgia – 1993

My weekly sessions with Anne kept me grounded during the next two and a half months as my father was dying. Old sibling rivalries were triggered as the weeks wore on leaving each of us exhausted and frayed at the edges. In therapy, Anne helped me avoid becoming entangled in the flare-ups that bounced from brother to sister to sister to brother and back again. At home, I stayed true to myself, resisting the strong family pull coming from Atlanta.

At his funeral, my mother thought people would "break down" if anyone mentioned my father personally. The church was packed with people who loved him, but no one asked—or allowed—to speak during the service. Only the

Monsignor, who'd known my father for twenty years, gave a eulogy, painting him in bold strokes.

The grief I felt for my father unleashed a torrent of emotion within me that was overwhelming in its ferocity. Eighteen years ago, I'd felt the same anguish so deeply and for so long that I never imagined I'd have one more tear left to shed. But secret grief doesn't heal. When the crying lets up and the secret is safely packed away, it simply waits. And waits. Then, one sad day, after a year or a decade or a lifetime has passed, we are cracked open and the grief that we've so neatly tucked away, submerged within our consciousness, breaks free. And it swims toward the light, thrashing and spiraling upward toward the surface, where it screams for compassion and healing.

The week that my father died just happened to be the same week—eighteen years earlier—that I lost my first baby. When I signed the relinquishment papers at the adoption agency all those years ago, the social worker told me I could not have contact with my baby or receive any news about her until she turned eighteen. All those years, I had loved her from afar. I worried about her and I wondered if she was happy. Was she loved? Did she need me? Now that she was eighteen, I needed to know.

CHAPTER 15

—···—

Changing

South Bend, Indiana – 1974

I had my future all figured out by the time I was twenty-one. I would marry my boyfriend Jack as soon as I graduated from college with degrees in both elementary education and special education. I would teach for several years. Jack and I would then have seven children—maybe even ten—to the joy and delight of our respective large Irish Catholic families. Of course we would raise our children Catholic, and I would do volunteer work in the church and community. We would remain close to our many college friends and see our families often.

I thought I was in control.

I believed that if I worked hard and did my best to make the world a better place that mostly good things would happen to me. If a person's life was filled with pain and suffering, it was probably the result of bad decision-making or laziness. I knew there were exceptions to this rule, like my good friend Georgeen who died of cancer when she was only nineteen. In high school, Georgeen dreamed of doing medical research to find a cure for cancer then, out of the blue, she was diagnosed with an aggressive type of bone cancer. The only way I could reconcile this was to conclude that she was too good for this world and God must have wanted her to be with him in heaven.

I also had trouble reconciling my philosophy while working in special education, but I had concluded that children who were handicapped were innocent gifts from God, serving to open our hearts more fully. As a healthy and capable young woman with a stable, loving family, I didn't realize how naïve I was. But my worldview was about to change once and for all and forever.

I was madly in love with Jack, the young man I was certain to marry, when midway through my senior year of college, I found out I was pregnant. When I told Jack, it turned out he didn't want to marry me after all. My neatly constructed world and the future I'd ordered up to match fell apart. I was devastated.

Although abortion had just been legalized, for me it was unthinkable. I believed what I had been taught—that life began at conception. Although St. Mary's and Notre Dame never openly banned unwed mothers from attending as students, I knew I would not be welcome on campus when I was visibly pregnant.

I got the news in mid-December of my senior year, the week before exams. In order to graduate from college, I needed to complete two more courses plus my second eight-week student teaching session. I convinced the Registrar that I had run out of money for college and could only stay for half of my second semester. It worked. My advisor scheduled student teaching early that semester. The two courses were set up as independent studies so I could take the final exams in early March, before I planned to disappear from campus.

I contacted my friend Shannon who'd graduated the year before. She offered to share her studio apartment in Chicago, where I could live from March until the baby was born in July. Shannon was my lifesaver.

I only told three friends at school. My roommate, Mary Meurisse, said she'd do whatever she could to help me out. Cathy, my best friend in the education school, listened silently and then never mentioned it again. My other friend, Mary Beth, was furious. When I slid into the pew next to her at an anti-abortion Mass at Notre Dame's Cathedral, she turned and looked me up and down. I was a living example of anti-abortion, but she leaned into me, narrowed her eyes and hissed, "What are *you* doing here?" She never spoke to me again. I was so hurt by their responses that I never told another soul at school.

After first semester exams, home for Christmas, I had to tell my parents. These were the messages I got: "You are on your own." "Don't tell anyone. No one can know." My mother said, "Don't you ever tell your little brothers and sisters or it will ruin their lives." I believed her.

My parents arranged a meeting with the Monsignor of their parish. I didn't want to go. He had been flirtatious with me and it made me uncomfortable. But there was no choice. My father drove me there and on the way he yelled at me, saying, "No bastard grandchild will ever step foot in our house."

I was in serious distress when I entered the Rectory and met with Monsignor B in his office. Right off the bat, he said I *had* to give up the baby for adoption. I could do this at a home for unwed mothers in Alabama and, he said, I would forget it ever happened. He counseled me to never, under any circumstances, tell any man I dated about the baby. Because a man who knew about my baby would never marry me.

These messages were branded onto my psyche. Shame filled up my entire being. My sin was unspeakable and unforgivable. My father was always lending a helping hand to people in need; yet now that I needed his help, I was unworthy. It was my problem—too shameful even for my parents to acknowledge.

Only weeks before I had felt very loved. Now I had lost my boyfriend, who I thought was the love of my life, and my college friends, who I couldn't talk to. I felt shunned by my parents and separated from my siblings.

But the worst blow of all was the dictate from Monsignor and my parents. All I had hoped for in life was to teach children and have children of my own. How would I ever give away what I considered most precious?

CHAPTER 16

—⁂—

Finishing

South Bend, Indiana – 1975

I kept my pregnancy a secret at school, physically hiding my growing waistline, pushing back "morning sickness" nausea, which lasted all day, and pretending like everything was just fine. I was a really good actress. When I immersed myself in coursework or student teaching, I could block out my challenging circumstances. Alone in my dorm room, I often sat in the rocking chair and stared out the window crying. Sometimes I'd talk to my baby or sing to him. I thought he was a boy and I called him Charlie.

I went to an OB/GYN because I knew prenatal care was important, especially vitamins. This was only the second time I'd seen a gynecologist. When I was home in Atlanta over the summer, I was having heavy periods every two to three weeks and the doctor had given me birth control pills to adjust a significant hormone imbalance. After the appointment, when I told my mother, she took the birth control pills from my hands, threw them in the trash and said, "Those could kill you."

I believed her.

Now I was in South Bend seeing an obstetrician. The doctor asked me if I knew who the father was. Before I could answer, he laughed and said, "Of course not." He sent an inexperienced medical student in to begin the exam. This student inserted the speculum incorrectly and I cried out in pain. The doctor didn't come in for another ten minutes to take it out, made no apology and was extremely rough with me. But he did give me the prenatal vitamins I came for. In my journal that night I thanked God for Dr. James and the vitamins he prescribed. I was so deep into my own shame that I thought I deserved the treatment I got. I never told anyone about what had happened.

As second semester began, there was one thing I was still hanging onto—my career. I loved the challenge and the fun of teaching. I was happiest when I was teaching, especially students who had special needs.

I was an "A" student, but my graduation from college and ability to earn a professional certificate hinged on a successful student teaching experience. Even though my life was a mess, I was still confident that all would go well. I thought I was ready for anything.

I was assigned to a class of fifteen students ages six to nine with mild developmental disabilities. According to the report, several students also had serious behavior disorders. The teacher was a matronly woman with a large, military body who wore her hair in a tight bun. Her name was Miss Wise. The first day

I learned the routine. The students did pegboards, wrote their names, wrote numbers, and then watched TV much of the day. I was horrified! I could see these children were bored and I vowed to save them.

Although it was unheard of for a student teacher to take over a class during the first week, I convinced Miss Wise that I could teach a simple art lesson on Friday. I planned to do sponge prints. The children would dip cut-up sponges into paint and press them onto paper to make a design. I thought this innovative idea showed my creativity and enthusiasm.

On Friday afternoon, Miss Wise headed to the teacher's lounge for a break and I began the art activity. The students were all excited as we pushed the desks together to make a long table and covered it with newspaper. I told them they could *only* do this special painting if they sat in their seats and behaved. Next, I laid out the aluminum pie plates, sponges, and paper. I talked about how great their pictures would look decorating the otherwise blank hallway. The children seemed really happy and they were doing a very good job minding me. *This*, I thought, *is why I want to be a teacher*.

Next, I asked the children to put their hands in their laps while I poured the paint into the small pie tins in front of them. I went over to the teacher's desk and very carefully opened the wide lid to the one-gallon jug of concentrated, liquid, red tempera paint. Every one of them sat still and quiet, just as I had asked. I lifted the large container of concentrated red paint and started walking over to the group of fifteen desks. When I was about a foot away, I tripped.

I held tight to the container, but the gallon of thick, red paint went flying through the air and landed directly on the heads and bodies of my startled students. Two children looked exactly like red M&Ms. Others had red blobs on their faces and in their hair. Some merely looked like they had been speckled.

Hoping to keep everyone calm I said in my teacher, sing-songy voice, "Woops I tripped, we'll have to clean up this paint."

The kids stared at each other in shock. Then they began chanting louder and louder, "Look at Willy! Look at Willy!" I calmly answered in my teacher voice, "Yes, I see Willy. We'll have to get that paint off, won't we." Then I actually looked at Willy. His head and upper body were covered with the thick red paint. He stared up at me in silence, his big brown eyes blinking through his shiny red coating. "So this is Art?" I imagined him asking.

My heart began to race. There was no sink, not even a pitcher of water in the classroom. The bathroom was way down the hall past the teachers' lounge where Miss Wise had gone to have a relaxing cup of tea. There was no way I could sneak her red students down the hall to get cleaned up.

Several students began getting out their seats. Two discovered that their shoes could make wonderful red prints on the floor. I commanded them to sit down. They ignored me. Others joined them. The students who remained seated tried desperately to wipe off the paint, which they spread and smeared everywhere. Finally they gave up and joined the others who were clearly having more fun. The class became one joyous red wild-ruckus free for all. My attempts to round them up and get control failed miserably.

As I frantically jerked open the classroom door and screamed hysterically into the hallway, "HELP!!! HELP!!!" my career—the future I'd imagined—passed before my eyes. Miss Wise marched quickly up the hall as I calmly informed her in my lovely, teacher voice, "Everyone is okay, but I spilled some paint and I need help." I still remember her face, ashen in horror, as she watched her painted students happily stamping their bright-red footprints all over her classroom.

It took me hours and hours to clean up the classroom. Late into the dark, alone scrubbing the floor with a sponge, a bucket of soapy water, and gallons of tears, I just kept repeating over and over, "One day you will think this was funny. One day this will be a funny story. One day you will think this was funny..."

Over the weekend I told a few other fellow student teachers about it while we ate dinner in the cafeteria. They thought it was hysterical. Word spread quickly and I ended up telling the story over and over, mostly to groups of education students. Even I was able to laugh a little at my ridiculous mistake.

However, my supervisor heard about the paint incident and she summoned me to her office the following Monday afternoon. She was not amused.

I was nervous. When I entered Sister Mary Catherine's office, she skipped the polite chit chat and simply asked me to drop out of student teaching. I felt like I'd been punched. Was I going to lose my career, too? The one thing I hadn't lost yet?

Somehow I had the wherewithal to say, "Are you *asking* me to drop out or telling me I *must* drop out?"

"I'm asking you," said Sister Mary Catherine.

I sat thoughtfully and took a deep breath. "Then I choose to finish my student teaching," I said, wondering where this voice of clarity and courage was coming from. That voice made me realize how much I wanted to be a teacher.

Because of "the red paint incident," I was given less opportunity to lead the class during the rest of my student teaching. This allowed me to watch and learn from both the teachers and the students. I came to further understand the life circumstances of the children when the teacher began sharing information about their home lives and medical issues. I watched to see what motivated these teachers, and I began to discern internally how I might approach different situations. The take-charge part of my personality was given a much-needed rest. I had enough to cope with in my personal life.

Luckily, I passed student teaching.

I also had to complete my last two courses. The professors had given me a full sixteen-week workload to complete in only eight. Given my heavy academic burden, my friends and acquaintances didn't question why I had completely withdrawn from all socializing. I spent most evenings alone in my dorm room silently talking to my baby, telling him everything was going to be okay, that he would have a good life. And I cried a lot, over my lost love and the separation from my family. And I worried. There was no one to talk to about all the many changes in my body. Were they normal? Was the baby okay? I felt utterly alone.

Some late afternoons I'd sneak over to the church where the nuns were singing Vespers. I'd quietly enter the back door and climb the steep stairs to the balcony, then lie down in a pew out of sight. As the sun went down I could see the colored lights from the stained glass windows making impressionist paintings on the ceiling. Then flickering candlelight would take over, not permitting the darkness here. I would pray desperately for help and then feel myself surrounded by the echoes of the beautiful music and chanting. I would imagine that all the nuns were singing to the precious baby growing inside me.

I finished college in March, having kept my pregnancy a secret.

I went to Atlanta for one very long week and applied and interviewed for teaching positions. Five months pregnant, I had not gained any weight. I wore little cardigans with my otherwise tight-fitting clothing, the style at the time, that hid the pregnancy for this one last week. I still didn't know if I was going to keep my baby or not, but I knew that if I did, I would never be hired to teach. Applying for jobs gave me an option in case I decided to give up the baby or in case I found someone to marry me.

CHAPTER 17

—ɯɯ—

Surviving

Chicago – 1975

When I finally went to Chicago to live with my good friend, Shannon, in her studio apartment, it was a relief to be in a big city where I didn't know anyone except her. At first, I hung out with Shannon and her friends, but I could tell I made them uncomfortable. I was a walking advertisement for the consequences of premarital sex. Her Catholic friends seemed uneasy around me, and my sad seriousness made it difficult to join in their fun. Instead, I worked odd jobs babysitting and cleaning houses to earn enough money to live on.

During my week in Atlanta, I found out that I needed three courses to earn my teacher certification in Georgia. Remarkably, I was able to sign up for all three courses during Northeastern Illinois University's summer session.

Whenever I could, I attended early morning Mass at a church near Shannon's apartment. I sat in the back, hoping no one would find out I was pregnant and unmarried. I assumed the Church wouldn't let me come if they knew. I thought about going to Confession but what would I say? I wasn't sorry for loving Jack or keeping the pregnancy. I hadn't used artificial birth control, which was a Church law. I had used "natural birth control" which, I later learned, was how most Catholic children were conceived. But because I couldn't think of what to confess, I became convinced that this "mistake" was somehow unforgivable. Unlike the guilt and regret I felt when I did something sinful, instead I felt ashamed. I was convinced that it wasn't that I'd *done* something bad, it was that *I* was *a bad person*—both unforgivable and unlovable.

With no health insurance, I found out I could become a clinic patient at the hospital. My medical bills would be covered for a flat fee, which I was working to earn. As an indigent patient, I never saw the same doctor or nurse. The mood at the clinic was cold and businesslike; everyone was overworked and too tired for kindness.

Shannon's apartment was across from Grey Park, a city park with several old shade trees and wooden benches. Next to it was an apartment-sized halfway house for people with mental illness. I started sitting in the park having friendly visits with all these people I felt sorry for. At first, I thought maybe I could help them. Instead, as I listened to their stories of survival from poverty, abuse, and heartache, I realized I was no different than them. I was looking for a way to survive too. I knew that come July, if I kept this baby, I'd never be hired to teach. I would probably find myself homeless and on welfare. I was one of them.

Shannon's sister-in-law told me about a private adoption agency called The Cradle, which supposedly had a fabulous reputation. I began seeing a social worker there every week or so. At first, Margaret answered the questions I had about the adoption process and then she began to do a bit of counseling. When she got around to asking how I was doing, I broke down. For the first time, with anyone, I was completely honest about my deep sadness over the decision I was making. I looked down at my lap and started crying. My heart was broken and I'd had no one to ask for help. I felt embarrassed to cry in front of the social worker, but I desperately needed support and guidance.

Margaret waited, and when I pulled my head up, she looked right at me and said in a snappy voice, "Why, you act like this is the worst thing that could happen to you!"

In my mind it was.

"What if you had cancer, or MS, or became a paraplegic from a traffic accident? Now *those* would be really bad things to happen to you."

I sat in silence. None of those compared to the heartbreak I felt at losing my first child.

She went on to explain that "all the other girls" that "went away" to have their babies, like me, simply returned to their friends and family and would "forget it ever happened." She compared it to a girl returning from an extended vacation—or studying abroad—unchanged, ready to resume her happy life.

In that brief exchange, she confirmed my two greatest fears. First, that no one could accept or love me fully—feelings, thoughts and all. If an adoption caseworker couldn't accept them, then no one could. Was I feeling sorry for myself like Margaret thought? I hoped not, but I would keep my distress to myself.

My second biggest fear was of making this important decision alone. My parents' message was clear: "You are on your own." But I desperately needed someone who might understand, who might help me figure out how to keep the baby and earn a living as a single mother—or just help me weigh each choice. Shannon and Mary Meurisse were great listeners, but ultimately they were too young themselves to know what advice to offer me. I tried not to burden them with my deep distress and confusion. Now even an adoption social worker couldn't help me. I became certain no one could.

I never mentioned my difficulties with the adoption caseworker again. I realized that *she* would choose the adoptive family if I decided to give up my baby. So the smarter, the healthier, the more emotionally stable I appeared, the better her family choice might be. I started bringing her small thoughtful gifts I'd made, to insure my baby got the very *best* family on the waiting list.

On the outside, I appeared to be doing well. Inside, I was tormented. I really wanted to keep the baby. But my father had said that the baby couldn't come into the house, and my mother said my younger siblings could never know about the baby, so I assumed my family would want nothing to do with us. I couldn't imagine raising a child without an extended family—no grandparents, no aunts, uncles, or cousins, and especially, no father. I had used what little money I had to pay my medical bills, tuition, and food. I would never be hired as a teacher. How could I ever support a baby financially? Where would we live?

Each time we met, the adoption agency caseworker would tell me about the wonderful couples who wanted children but couldn't have them. The families on their waiting list were financially stable and could provide good homes with two parents and a loving extended family. I loved my baby too much to keep him from one of these perfect families. By May, I knew I would give the baby to a family with two parents, a house, and loving relatives. I was devastated.

I made one stipulation with the social worker. I told her that if the baby had any handicap at all, I would keep him. With my background in special education, I knew that children with disabilities were not adopted; they were put into institutions. I had worked in two of those institutions, and I knew that no matter how difficult my circumstances were, I'd take better care of the baby than any institution ever could. But the pregnancy was going well and the baby, it was assumed, would be healthy.

I started worrying about work. I contacted the Atlanta schools that I'd applied to in March. There was a glut of teachers in 1975. Public law 94-142, which gave all children including those with disabilities the right to an appropriate public education, had been passed but not implemented. Most children with special needs stayed at home or attended non-accredited day programs. Special education jobs were scarce, so I had also applied for elementary education positions. The public schools said they wouldn't be notifying me until August. That seemed like a long time to wait.

In mid-June, I was offered a second-grade teaching position at the Immaculate Heart of Mary Elementary School, where my sister Mary Pat would be in fifth grade, and sister Kathy in seventh. Monsignor B, who had told me to give up my baby, was in charge of both the church and school. Afraid that this might be my only job offer, I accepted.

As I began preparing for my teaching job, creating games and materials, I also started another important project—praying that, after my baby was born, I would die.

As an unmarried pregnant young woman, scared and overwhelmed, without resources or support, I had convinced myself that I wasn't worthy or able to raise my baby on my own. All I had ever wanted was to teach and have children. I believed the messages coming from my parents, the priest, and the adoption caseworker. But I'd also decided that the shame of giving up my precious baby would leave me unworthy of life itself.

CHAPTER 18

—◊—

Reliving

Richmond, Virginia – 1993

The pain that seared my psyche eighteen years ago was burning again with the same white-hot intensity. I'd told a few close friends over the years that I had given up a baby for adoption, but I never told the emotional side of the story. Back when we were dating, Dan received my confession with complete acceptance. But my shame was so deep that I never sought his emotional support. I couldn't fathom that I might warrant compassion, too.

But the pain of my past was now wreaking havoc on my life in the present. Every morning, I woke up fully aware that I was a wife, a mother, and the year was 1993. I talked to my husband, got my children off to school, and went to the Jewish Community Center to swim laps. I'd run a few errands and then, just when I was coping pretty well, a memory would come flooding in and drag me back in time. My stomach would tighten as a wave of shame rippled through me. I could be buying stamps at the post office, and suddenly I'd be back at The Cradle, my social worker dismissing my tears, or at the clinic facing a new doctor who might hurt me. Or I'd hear my mother telling me my pregnancy would ruin my little sisters' lives.

I felt these flashbacks more vividly than my own here-and-now. And with them, the truth I'd once held deep in my bones: No one loved me and no one could help me. I was completely and utterly alone.

Anne had given me some tools to help me push through the memories and return to the present moment, but it was a struggle. Sometimes I simply went home, got into bed, and didn't budge until it was time to pick up the kids. When my children were around, I could stave off these episodes. My deep desire to be a good mother to my children motivated me to keep moving through the healing. I was convinced that this healing work would free me to be a better mother.

I couldn't seem to control the triggers. Each flashback was a surprise, so I never knew how or when I'd be overwhelmed by feelings from my past.

Anne finally named it for me. I was experiencing *post traumatic stress disorder*, or PTSD. The diagnosis was relatively new and it usually applied to Vietnam War veterans, whose past trauma would trigger vivid scenes of war in their consciousness. At least I'd found an explanation for the internal battle I was waging.

At the same time I was uncovering some of my most difficult memories with Anne, I discovered a lump in my breast.

In the doctor's office, I found myself remembering the doctors in Chicago and my body panicked. I could hardly speak to the surgeon. I needed to tell him that this was my third breast tumor, that my father had just died from cancer a few months ago, and my mother's identical twin was scheduled to have a double mastectomy the next week. He scheduled the surgery for me. "I think it is probably another benign tumor like you've had before," he said.

"Oh good," I said out loud. Internally, I was convinced I had cancer.

Week by week, I opened up more of my story to Anne. She knew it was tough to go back and remember; she knew my healing depended on letting go of this long held secret. And there was more.

CHAPTER 19

—⁓—

Losing

Chicago, Illinois – July 1975

During the last month of my pregnancy, I had a lot of trouble breathing, especially in summer with no air conditioning. I didn't know what was wrong with me. During a regular clinic appointment, they took my blood pressure and noticed the swelling in my hands, feet, and legs. I was diagnosed with toxemia, a complication in pregnancy caused by an abnormal protein, which causes high blood pressure and can lead to seizures or convulsions if not treated.

One day, as my breathing became even more difficult, I asked Shannon if she could drive me to my appointment. I wasn't sure I could breathe through the bus ride and walk in the heat. When I arrived at the hospital clinic, they took one look at me and admitted me. My blood pressure had skyrocketed and my skin had turned gray. They broke my water to induce labor. My baby and I were in danger. My friend Shannon was ordered to leave the room.

As I began labor, the doctor said my blood pressure kept maxing out and my toxemia was very serious. "No anesthesia," was his command. A male medical student was assigned to me. Neither of us had been to childbirth classes. Over and over I silently prayed, "Please let me die. Please let me die as soon as I deliver this baby." I was ready.

They wheeled me into the delivery room crying in pain. The medical staff was very professional and concerned. I was not well. Time passed slowly, the pain excruciating. Finally, my baby was born. It was a girl. A girl. All along I had thought it was a boy, but now it was a girl. She was healthy and beautiful with bright red hair and pink cheeks. But because she was perfect and healthy, with no handicaps, I would give her away. My heart broke.

They offered to let me hold her, but the adoption social worker had said not to look at or hold the baby because it would just make it harder. I was already falling to pieces, so I was afraid that I wouldn't have the strength to give her away if I touched her or held her. I turned my head away from her tiny cries and sobbed.

Following the delivery I was taken to a room, sick to my stomach the whole way. They dropped me off without a word.

My roommate was smoking a cigarette and had just delivered her fifth child. When the nurse walked in with her baby, the woman said, "Keep the damn baby in the nursery would ya? I'll have him for the rest of his life for god sakes. I need a nap."

After the nurse exited, my roommate turned to her man and said, "Bobby, go get me a beer would ya?" Was this lady really a better mother than me? I couldn't even look at her.

A few hours later, a bossy irritated nurse poked her head in the room, pointed at me and ordered, "Get your things, we're moving you to another room." She left without any further explanation.

I got out of bed, shivering, head spinning, my legs like jelly. As I reached down to pick up the paper bag that had my belongings, my lungs closed in on themselves. There was no space for air. No matter how hard I focused I could not get a breath. I tried to say "help" but nothing came out.

Within moments, I found myself looking down at my melted body in a heap on the floor, and I began floating out of the room through the hospital corridors. I saw the red flashing lights and heard emergency alarms beeping as people rushed to that collapsed body. I had not a care in the world as I floated toward a bright light at the end of a long hallway. I floated around the hospital, and some time later I noticed a whispery voice in the distance. What was it saying? I couldn't quite hear it, but I knew it was telling me to go back. I *needed* to go back. Apparently I had more to do.

Then, with a jolt, I slammed back into my body and awakened. Almost a full day had passed. A nurse, sitting in a chair beside my bed said, "Oh honey, you scared us half to death last night. We all thought we had lost you. Let me go tell them you are back."

You did lose me, I thought. I am lost. Why am I back? Why am I alive? A vague answer to that question was inside me somewhere. A very faint pilot light flickered within me, holding the answer to why I was alive. For the moment, though, I was merely existing, lying in bed, breathing, lost in the deepest grief and heartache. I had come back, but I had no desire to live.

The day I came back from the dead, I talked briefly to my parents. *Yes*, I was okay, I told them, and *yes*, I was still giving up the baby. I also spoke to Shannon and Mary Meurisse. They were very loving and I was a mess. I felt a hundred years old. Their joyous youthfulness seemed naive to me. I didn't want to bother them with my heaviness, so I said as little as possible. "I'm fine," I said. "The baby is fine."

My former boyfriend Jack called from New York to say he loved me. Of course, love to him did not include marrying me so that I could keep our baby. Jack had promised himself long ago that he wouldn't marry until he was thirty years old. At the age of thirty his father had committed suicide and he was determined not to follow in his footsteps. Jack was five when his father was found "asleep" in the car in the garage with the engine running.

These few phone calls, received on the first day, were my only communication with the outside world during the seven long days and nights I spent in the hospital.

A doctor with a group of medical students came in each day. He'd state my name, age, the fact I was giving up my baby for adoption, and then lift up my hospital gown and direct this young, all-male group of medical students to look at my private parts and supposedly "check my stitches." I was humiliated. One day a doctor came in with about ten male medical students and laid a stack of birth control pamphlets right on my abdomen, right where my baby should have been. He began rattling off information about each type of birth control. I kept my eyes down and prayed they would leave me alone, leave the room before I started crying. I wasn't listening to a word he said. I took the pamphlets off my belly and put them on the nightstand.

"What, you think you won't have sex again and need this information?" All the young male medical students laughed.

Endless days followed sleepless nights. Three night nurses came one at a time to keep me company throughout the week. They told me stories about choices and courage and the hope that arises from difficult circumstances. One night at three a.m. the nurse named Janine told me that her first baby had been stillborn. She shared how her body didn't know the baby was gone. She wanted me to know about the hormonal and physical changes I would be experiencing when I left the hospital without my baby. And she wanted me to know before I went to Atlanta, where I'd have no one to talk to. She said she didn't want me to be scared of my body. Janine was so kind to me.

My sense of loss was overpowering. Not only had I lost my baby, I had lost the man I loved and all but two of my friends. My family felt lost to me because I had to keep this deep dark secret or their reputation would be ruined. I had lost the strong sense of belonging I'd felt in the Catholic Church. I had lost my outgoing happy nature, my optimism, and my sense of fun. I had a trunk and a suitcase with all my worldly possessions, mostly clothes and books. None of these mattered. I had lost everything.

I did some deep soul searching wondering what, if anything, I had not lost. I could not think of a thing. I laid in the bed staring into space. I continued to wonder about this.

During those silent endless days alone in the hospital, I kept searching for what was not lost. What was left of me? What was left *for* me?

And then, finally, one day I knew what had not been lost. It came to me as a simple sentence—a sentence that seemed true.

I could still love.

Was this the small light that flickered in my soul, the one I'd been aware of when I'd first woken up? I'd "lost" so many things *outside* of myself that I had, maybe for the first time, connected with a core part of myself, *within.* Something no one could take away. This was the *me* I hadn't lost. I could love. It was true. It began to fill me up. I thought of how much I loved my best friends, Shannon and Mary Meurisse, all the many children I had worked with, and these night nurses. No one could stop me from loving. I had the power to love.

This inner knowing gave me permission to live so that I could teach and love my students. I could continue loving friends and family and accept and love people even if they hurt me or didn't love me back.

I was able to tell the night nurses my story. During their gentle listening, I felt cared for and accepted. I told them that I had woken up from that "close to death" experience with the faintest feeling that I was meant to live and there were things for me to do. I believed there were children out there who needed me. Now I knew that I could love them. The nurses helped me restore my belief that I would be a good teacher. They also checked and confirmed that my baby was healthy and would be with her new family soon. These nighttime counseling sessions gave me back my life.

When I got out of the hospital, I had a plane ticket to Atlanta and ten dollars left to my name. I went out and bought a small bouquet of flowers and a box of candy. I addressed the card to all the nurses who helped me, but especially Janine, Janet, and Karen, the three night shift nurses who had talked to me for hours. When I handed it to the receptionist at the nurses' station on the floor where I'd been, she thanked me and looked at the card. "We don't have any nurses named Janine, Janet or Karen."

I said, "Oh, they were on night shift; maybe they were part time."

She had a unit staff list in her hand, "I'm just telling you— we don't have any nurses here by those names on any shifts."

"Well anyway I hope your staff enjoys the candy and flowers," I said. As I left the hospital, I wondered where they had come from? How had they managed to spend so much time with me? Who had told them to come sit with me?

Five days later I had to go back to The Cradle to sign the formal relinquishment papers. I took a bus then walked another mile to get there. As my body very ably moved forward on the sidewalk toward the adoption agency, I had the sensation of floating above myself watching. I thought maybe I was losing my mind. There seemed to be two of me. I did not want to sign those papers, and yet I knew I must. Although my body walked into The Cradle and signed, my spirit waited outside for me.

It would take time to reunite the two.

CHAPTER 20

—※—

Appearing

Richmond, Virginia – November 1993

In November, I had hit a low point in therapy while remembering what it had been like to feel so alone and unloved, and to feel the grief and shame of giving my baby up for adoption.

My father's death only four months earlier was also causing difficult shifts in family dynamics. And my eight-year-old son was having his own serious health and school issues. The surgery to remove my breast tumor was scheduled for the following week. With my father's recent death, my mother's identical twin recently diagnosed with breast cancer, and this being my third breast tumor, I expected the worst.

But it was at this time that the most defining moment of my life occurred. There were no witnesses. I could not have photographed or taped it. I could not prove it to a soul. Yet, I would never be willing to deny it. And although it took place in only a matter of minutes, it would begin a whole new way of being in the world.

Anne had suggested that I continue the practice of doing something just for me. I had really enjoyed the class I had taken on midlife back in the spring so when the fall came, I signed up for another evening course taught by the same teacher at the Women's Resource Center, Nancy Millner. This course was on the Psychology of Carl Jung. I was fascinated by how he had explored his own inner landscape and the way he considered consciousness, personality, and even dreams. Nancy approached me after class one night to tell me about a "labyrinth" experience she was going to be offering.

She explained that the labyrinth was a replica of the walking meditation made of stone in the floor of Chartres Cathedral in France that pilgrims journeyed to back in the thirteenth and fourteenth centuries. Apparently she and a small group of others had recently made this replica, the exact size and design of the original, from a big piece of canvas that they had painted. I was intrigued and told her that I would come.

I wondered why I had agreed to go since this was a replica of a "Catholic" walking meditation. Plus I had totally lost the ability to pray or even spiritually connect through nature like I had been doing for years. Nothing felt right in my life. So why was I going to try meditating on a piece of painted canvas?

I showed up at seven o'clock and joined about fifteen others in the circular lobby of a small old Gothic-style classroom building at the University of Richmond. We sat on wooden benches along the perimeter of the lobby, where we met to talk before entering the space that held the labyrinth. Nancy shared some of the history of the labyrinth and then said, "This will be a silent walking meditation. Just follow the path and it will lead you to the center. Feel free to just sit or stand in the center for as long as you want. Then follow the same path on the way out. If you meet someone on the path, just step around him or her." She also gave detailed information about how one can experience the labyrinth from a psychological perspective, but my own busy mind and depressing thoughts kept me from listening.

"Ready?" she asked as she opened the doors to the room where the labyrinth had been laid and we entered in silence. It was a beautiful big open space with high ceilings and soft lighting. Except for some gentle flute music to accompany us, it was quiet. And there on the floor was this rather interesting circular design painted on a forty-foot square piece of ivory canvas. I stood for a moment at the opening of the labyrinth, and then as I had watched a few others do, I began walking the path. With each step I felt my sadness, my self-hatred, my desperation. As I followed this path, I thought to myself, Surely, walking this painted canvas has to be the stupidest thing I have ever done. To me it was a sign of just how pathetic I was. When I got to the center I sat in one of the six petal-shaped areas. I put my head in my hands and silently wept. I felt completely alone. "God, where are you?" I asked. I couldn't find him or feel his presence anywhere in my life. My insides began wailing. With my eyes closed and in my loudest inner voice I inwardly cried out, "God, I need you! Please, please help me!"

Suddenly, in the silence of the moment, a woman appeared sitting before me. What was this? I was mysteriously being given her name. Into my mind seemed to come words from her, yet not spoken. Compassionate Goddess she was calling herself and my inner voice was saying, "Oh Compassionate Goddess," as I might have invoked Mary or Jesus in my childhood prayers.

She sat cross-legged in a meditative pose. I was struck by the velvet soft violet robes covering her head and draped over her body, which had a multitude of bright pink stars shining through. Her beautiful ageless face was framed by long dark flowing straight hair. She herself seemed to be emanating the pink light of the stars, as if her heart was made of pink star-light. She was the most strikingly beautiful sight I have ever held.

I opened my eyes, but she was not outside, and no one else in the group seemed to be experiencing anything out of the ordinary. I closed my eyes and she was still there sitting in front of me. Shaking my head, I tried to clear what surely had to be a trick of my imagination. But she remained, as real as anything or anyone I had ever seen with my open eyes.

I sat perfectly still before her, just being with her beauty. My attention focused and my mind quieted. Then, the pink starlight from her being stretched out and came over me. Very slowly and gently, beginning at the top of my head, my entire body was bathed in a feeling of warmth, filling me with a sense of complete contentment and peace. Every cell was washed in this pink light. I was totally loved in that moment. There was no fear or anxiety, powerlessness, or depression. I felt like I was enveloped in a pure state of compassion. I had never known a love like this. The power of it held me.

In silence I began to tell her how troubled I was. But some-how this woman already knew. I told her how much I had worried about my daughter whom I'd given up for adoption. I then asked if she would help me find her. I wanted to do a search. I needed to know if she was okay. Without words, I sensed her communicating to me that she would help me and be there for me. I was grateful.

Neither of us spoke out loud, but as she continued to sit there before me, I realized that she had one more thing to say. This time she voiced it in words. Seven words. There I sat cross-legged in the middle of the labyrinth, and she said, "I am you and you are me." Then she faded before me. However, the feeling of her loving kindness remained. Her light gently held me as if I were swaddled in a warm pink baby blanket. I still felt sadness, but I was no longer so tormented and full of self-hatred.

Opening my eyes, I realized I had no idea how much time had passed. Was it five minutes? An hour? I looked around and saw the others still in the room. As directed earlier, I stood up and followed the path back out. I walked over to my backpack, took out my notebook, and tried to write about what had happened. But mostly I wanted to simply sit and feel this sense of compassion forever.

Nancy directed us to return to the lobby area where she then offered us an opportunity to share with the group anything we wanted to about our experience. I was silent.

The group ended and Nancy came up and asked, "Is everything okay?"

I said, "I had a big experience. That's all."

"Please feel free to stay for a while if you want. You may want to write as much as you can so that you'll remember the details. Writing is also a good way to honor an experience."

"Thank you," I said. I couldn't imagine that I would ever forget, but I did sit and write in my notebook before leaving.

I drove home, still in a daze. When I came in the door, my husband asked, "So how was the walking meditation?"

All I could seem to get out of my mouth was, "It was different than I expected."

This experience threw me into inner chaos. I had nowhere to put it. Not only was there no one to tell, I didn't know what to tell myself. I had always been taught that God was masculine, yet a divine emanation appeared to me as a woman. Also I could barely admit to myself that I'd had—what I guessed would be considered—a vision. My only knowledge of visions was from the stories of the saints. But I was no saint. I was still an ordinary mother and wife with carpools and laundry and dinner to fix. Besides that, the saints had *Catholic* visions of Mary or Jesus. Mine was no Catholic vision.

Though there was much I didn't seem to know, I did know this. For the first time in my life, I knew the feel of being held in complete compassion. I experienced the power and healing ability of it. I knew I was loved. I still couldn't love myself, but this vision—my Vision—had come with a Compassionate Goddess who loved me for who I was, including my most shameful parts.

What I also experienced without a shadow of a doubt in that timeless moment in the center of the labyrinth was the ultimate confirmation that there was a spiritual realm that I had only imagined or prayed to but had never experienced directly. And this awakened in me a curiosity and deep yearning to know more about it. Who was this woman? What did it all mean? What was I supposed to do with the Vision?

A week after walking the labyrinth, this same beautiful violet-robed woman from my Vision appeared again when I had surgery to have the breast tumor removed. I was very frightened as they rolled me into the operating room; sure I had cancer. But when I awoke from the anesthesia, alone in a curtained cubicle and wrapped in warm blankets, the same beautiful woman was once again sitting before me. Calmly sitting, wearing her violet robes, emanating her pink light, she assured me without words that I was going to be okay. I was greatly relieved and instantly felt that same calm and peace in my body. She quietly faded from my view.

The nurse came in and said, "Good news, dear. The doctor is ninety-nine percent sure that it was just a fibroadenoma. You are going to be fine."

"I know," I said before I realized what I was saying.

"What?" she asked.

"I'm so relieved," I replied quickly, definitely not wanting to explain how I already knew.

Following this, I found myself consumed with wondering who this Compassionate Goddess was. Had anyone else ever met her? Who could I tell or ask? Only a week before I would have told anyone that I didn't believe in visions or Goddesses. I was totally ignorant about Goddess religions. I had never even studied Greek Mythology because Catholics considered it pagan and therefore evil. I searched through books on Goddesses at a Unitarian Church and the public library. There were so many Goddesses, ones with extra arms, standing on snakes, intertwined with masculine figures, naked ones with large bellies and breasts. Some were shown in bright reds and oranges, others in soft blue. Many were shown as sculptures, made of stone or metal. But I never saw any depicted with purple robes or with her beautiful ageless face and long dark hair. I didn't find any images that showed a goddess that emanated the pink light of stars. None of them seemed to be the woman who had appeared to me.

I wanted to tell a friend. I was surprised how vulnerable I felt about telling anyone. It was such a sacred experience that I wanted to protect it. I couldn't afford for someone to dismiss it or act like it was only a dream. I needed it to be just what it was, a beautiful and powerful healing experience. Finally, I decided to share the experience with Mary Meurisse. Surprisingly, she told me she was taking a course on the Goddess traditions at the Unitarian Church in Atlanta. She was touched by my experience and began looking for my "Compassionate Goddess" too.

Although there was confusion over what I was to do with the Vision, one thing had become very clear to me. I would do the search for my birth daughter. I needed to know if she was okay.

CHAPTER 21

—⁓—

Supporting

Richmond, Virginia – December 1993

December was hardest. Every year, for the past eighteen years, it left me feeling alone and unloved again. For eighteen Decembers, I'd fought the feelings off. Now, the depression was severe, and it was time to tell Anne I was feeling desperate. Normally, I resisted medications, but when she referred me to a psychiatrist to be evaluated for antidepressants, I didn't argue.

Dr. Z had a beard and kind eyes. He listened as I told my story and then very gently said, "You have every reason to feel depressed. Sometimes sadness and depression are there to tell us we have something to heal." My feelings were real; I'd earned them the hard way he was telling me. If I could stay with them, feel the pain just a bit longer, the healing work I was doing with Anne would, over time, release me from the depression.

He didn't tell me I should be grateful, or that I was ruining my children's lives, or that my husband deserved better. He didn't tell me to put on a brave face. Instead, Dr. Z gave me permission to believe my own truth—even if that truth was miserable. The hope and support he offered were exactly the medicine I needed most.

Before I left, Dr. Z did scribble out a prescription and hand it to me, in case the dark, suicidal thoughts became more than I could handle. I never filled it, but when things got tough, I'd hold that prescription in my hands and repeat Dr. Z's words: "You have every reason to feel sad and depressed." If I could believe I had a right to my own feelings then maybe, just maybe, I could begin to accept myself—all of myself.

In therapy, Anne wanted me to explore how I'd coped after I gave up the baby. What helped me go on? What qualities had I found in myself that carried me through the next days, months, years? I'd lost everything, and looking back I didn't know how I'd survived. I was at a loss. The only thing left in my life was "being able to love," but I couldn't imagine how that had pulled me through. When I couldn't think of a single quality that helped me survive, Anne asked me to tell her what happened after I left Chicago.

CHAPTER 22

—⚏—

Teaching

Atlanta, Georgia – 1975-1976

On August seventh, just days after signing the relinquishment papers, I boarded a plane in Chicago bound for Atlanta.

My parents met me at the airport.

"You look great honey," my father said as he hugged me.

"You can't tell at all," my mother whispered in my ear.

That was the one and only reference they ever made to my pregnancy. The three of us had made an unspoken pact to keep my secret and pretend like nothing had happened. They assumed I'd left my past behind or would soon "forget" as Monsignor B had predicted. On the ride home, my parents chatted about my brothers and sisters and caught me up on family news.

Mary Meurisse had also decided to live in Atlanta, and over the summer, she'd found an inexpensive two-bedroom apartment for us to share near the school where I'd be teaching. I borrowed money from my father until I got my first paycheck.

Two weeks and three days after I had delivered my baby girl in Chicago, I walked into the Immaculate Heart of Mary Elementary School in Atlanta "ready" to teach second grade. My sisters filed into their fifth and seventh-grade classes. And Monsignor B, head of the parish, welcomed everyone on that first day of school, including me.

In addition to teaching, I had a second full-time job—pretending that the last nine months never happened. Once again, I discovered that I was a talented actress. Sometimes, I even fooled myself.

During the day, I was a cheerful, enthusiastic first-year teacher. I had a wonderful group of students who loved coming to school, enjoyed all the creative activities I dreamed up, and were generally enthusiastic about learning whatever I presented. As long as I was teaching, helping children or preparing lesson plans, I was well. After all, I knew I could still love. And I loved my students.

But the minute I went home in the evenings, I entered the dark cave of my inner world, filled with unspoken thoughts and feelings. At first I had terrible separation anxiety, physically missing the feeling of my baby with me, in me, all the time. A part of me had been taken away, and I no longer felt whole. I longed to cradle her, check her breathing, find out if she was okay. I sat on my mattress hugging myself, rocking back and forth and reminding myself over and over that I had given her up because I loved her and wanted what was best for her. The separation anxiety kept me awake at night. I prayed endlessly for my baby. I prayed that her new family was welcoming her into the world and that they loved her as much as I did.

These nights were long and lonely. When daylight came, I'd become Miss Conboy, perky first-year teacher.

As the weeks passed, this split got harder rather than easier. I was exhausted—both physically and emotionally. My close proximity to the Catholic Church, Monsignor B, and my parents was only rubbing salt in my wound of shame and grief.

Also, although Mary Meurisse and I lived in a nice apartment on Briarcliff Road in suburban Atlanta, I was not safe. It started with obscene phone calls in the middle of the night while she was at work. The police came; we had our number changed and unlisted but within a month, they began again. We changed our phone number three times that year.

Also, on two different occasions, men followed me as I left school and forcefully tried to pull me into their cars. I'd torn myself loose and run quickly to the nearby busy street. But I was being stalked. The police didn't know if these instances were related, but they suggested I stop walking everywhere, which was difficult since I didn't own a car and Atlanta's public bus service was limited. They said my long blonde hair and daily routine of walking to and from work made me an easy mark. They implied that I was responsible for avoiding situations where these men could bother me again.

I needed a fresh start, and by January I knew without a doubt that I had to get out of Atlanta. I was willing to go far, far away. My plan to get married and set up housekeeping near my family had loosened its grip on me. Now, it was obvious that all bets were off. I had no idea where my life was going and I wasn't attached to anyone—not even my family. I had no particular place that felt like home. I'd lost touch with my old friends in New York and I'd cut myself off from my college friends—all except Mary Meurisse and Shannon. I knew I'd miss Mary Meurisse if I moved, but she'd already helped me so much. I was tired of feeling like a burden to her.

Swept clean of all expectations, I felt a peculiar lightness. It was freedom. I was free to go wherever I wanted. Free to do anything I chose to do. I'd shed the dogma that dictated every facet of my young life and now it lay in a heap at my feet like a burlap hairshirt. I was free—and my world had suddenly expanded. I mailed applications to the Peace Corps and several Catholic missionary groups, daydreaming about exotic corners of the earth and wondering to myself, *Where could I be most helpful? Which children need me the most?*

Apparently, somewhere else in the universe a benevolent spirit must have been asking, *Let's see, which children will help Peggy the most? Where could she go to find healing?*

—⚭—

Experiencing

Atlanta to Jasper, Georgia – 1976-1978

By April, the Peace Corps was offering me three placements in Africa, and the Catholic Missionary group had two posts in Brazil they hoped I'd consider. I was weighing my options when I met Larry, a young man from the north Georgia mountains. We were volunteering at a weekend camp for children with special needs. During a break, I was talking to a group of counselors, all young professionals, about the decision I needed to make, when Larry overheard me and interrupted.

"What are you *thinkin'*?" he asked in his slow Southern drawl. "Travelin' all the way to Africa or South America to help needy kids? Shoot, we don't have special ed in Pickens County! That's only two hours from here."

"What do you mean?" I asked, startled by his comment.

"I mean, only 'bout ten kids are in special ed and they have a crazy ol' teacher. The rest of the special ed kids don't bother comin' to school or they sit in the back of the classroom makin' F's or getting paddled for bein' stupid."

"Larry, that's hard to believe," I said.

"Why don't you come see for yourself? Whatcha doin' next weekend?" he asked me.

Sheer curiosity led me to Jasper, a tiny town in Pickens County Georgia. Larry introduced me to the principal of the elementary school, Mr. Jones, who proceeded to interview me and confirm Larry's claims about special ed, or the lack of it. Among Jasper Elementary's one thousand students in grades K-8, just ten of them were receiving special education services. There was no funding for new programs, but Mr. Jones wondered if I'd consider teaching first grade instead, adding, "I'm right impressed with your cree-dentials on this here resume."

I was right impressed that an impoverished community with virtually nothing to offer school-aged children with special needs was only one hundred miles from Atlanta.

I drove home thinking about whether to teach at Jasper Elementary or take one of the jobs in Africa or Brazil.

On Monday night at nine o'clock the phone rang. I was tired from my school day and busy working on Tuesday's lesson plans. "Hello?"

"This is Mr. Frank Jones, the principal of Jasper Elementary School."

"Oh, hello sir," I perked up, what in the world was he calling about?

"The Pickens County School Board met this evenin' and I called to let you know that they unanimously voted to hire you to teach first grade next year."

"Well, thank you sir," I said.

My mind raced as I noticed the application, still sitting on the floor next to my purse. I hadn't even filled it out. What was I going to say?

"So, do you accept?" he asked.

"I need to think about it. I've been accepted into these teaching programs overseas with the Peace Corps," I said.

"You know our kids could really use a good teacher like you. We don't want you to teach any ol' first grade. We want you to teach the Follow Through Class. It's federally funded for disadvantaged kids, got extra teaching materials and teachers' aids. Lots of these kids don't even have runnin' water in their homes and their parents are young and most are illiterate. It would mean a lot if you could teach these kids to read."

It was powerful to hear him say that these kids *needed* me. I was quiet.

He added, "You know while you're teachin' first grade next year. You an' I can figure out these ideas of yours about special ed classes."

That clinched it for me. I accepted.

By August of 1976, after a year of teaching in Atlanta, I had saved enough money to buy a small used car, and I was ready to venture into my new life.

I was twenty-three years old, and I didn't know a soul in Pickens County. Larry, the friend who'd arranged my job interview, had packed up and left for California.

Once I exited Interstate 285, the highway circling Atlanta, I was driving through the country, passing through quaint towns like Alpharetta and Roswell with antique shops and a stoplight or two. But continuing northwest, I saw only farms, pastures, and woods with an occasional stop sign when the small highway crossed another two-lane thoroughfare. As the road wound around hairpin curves and traversed more and more hills, I felt as though I was riding a luscious green roller coaster. I cranked down my windows and let the hot humid air envelope me. On this sultry August day, for the first time since I'd sealed a secret inside me, I found my voice and began to sing my favorite songs out loud, knowing no one could hear me.

I was starting fresh. A clean slate. I could be whoever I wanted to be. There would be no one to say, "You don't seem like yourself." No reminders to surround me. For the first time in a long while, I felt an inkling of freedom. I could breathe.

Although I would catch occasional glimpses of the distant mountains between trees or on small rises on the roadway, it wasn't until ten miles from Jasper that I could see Sharp Top and her sister peaks. Jasper lay at the foot of the southern tip of the Appalachian Mountains near the start of the Appalachian Trail. The soft green hills, the mountains, and the fresh air felt familiar, somehow. I was surprised by a strong pull within me, and I felt like I was coming home.

I knew I was approaching Jasper when I passed the Dairy Queen, then the laundromat, and several old service stations with groups of men hanging around talking. The blinking yellow light marked the crosswalk on Main Street.

Main Street in Jasper was home to a gift shop, a diner, a Woolworth's 5&10, and a small granite courthouse. Across the street, behind the county lock-up was the Pickens County Bank. I parked my little yellow Toyota out front, took a deep breath, and walked inside where two lady bank tellers glared at me from behind the counter. Larry had warned me that people here were highly suspicious of outsiders.

"Hi! I'm Peggy Conboy, the new school teacher in town," I greeted them enthusiastically.

"Oh yeah. I heard about you. Yer from the city," she said.

My breath caught. The city? How did they know I was from New York? Rural Georgians can't stand Yankees, but before I could work myself into a full-blown panic, she continued. "Yeah, they say you're from Atlanta and even went to some fancy college out of state."

"Yes, Ma-am. Well I was wonderin' if y'all might know of any place I might live 'round here?" I said in the best fake southern accent I could muster.

The two began a chatty dialogue. "What about Jimmy Smith's place, LeAnn?"

She gave a disgusted look, "No, it's a mess. She'll want somethin' nicer 'en that, Becky!"

Becky looked back at me. "Did ye chick the apartmints?"

The principal had told me about the county's cinder-block apartment complex with ten units. "They're all rented," I answered, wondering just what I was going to do if there was no housing in this county.

Then LeAnn's eyes perked up, "Hey what about Reverend Owens' place?"

"Yeah, I heard they just threw Janie out. Too many boy-friends visiting. She was lettin' men spend the night. That is just dis*gus*ting. Pretty little thing like her? Is she still workin' up at the shoe factory?"

They were about to get sidetracked with gossip when I interrupted.

"Where is Reverend Owens' place?"

"Just up the road a piece. Here, let me write his number down for you," Becky said as she pulled out the flimsy Pickens County Phone Book, and copied it for me. I thanked them and headed up to the pay phone by the County Courthouse where I called the Owens. The house was two miles from town on the main road. The Reverend told me to come right on over; he and "Mother" would be sitting out on the porch swing looking for my yellow Toyota.

Rev. Owens, as it turned out, was an eighty-year-old retired Southern Baptist minister. Pretty much the first thing he said was, "Well young lady, if you was to rent here there would be no drinkin', parties, or overnight male visitors."

"That's fine by me," I replied.

"Well Mother," he said to his wife, "I believe we got our-selves a school teacher for a neighbor." They had divided their small frame house to create my small two-room furnished apartment which had running water, electricity, and heat. For eighty dollars a month, I had everything I needed. I would live like one of the wealthy people in this county.

As I was unpacking my things, I came across my father's letter asking me to move to Georgia with the family for my senior year of high school. As I reread the letter I was shocked to read his recollection of something I'd told him when I was just nine: "One day I will teach in Appalachia." And here I was. Had I really known? I had forgotten all about my father's letter and how he'd used my dream of teaching in Appalachia to convince me to move to Atlanta.

Most of my students came from basic means and gorgeous land. The lucky ones had parents who worked at the shoe factory or the carpet mill; the rest of the families were on welfare. My students had electricity at home, but six out of twenty-four had no running water. Many lived in trailers or small cabins.

Although I arrived thinking I'd come to save these children, on most days, it was clear that I'd learn from them, too. The Follow Through Program required teachers to make home visits, so thanks to them I tasted my first acorn squash, learned to can summer beans, and even fed some pesky pigs. One time, I was even invited to stay for supper when the main course was squirrel.

Most of the county's dirt roads didn't have names or route numbers, so driving directions always included natural landmarks like trees, rocks, and creeks. Once I received directions that read: *Turn right at the barking black dog*, and sure enough, just at that curve in the road a black dog ran at my car barking and jumping, and I knew I was almost there. When I arrived at that particular home, James' daddy was settin' on the porch holding his shotgun, just waitin' to welcome me.

I quickly figured out that everything was "over yonder," relatives were all "kin," and any kind of bag was a "poke." Instead of saying good-bye, people in Jasper said, "Stay with me." I'd make lame excuses about needing to leave until another teacher told me that the polite response to "Stay with me" was "Come see me."

In the classroom, show and tell became my favorite part of the day. One Monday, Billy stood up and proudly explained that he'd been "pilferin'" the past Friday evening and held up a straggly big brown teddy bear for all to admire. "Wow," was the crowd consensus. I turned back to Billy clearly needing an education here. "I'm sorry Billy, where did you say you got the teddy bear?"

"Pilferin'," he answered loud and clear.

"Where's Pilferin'?" I asked.

They were incredulous.

"Pilferin' is at the dump," Billy said. "Ain't you never been?"

When I told him I hadn't, the whole class competed to tell me about all the toys, toasters, bikes and chairs their families had picked up for free, all while "a pilferin at the dump." Apparently, the first Friday of the month was the best day.

Then there was the tellin' part of show and tell. People in Pickens County sat on their porches and traded stories most evenings and these children were experienced storytellers. Chris, a stocky boy with a crew cut, shared his bear sightings. He lived up on the side of the mountain, and now that he was six, he was allowed to go huntin' with his Daddy, uncle, and cousin. He'd have us all in suspense as he spun a yarn about the "bars" as he called them.

Michelle told us about her dog having a litter of puppies and how they drank from the momma dog's titties. She explained it was better for the momma dog to feed the six puppies because the daddy dog only had one titty. When I told her that actually daddy dogs have *zero* titties, it kicked off a rather lively classroom discussion!

The Follow Through Program provided extra services, like dental care, for my students. A traveling dentist visited my class one day to teach basic dental hygiene and give each student a free toothbrush and toothpaste. He then did basic screenings, for which I was grateful because I'd noticed that the children's teeth were dirty and their breath was sour. He suggested I sit beside him as he checked their teeth. One at a time, they approached, and he looked in their mouths, counted, and wrote a number beside their names on his clipboard. In between students I quietly asked, "What's all the brown stuff on these children's teeth?"

"Tooth rot," he said. "The mommas put Coca-Cola in their bottles when they're babies. It's cheaper than milk and keeps them quiet. Young children love sugar. They'd probably all tell you they drink Coke at home, not milk."

The next student was Jason, the smallest child in my class who had great big curious eyes. When he opened his mouth, I saw that all of his molars were rotted straight to the gums. His front teeth were not much better. Even the dentist shook his head. "Do your teeth hurt when you eat Jason?"

"No sir. Only if I chew hard. I like soft food," he said.

My face fell and my heart sank. This would be just one of many heartaches I would feel for my students.

The Follow Through Program also provided free breakfasts and lunches, a clothing bank, and social services, while I received extra teaching materials and two full-time teacher's aids. The program had arisen from the generosity of the '60s and now fully matured in the 1970's, it was a great gift to the children of this Appalachian community.

About once a month I'd go to Atlanta to visit Mary Meurisse and stop by to see my family. Each time, my parents stuffed my car full of donations from people in the parish or the neighborhood who'd heard I was teaching in Appalachia. My parents' garage became a "Goodwill" center where they collected clothing, blankets, toys and books for my students. At Thanksgiving, with lots of assistance, I organized a large food drive for Follow Through families through the Immaculate Heart of Mary where I had taught the previous year.

My father and my Uncle Howard, who was visiting from New York, drove the two hours from Atlanta to Jasper to deliver some of the food baskets to the Follow Through Office. They peeked into my first grade classroom at the end of the day and joined in the singing of, "Let's Go on a Bear Hunt." After each student hugged me goodbye and ran to the buses, my uncle looked over at my desk and said, "What's with all the rocks?"

There on my desk was my usual pile of twenty to thirty rocks. I just laughed and explained that one day after coming in from the playground my student Sally, a bright little girl with straggly brown hair who always wore faded cotton dresses, told me she had spent all recess looking for a special gift for me. Then with her eyes twinkling, she drew her hand dramatically from her back and opened her palm to reveal a sparkly mica covered rock. I hugged her and thanked her for this generous surprise.

The next day three students presented me with gifts of beautiful rocks and the idea grew from there. When the bell rang at the end of recess, the teachers assigned to playground duty recognized the students in my class because they all carried rocks, which they each presented to me with a smile and a hug as they reentered the classroom. Whenever I'd get discouraged with slow progress or the sheer neglect these children faced, I'd look over at that pile of rocks and realize that, while they lacked plenty, my students never lacked for heart. And it was in the presence of their wide-open spirits—and this daily pile of rocks—that my own broken heart began to heal.

In the meantime, the well-intentioned adults in Jasper were looking at heart from a whole different perspective. Back in Atlanta, my friends and family wondered out loud who I'd find to marry up there with all those hillbillies. Little did they know that in Pickens County, my social life would become everyone's business. At twenty-three, I was the oldest single woman in the county, not openly condemned to the ranks of old maid, but close. I needed "to find me a man" they'd decided and, one at a time, I was fixed up with each of the county's seven eligible men. When the seventh one showed up with a bible—and proceeded to preach to me on my porch all evening—that was the last straw. Before they could explore neighboring counties, I spread the word that I actually *enjoyed* living alone and didn't care to meet any more potential suitors. The county matchmakers let up on me, for a time.

Later that year, four eighth-grade boys I had tutored came in one day wanting to talk. They had apparently spent a lot of time concerned about my social life. J.L., a tall handsome blonde young man spoke up first.

"Miss Conboy, we've been thinkin' 'bout why a pretty teacher like you ain't married and we done figgered it out."

I stared at him wondering what in the world these pubescent boys were going to name as my flaw!

He continued on in utmost seriousness, "It's yer car!"

"My car?" I laughed. I loved my little yellow stick-shift Toyota I had nicknamed Daisy.

"Yes," they all chimed in dramatically. I wiped the smile off my face.

"You need you a red corvette with souped up tires!" They went on to explain where I could purchase this new red hot rod and how beautiful I'd look in it. All the men would be after me then, they assured me.

I graciously accepted their suggestion and told them I'd think about it. Here was yet another group watching out for me. After they left, I realized that on a deeper level these boys wanted me to fit in and make a home here in Pickens County with them. Maybe the local parting expression of "stay with me" meant more than I knew at the time.

CHAPTER 24

—⚍—

Appreciating

Jasper, Georgia – 1976-1978

It wasn't just Pickens County's people that helped heal me. It was the land. Alone in the mountains, the natural world was extending an open invitation to come outside and play. And I did.

When I first moved in, I romped and roamed and wandered, getting to know every rock, tree, and stump around the house. The horse next door became my sunset companion. Each evening I'd climb the fence to bring her some sugar cubes or an apple. Then she'd follow me up the hill through the pasture, past a row of trees to a small clover-filled meadow, which faced west overlooking two calm green mountains. We'd stay and watch the sun gently set over the ridge, splashing the sky with peach, pink and golden light. Sometimes, I'd lie on the warm ground and feel the cool night air wash over me.

I still thought about my baby girl and prayed every day that she was safe and being loved and appreciated by her adoptive family. I reminded myself repeatedly that I had given her up in love. And it helped that my work in Pickens County seemed meaningful.

At night, the crickets and toads sang me lullabies and I never felt lonely, bored, or afraid. As I got more comfortable, I began exploring. Local folks were always happy to tell me about a certain overlook or a fresh-water spring I might want to check out. I took long hikes up nearby mountains. Sometimes I'd stop and hug a big old tree, and I would feel her hug me back. The sky seemed bluer, the clouds fluffier and softer than I had noticed before. The intricate beauty of the wild herbs and flowers filled me with awe. Sometimes I would get to the crest of a peak, find a perfect overlook and sing to an audience of trees and wildflowers. The wind encouraged the leaves to applaud me.

Following creeks and looking for waterfalls became a favorite past time. When the weather was warm enough I'd actually walk in the creek, using it as a trail. "Creek walking," as the folks around here called it, loosened my long tightened nerves and freed me to listen to the healing waters as they spilled over solid aged rocks. Time stopped as I sometimes stood under a waterfall as it pounded out the old fear, grief and rigid thinking from my body and helped me experience freedom of movement and spirit.

The nearest Catholic Church was small and modern, an hour-long drive away. When I attended Mass there, I felt the same old judgment and shame. By this time, I disagreed with the Church on so many basic issues that I knew it was time for us to part ways.

I was no longer willing to tolerate the male chauvinistic attitudes of Catholicism. I was clear women should be priests. And after giving up my baby, I had become pro-choice. I knew firsthand that for younger girls, or victims of incest or rape, abortion was the healthy and right decision. The bottom line was obvious: We could only truly understand our own circumstances, therefore, choice should be a personal decision.

The more closely I paid attention to the wording of traditional prayers and listened to the priest's sermons, the more rigid and judgmental Catholicism seemed. I never brought it up with my family, but eventually, I stopped attending altogether. Instead the earth became my church. I'd discover an emerald field of ferns, a spray of pink wildflowers beside a boulder, or step into a silent meadow facing a fawn eye-to-eye and know God. The sheer abundance of life in the mountains was testimony to the grace of a most generous creator. The mountains didn't have rules and requirements or mortal and venial sins to worry over. The only two guidelines I set for my church were to appreciate the earthly gifts surrounding me and to love others.

Those rocks and trees, trails, and waterfalls became my spiritual home. They accepted me with my past, in my present, and for my possibilities, and that made all the difference in my life.

CHAPTER 25

—⚭—

Searching

Richmond, Virginia – 1994

The two years I'd spent in Appalachia had helped me heal. I'd
met Dan in Atlanta during the summer while I took graduate
courses preparing to start the special education program
at Jasper Elementary. Dan, a third-year law student at the
University of Virginia, had come to Atlanta to clerk for a law
firm. After dating for the summer, we fell into a comfortable
long-distance relationship. But when he accepted his first
position as an attorney in Dallas, Texas, I moved away from my
mountain home to be with him. We married two years later
and moved again to his hometown, Richmond.

When we had first dated, Dan had listened quietly with
gentle eyes as I told him about my birth daughter. For the first
time in a relationship with a man, I felt heartfelt acceptance. And

I felt safe. Later, after we had our two children, Dan saw how much I loved them and he understood, even more fully, my loss.

Telling Anne about my time in Appalachia and my relationship with Dan gave me strength in my present-day life. I knew I was ready to begin the search for my birth daughter.

I poured over every book I could find about adoptions, searches, and reunions. I spent weeks trying to figure out where to start and how to go about searching.

When I signed the relinquishment papers in August of 1975, I was told that the agency would send me non-identifying information about the family who adopted my daughter, but under no circumstances was I ever to try to find or contact her. They said it would be devastating to the adoptive family and to my daughter. It was also against the law. But before I agreed to sign the papers, I'd confirmed what the caseworker had told me: When my birth daughter turned eighteen, I would be allowed to look for her.

The books about adoption searches warned that oftentimes agencies were not very helpful. They tended to believe that reunions were unnecessary and unhelpful, although I couldn't imagine why. I only hoped that, these eighteen years later, The Cradle still existed.

One morning after I got the kids off to school, I decided to make my first move. I took some deep breaths, steadied myself, and called Directory Assistance in Chicago.

"Yes, do you have the number for 'The Cradle?' It's an adoption agency." After a brief pause, the operator read out the number.

I stared at that number and wondered if I really had the nerve. I was simply asking for information, right? This call was routine for them, I told myself.

I sat at the table clenching my pen and pad and dialed The Cradle. A woman answered.

"Hi, may I please speak to an adoption caseworker?" I said.

"Yes, just a moment please."

A moment later I heard, "Hello, this is Margaret Bartosik. May I help you?"

Oh my God, *Margaret*—the same Margaret who'd been my caseworker eighteen years ago. Just hearing her name, I broke out in a sweat, afraid. The sound of her voice triggered a flashback, and I found myself back in her office.

"This is Peggy Conboy," I hesitated. "You were my caseworker in 1975?"

"I remember you," she said. What would she remember about me? What had she thought of me back then? Had she continued to think that I felt sorry for myself? Had she figured out why I gave her all those gifts? My stomach knotted up.

"I'd like to reconnect with my birth daughter," I explained.

"Why in the world do you want to do that?" She spat out the question as if I was the first birth mother ever to suggest such a thing. The tone of her question threw me right into shame, and I had to quickly steel myself to her insensitivity.

I said, "I've worried about her over the years, and I want to see if she's okay."

"I'm sure she's fine. Don't worry."

I couldn't believe my ears. Here was an adoption caseworker, apparently oblivious to the emotional issues surrounding *adoption*. I wanted to send her the books I had been reading like *The Other Mother* and *Adoption Reunions*.

Instead I asked, "Does the Cradle have a registry?"

"Yes."

"Can you tell me about it?"

"How it works is that one day, if they notice that both you and your birth daughter are listed in the registry, they will notify your birth daughter and counsel her about the pros and cons of reunions. If she is interested, they will give *her* your address and phone number."

"One day if they notice..." was all I heard. I knew their registry wasn't going to help me.

"Could you please send me those forms?" I asked.

"Yes, but really don't worry. She's fine." She said this in such a definitive way. I got excited. Maybe someone she knew had adopted my baby and she had been able to watch over her for me.

"Have you seen her or talked to her parents recently?" I figured maybe Margaret knew the family who'd adopted her, and she'd seen firsthand there was no need to worry.

"No," she replied, "but didn't you get the letter we wrote you?"

"What letter?" Had I missed out on information about her?

"We sent you a letter telling you about the family who adopted her."

"Yes, of course I got that letter, but it merely said the father was a businessman and the mother had been a teacher before becoming a full-time homemaker."

"Well wasn't that enough?"

Not quite, I thought, but did not say. How was this woman making me feel so bad all these years later?

I gave her my address for the registry papers and hung up, knowing full well that their registry was not going to help me reunite with my birth daughter in any way. I was disappointed.

A few days later, my determination kicked in again. The books I'd read said that hospital records sometimes provided information about the baby. I sent the hospital in Chicago a formal written request. The response took weeks, and when my records arrived, I was stunned to find no complications mentioned beyond the word "toxemia" in one of the blanks. Yet, right there, my eight-day stay was documented. At that time, the normal stay for a vaginal delivery without complications was three to five days. Most disappointing, the hospital records held no information at all about my baby.

Next, I made repeated attempts to access her birth certificate. Nothing worked.

With each small step of the search, I prayed to the woman from my Vision. I asked her to be with me and give me the courage to continue. If I sat very still and quiet and prayed to her, I could sometimes feel her with me. I would remember her loving presence and how she offered acceptance. I was reminded that she seemed to understand why I needed to do this search. It was enough to know that she had promised to be with me. Her loving presence didn't make any part of the search easy, but it filled me with the certainty and the courage to take each step as it came.

And the next step would be the most important.

After hitting three painful dead ends, my husband and I talked at length about what I should do next. He supported the work I was doing in therapy and he understood my need to search. Together we decided that I should hire a professional search consultant, even though it was expensive. I contacted a woman who had been written up in an adoption search magazine. She was very kind on the phone and briefly told me about her experience with searches. She lived in Arizona, but she did searches nationally and we could work by phone. She was sensitive to my issues as a birth mother and made sure I was seeing a therapist to support me through the emotions that were sure to arise.

The first piece of information she located was a copy of the birth certificate. When the mail arrived, I ripped open the envelope and there was my daughter's name: Lisa. As I scanned the birth certificate over and over, I began crying. I knew I wouldn't be listed as mother. Didn't I? Then why was I crying? The birth certificate made no mention that Lisa had been adopted by the man and woman listed as her mother and father. There was no acknowledgement of me whatsoever. I couldn't breathe. My heart ached. How could I still feel this bond so strongly when no evidence of it existed?

But now that I knew her name, I could think of her and pray for her by name. This was a big step but the consultant had other surprising news she'd uncovered along with the birth certificate. My baby was adopted by a family who lived in Connecticut. How could that happen if she was born in Chicago? How could the agency have conducted a home visit? How could they have checked on her like they said they would? They'd told me they would make several home visits to assure that the baby was safe, well, and happy. I felt betrayed.

Two months after I'd hired the search consultant, she located the family in Connecticut. My daughter was a freshman at Duke University. Finally, I knew that she was alive and well enough to be in college. I was so relieved and happy.

With this wonderful news, I could finally put down on paper the love letter I had written over and over in my heart. The reunion books suggested making the initial contact in writing so that Lisa could get used to the idea and respond when she was ready. It also gave her the option to write back or to call. I mailed my letter right away, anxious to finally connect. In it I told Lisa the circumstances of her adoption, a little bit about myself, and asked her a few basic questions.

Now that I'd found her, I knew I needed to tell my family. First, Dan and I would talk to Tommy and Julia. During the past year, we'd begun having weekly family meetings where we compared calendars, discussed family issues, and ended by giving each other compliments. We thought their upcoming spring break would be a perfect time to hold a special family meeting to share the news. They'd have the downtime to let the information sink in and to ask questions.

But as our meeting date approached, I felt my anxiety building up. Would they understand? Would they make the same mistakes I had? Would they still love me, knowing this? How would I tell them simply and honestly?

As planned, Dan came home from work during lunchtime on Monday of spring break and we held a family meeting at the kitchen table. I wondered if anybody could hear me over the pounding noise of my heart. "We are having this special meeting because there is something I want to tell you about," I began, slowly. "Some of it is sad and some of it is happy," I paused as my children's eyes grew wide in anticipation. "A long time ago before Daddy and I met, I fell in love. I got pregnant but my boyfriend didn't want to marry me. I was finishing college and I had no money, no job, and I had no place to live. I loved my baby, but I believed that I could not take care of her. So I decided to give her up for adoption. It was the saddest thing I have ever done."

I stopped to take a deep breath. "There are laws that said I was not allowed to find out her name or where she lived. I could never check on her to see if she was okay. That is the sad news." I quickly went on, "This year, when she turned eighteen, I was allowed to look for her. I hired someone to help me find her." A big smile came across my face as I added excitedly, "The good news is that I found her! You have a half-sister named Lisa, who is eighteen years old and lives in Connecticut."

Julia's face lit up. "Oh boy, we have a sister! You definitely made the right decision," she said emphatically. "If you hadn't married Daddy, you wouldn't have me and Tommy."

I hugged her and turned to eight-year-old Tommy whose eyes had filled with tears. "That's sad, Mommy. I can't believe I never knew that." I acknowledged that it had been very sad. But I reassured him that she was probably happy in her new family, and I was happy now that I had found her.

Then their questions began: What does she look like? How big is she? Can she come visit us? Can we bring her to the pool this summer, so we can introduce her to all our friends? Can we be friends with her family?

Later Tommy remarked, "I can't believe I have a *sister-in-law*."

Among my six brothers and sisters, four had no idea I'd had a baby almost nineteen years ago and the other two knew nothing beyond that simple fact. I wrote to tell them about what had happened, the circumstances surrounding my decision to give up the baby, the search, and what I knew about my birth daughter so far. To me, writing the letter was a bit like sharing news of a pregnancy. I was letting them know they'd have a new family member to welcome.

I'd wanted them to say "I am so sorry for your loss" and "I am so happy for your reunion." Unfortunately I didn't *know* this until I got a radically different response.

My letters were not well received. My siblings were either silent or they excused the way the family and the Church had handled my situation. They were circling the wagons, protecting the family, my mother, the Church.

I was deeply hurt—too hurt even to ask for what I needed at the time. What I really needed was support for the reunion and a word of welcome if Lisa wanted to meet them. Clearly I wasn't going to get it.

I tried to stay focused, looking forward to my reunion. I had grand visions of talking to my birth daughter, seeing her soon, getting to actually touch her and hug her. I was sure my love would somehow make her life better and more complete. And I knew that a reunion would cure all my ills.

Two days after I mailed the letter to my birth daughter, I found myself trembling whenever the phone rang. I'd break into a sweat at the sight of the mail truck. A week went by. Then two. I worried I wouldn't get a response. By the third week, I was distraught.

Finally, after four of the longest weeks of my life, the mail came and there it was, the letter from Lisa. It was May 17, 1994. Briefly, she shared where she lived, which boarding school she'd attended, and the sports she'd played. The note could have been written to any stranger. Her life was busy, she said, and she didn't wish to correspond any further. She closed by thanking me for giving her up eighteen years ago and wishing me and my family a lifetime of happiness.

I was devastated. I honestly didn't believe my heart could break again. I'd read every encouraging word in *People Searching News* and in books like *The Other Mother, Synchronicity and Reunions, Birth Bond,* and *Adoption Reunions.* I reminded myself that our relationship might be *limited*, but *no contact*? I had never allowed the pain of that thought to do any more than tiptoe across my mind.

I decided the search had been a waste of time, money, and energy. I hated that people who were unsupportive of the search would think they'd been proven right. "See? She didn't want you in her life," their cruel voices scolded. I wanted to choke Ann Landers who never missed an opportunity to speak out against reunions in her column.

During the search, I sometimes fantasized about speaking publicly about searches, reunions and open adoptions. Instead, I was so hurt that I actually thought that maybe I'd made a mistake—maybe I should've had an abortion. All these years of pain for a person who doesn't seem to care that I existed. The hurt felt overpowering.

It was midday and the kids were still at school. I carried the mail upstairs to the guest room, my private space. I cried for hours, hoping each tear would wash away some of my pain and sadness. That's when I noticed that a small package had arrived in the mail the same day. I ripped it open, and found a book about Kuan Yin, Goddess of Compassion in the Buddhist tradition. Mary Meurisse had sent it, and in her note, she explained that Kuan Yin might be my Compassionate Goddess. The book said her name means, "She who hears the

cries of the world." Was this the woman in my Vision? The
book described the same compassionate care I'd been offered
on the labyrinth.

In the Vision, I had asked for her help with the search.
Although searching had been difficult, I had felt supported
and clear that I needed to do it. I recalled the feeling of being
washed in pink light, and it had given me courage. I sat with
the book and prayed for her help with my grief. Could she
make it go away? No, but I felt reminded that even though I
was heartbroken, I was loved.

Later when I told Dan and the children that Lisa didn't
want to meet us, we cried together and hugged one another.

Since my brothers and sisters hadn't approved of my search, I
couldn't bear to tell them that Lisa wanted no further contact.
I assumed they'd claim they were right, that a reunion wasn't
a good idea.

In the days to follow, I fell into episodes of depression and
self-hate. At times everything felt dark again. I was tired and
unmotivated. My mind berated me for feeling sorry for myself,
for not earning money, for being self-centered. The voices
would not quit. I wanted to kill myself just to stop the inner
pummeling. I prayed for help.

Finally, one day, I knew what I had to do. I was absolutely
certain, and I also knew no one would understand. It sounded
irrational, but it would save my life. I had no other choice. *Are
you sure?* I asked, speaking to wherever the certainty had come
from. *Yes.* It was definite and clear. I needed to separate from
my mother, brothers and sisters, and their families. I had to
step away from my family.

We lived five hundred miles apart, so it was easy not to visit. But I needed to cut off all contact. To my surprise, my body relaxed at the thought of a separation. It felt like a relief. My mind, however, hated the idea. How was I going to explain this? I had a really nice family. They might have different ideas about adoption reunions, but they were nice people who probably loved me. Right? How would I announce that I was cutting them off for a while?

I knew my choice would be misinterpreted. Still, I had to risk it; otherwise it felt like I would die. It was hard enough to understand my emotionally fragile state, much less explain it. I wish I could have asked my family for what I'd needed. But maybe I knew they could never give it. Not because they were unkind, but because what I needed could only be found within. I could only get there alone, with the loving support from my own family—Dan, my children—and my close friends.

I truly felt sad about the separation. I knew it would cause pain, and the last thing I wanted to do was create heartache for someone else. Rationally, the idea didn't make sense. But it would save my life. This message came from an internal source that was certain. And certainly, it was mysterious.

The next week I told Anne about my plan. She challenged every aspect of my decision: What if someone gets sick? How about your children, can they contact their cousins? Can your mother have contact with your children, her grandchildren? I had decisions to make. Why did I want to separate, Anne wanted to know. I told her that I had gotten very clear that I couldn't both get well and be in contact. I had work that could only happen during a separation from them. Anne finally accepted my decision and later that day I wrote a simple letter to my mother, brothers, and sisters, asking them for a time of separation while I did some personal work.

It was May and I thought the separation would last for the summer.

Over time, in the presence of loving kindness from the Vision, from my husband, children, and close friends, I decided that the search had been the right thing to do. I had received exactly what I needed. I'd wanted to know if my daughter was okay and if she needed me. I'd learned that she was in college; she'd always felt loved by her adoptive family, and that she didn't need me. Although I didn't get the prize I had hoped for, I got something else: *I got me.*

I'd worn the shackles of shame and secrecy for so long, and they had weighed me down. I was healing the depression that I'd silently endured throughout adulthood. I could stop worrying now. My birth daughter had my address and phone number; she could contact me if she needed me. I knew my husband loved me enough to support me through my grief and depression, and I trusted him more than ever. My close friendships took on a deeper level of trust. And, finally, I'd always thought nobody would love me if my secret came out. But I was wrong; I was loved.

Because I had always valued my ability to love and help others, the most painful suggestion anyone could make about my search was that it was a selfish thing to do. In the end, the hardest thing I had to admit was that it didn't directly benefit anyone but me. I'd had to discover I was worth it.

Part II

1994-1998

IN HONOR OF THE CHRYSALIS

No one understands
how a butterfly is made.
Yes, we can name the stages:
egg
larvae
caterpillar
butterfly
But, how does a caterpillar know
to shed its skin and be wrapped
in self-created darkness?
How can it let itself liquefy
in order to be made anew?
This we do not understand.
But, we know how essential
the chrysalis is,
this place that holds,
gentle and firm,
for the mystery to play out
until we get our wings.

Joan Garrabrant

—⚬—

CHAPTER 26

Questioning

Summer arrived. Waves of grief washed over me occasionally, as the dream of meeting my birth daughter faded. Still, I was healing.

This June afternoon reminded me why I loved summers as much as my children did. We'd hang out at the pool, explore a park, or invite neighborhood children to play. The long days unfolded at a leisurely pace.

Today the kids were using a refrigerator box from the nearby appliance store to build a fort in the backyard. I took my journal to the screened porch and sat down at the picnic table to write.

As I sat looking across the yard at our tall sycamores in the back yard, a question that had pestered me with sneaky insistence came back to me. I wrote it down in my journal.

Is that all there is?

I had arrived for my first appointment with Anne with this question haunting me. But I was too ashamed to tell even a therapist. The question seemed greedy and unappreciative. There was an implicit assumption of wanting more. I had so much to be thankful for—kids, husband, house, and meaningful work. How could I presume to ask if that was all there was? Appreciate your life, I had told myself.

Forced gratitude led me instead to feel ashamed and stuck. I couldn't allow myself to look for what was missing, and more importantly, I couldn't begin to look for what *else* was *possible.*

Eighteen months later this question felt completely different.

There was no shame or need to push the question away. I even knew the answer.

I looked down at my journal where I had written, *Is that all there is?* and simply wrote,

No. There is more.

I had barely begun to understand my Vision of the goddess, much less her message. *I am you and you are me.* She hinted at a spiritual realm beyond our physical reality, and through her I saw our innate capacity for love expand beyond imagination. Love comes at us from all sides. And more love was coming my way than I'd ever thought possible, love I'd dismissed or disregarded before. Through my healing work life felt larger, more joyful, free. I was still raw from the search for Lisa, but I felt alive and craved knowing what "more" was waiting for me to learn and experience.

But as I wrote, I wondered if the question was directed at me. Is that all there is *of me?* Am *I only* who I've been so far?

Here too, the answer seemed simply,

No, There is more.

I am still becoming.

I looked forward to exploring this, but being well aware I was still a mom, I looked at my watch and realized that it was time to begin exploring dinner.

CHAPTER 27

—٭—

Knowing

Later when school supply lists intruded on summer, I was anxious to get back to work that fall. I'd only briefly cut myself some slack, putting my adoption search and therapy ahead of teacher-training and volunteer duties. Now that the search was over and my sessions with Anne were winding down, I assumed I'd find a job teaching at VCU or training sex-education teachers. But whenever I pictured myself in those jobs, the cheerful willpower that always propelled me into helper-mode would collapse under the weight of a strange dread and exhaustion I'd never associated with work before. From deep within, my once-dying soul was sending me a clear message: *Not this, not now.*

The "old me," the can-do helper, was the only me I'd ever known. So what was this strange new message? Where was it coming from? I'd always looked outside myself, scanning the horizon for people who needed my help, looking outward for feedback and approval. But now I was curious about this inner voice and what it could tell me. Was a guardian angel directing me, I wondered? If so, why did this message, this *knowing*, seem so firmly rooted in myself?

Looking back, I'd known that my work felt more like a chore than a joy. But I was so skilled at dismissing my own feelings that I never noticed this simple truth which, when ignored, had tunneled deep within me where it conjured night-mares, headaches, and stomachaches. I had been sleepless and empty inside.

The same internal stirring had prodded me to search for my birth daughter and pressed me to separate from my fam-ily. Guided from a place of inner certainty, beyond words or explanation, I had done the unthinkable—twice. Had it been there all along, I wondered? Did the same inner-knowing guide my dolly tea-party baptism so God could welcome my Jewish playmate in heaven? Did it allow me to accept Dag Hammerskjold's "say *yes* to life" invitation as I contemplated suicide at fifteen? And when I almost died after giving up Lisa, did it convince me that I was still capable of loving and being loved?

I believed it was. So the next logical question was this: If my internal compass had helped me navigate crises, could it guide me through peaceful times? If I listened carefully for signs about my work, would it help me find my way? For now, I could only see where *not* to go. But I vowed to keep listening. I wouldn't shoehorn myself back into my old career, even if I couldn't see what was next.

CHAPTER 28

—⚇—

Moving

Once I turned down the volume on my helper-voice and got comfortable with "not knowing," I became clear about what might come next.

First, we needed to move. We loved our city neighborhood with its maple tree-lined sidewalks. We belonged to a babysitting co-op of twenty-four families. The library and pool and a park were nearby. I'd imagined our small brick cape cod would always be home for me.

But Dan and I needed some relief from private school tuition, and the kids needed more diversity in middle and high school. We wanted a neighborhood where they could walk to a friend's house or hang out at a park without our constant supervision. These practical realities supported what had preceded them—my own knowing that it was time to move.

Dan and I drove around considering different parts of town until we finally found the kind of neighborhood we were looking for with good public schools. By the end of August, a house in that area came on the market. It was only two blocks from a neighborhood pool and Bandy Field, a public park that was open green space. In addition, the brick ranch was close to the campus of the University of Richmond, which had a lake with pretty walking paths. Tucked behind two giant magnolia trees, the house had a full basement playroom that opened under the canopy of a two-hundred-year-old willow oak tree. The house was secluded, private from the street, and matched my own desire to go within.

It was settled then. My work for the fall would be to get the old house ready to sell and begin readying our new house for our eventual move.

CHAPTER 29

───ᴡ───

Converting

Although my soul was no longer dying, I didn't really know
how to keep it alive. Could it start to die if I didn't pay attention
to it? How would I nourish it? *Could* I nourish it?

I missed belonging to a spiritual community. I missed the
prayers, the hymns, the sacred texts, and stories. I wanted to
explore spirituality. My Vision made it clear that the physical
world was just a glimpse of our world. It had been a long time
since I grappled with spiritual questions. Was there an afterlife? And who was Jesus, really? I longed to search and explore,
to read and discuss different viewpoints. Although nature was
still central to my life, it had become a very lonely way to find
a connection with God.

Recently I had visited a local Unitarian Church. I loved
their open-mindedness, inclusiveness, and social activism, and

the sermons oftentimes gave me food for thought. I met like-minded people. After a few months of attending on a regular basis, I felt ready to join. I enrolled in the New Members Course led by Reverend Rolfe Gerhardt, the minister. During the four evening sessions, we learned the history of Unitarian Universalism and the seven principles upon which UU Congregations were based. They included such notions as valuing the inherent worth and dignity of every person, encouraging spiritual growth, and supporting individuals in a free and responsible search for truth and meaning.

The message was clear: Unitarians believe that spirituality is a personal choice and ultimately a lifetime search. This church was exactly what I was looking for at this point in my life.

At the end of the final class for new members, Rev. Rolfe announced, "We'd be delighted to have you join, if you feel that First Unitarian Church is for you." He smiled and passed out membership forms to those interested. As I was given mine and began writing my name and address, I broke out in a sweat and started having difficulty breathing. What is wrong with me? I wondered. Fear and panic set in.

Thoughts and images flooded my awareness. I imagined the nuns telling me that I was going to be struck by lightning for joining this pagan religion. I was becoming a heathen. Was I really? Would joining this pagan religion damn me and keep me from everlasting life in heaven? But I didn't really believe in heaven, did I? Was it really okay to join this church? What if my brothers and sisters, or my mother found out?

I read over the basic principles of the church once again and thought about the nice people I'd met at services. I forced myself to override my fear, fill out the form, and turn in my dues. I kept breathing.

I had to keep telling myself that these old voices trying to stop me were ridiculous and childish. Of course I wasn't going to be struck by lightning. Okay so an electrical storm was flashing outside, but I was safe inside a building. Right? I collected my belongings as the thunder rattled the windows and walked up to the Minister to turn in my form and pay my dues, still sweating profusely and feeling anxious. I told Reverend Rolfe that I was having a big body reaction to joining the church.

"Have you ever had anyone ever tell you how hard it is to join this church after being raised as a Catholic?" I asked him.

"Oh yes, Catholics, Baptists, really anyone that grew up in a religion with a lot of dogma," he said.

"Did they mention the body feelings of fear? I kept thinking I was going to be struck down by lightning as I finished filling out the form and even as I handed it to you." I laughed as I said this, making light of it. It seemed so ridiculous.

Another new member overheard me and said, "Oh, I'm so glad to hear you say that. I kept imagining my mother repeating over and over that I am going to burn in hell for sure now."

I turned to her and said, "Do you feel all nervous and like this is a really big deal?"

"Yes, this *is* huge for me to join a non-Christian religion."

Rolfe said that others had told him about going through a lot of fear and doubt but that he never quite understood the big deal about it.

"I mean it's not like you've agreed to a set of beliefs or anything. You've just filled out a form with your contact information and paid a basic membership fee."

The other woman and I just looked at one another. Then what *is* the big deal here? I wondered.

Months later I approached Reverend Rolfe with the idea of designing a six-week course to assist those members transitioning from a religion with dogma to this religion based on personal searching and spiritual freedom. He liked the concept and together we created and co-facilitated the course, which I entitled, "Recovering From Controlling Religions."

Although I designed the course to help others, it gave me the opportunity to begin coming to terms with the impact of Catholic teachings and understand the origins of the fear and guilt I often experienced. I re-examined basic beliefs. I knew that I did believe in a God. I believed that Jesus was a great teacher and healer but not that he was God's only son. I no longer believed in heaven and hell. I believed that at death we returned to the earth. I believed men and women were equal and that therefore they should have equal responsibility and leadership roles in religious institutions. Possibly the most important aspect of the class was being with a group of others who were new to the experience of spiritual freedom. We told stories and laughed about our childhood ideas of spirituality while offering one another support in coming to our own present truths. This was a relief to me.

I still had questions and didn't know how to define "soul" really. And I wasn't sure if I was to *do* anything about my Vision. But as a member of the Unitarian Church there was encouragement and acceptance for what now felt like a spiritual journey. And I liked the company of my fellow travelers.

CHAPTER 30

—⚉—

Asking

That fall I spent long hours clearing, straightening, and packing up our old house and cleaning and painting the new house. Our old house was taking longer to sell than we had expected. I had lots of quiet time to ponder things.

One day as I painted Julia's bedroom, I was reminded of a central component of the Midlife Class I'd taken the year before. In one exercise, our teacher Nancy asked us to tease out our Life Question. "It's an internal question that drives us to live our lives a certain way," she explained. "We can live our whole lives without articulating this question. By identifying it, we're empowered to choose."

Initially this question was hard for me to access. Then it hit me. For as long as I could remember, I'd lived the questions: *How can I help? Who needs me? Who needs me most?*

But I felt changed. At any time I could certainly see where there was a need, where I could go help. But that was an outward-focus. I was different now. And as a matter of fact, a moment of clarity had happened just the day before.

After I dropped the kids off at school, I came home to the old house where we were still living and got lost in thought wondering about these internal silent changes and no clear pathway ahead. I prayed that I would know what was happening to me. As I was thinking about my life, I was going through the motions preparing to work on the accounting and shipping aspects of my book business. I had self-published my books on puberty and sold them to distributors, bookstores, schools, and individuals.

I laid out the envelopes, labels, packing tape, and boxes on the dining room table. Then I went upstairs to the playroom where there were boxes holding several thousand books. I counted out fifty girls' books and then gathered the fifty boys' books that I needed to fill today's orders. In the trance of a routine, I came downstairs and stacked the one hundred books on the dining room table all the while lost in thought wondering about my life. Should I do that parent program I was asked to do? Should I get involved with the kids' soccer league again? What kind of work could I possibly do now if it's not teaching or teacher training?

I sat down and began labeling envelopes and boxes. As I went to count out twenty books for an order, I paused and stared at my books.

It was then that I *first saw* my books. I sucked my breath in.

It wasn't like I hadn't been looking at them almost on a daily basis for the past few years as I packed them up for mailing or brought them to workshops I taught. Not only that, the creation of the book had taken painstaking visual attention to detail for layout, artistry, design, paper quality, font, cover design, and color, etc. But when I wrote the books, I was totally driven by the *need* I saw in the community for books like these on puberty. I was committed to providing sex education for children with special needs.

Although I had paid close attention to the creation and marketing of these books, I had never once thought about them in relation to me *personally*. Here I was, only minutes before, praying for help to understand what was going on in my life. And there on the table were one hundred books, each cover and binder now announcing in neon blue and hot pink typeface:

Changes in You
Peggy .C. Siegel

I had to laugh.

I had spent several years writing and producing these books, and now for three more years, I had sold them, done public speaking, taught and trained teachers. At the moment with the recent delivery of my second printing of the books, our small house had almost four thousand copies of *Changes in You*. In sex education circles my name was synonymous with *Changes in You*.

After focusing for the better part of five years on the *external* project that I had named *Changes in You*, here I was wondering how to deal with my very own *internal* and inexplicable changes in myself.

I considered the possibility that one of the changes in me was my Life Question. But what was it now? Was there a question that was nudging me to paint our new house, leading me to fill book orders, but directing me *not to* return to teacher training? A question that would help me know what to do next for work?

No longer was I driven to see where conditions or policies needed to be changed, or who needed to be taught what in order to make the world a better place. There was no looking around to see who or what organization needed my help. My old life question apparently had left.

I needed a new life question.

I liked this premise that we have an underlying life question that directs us. It seemed true to me. I wanted to figure out what mine was. I pondered this as I continued painting. Nothing sensible came up, so I put on some music and forgot about it.

But later when I went for a walk, a question came to mind. It was:

What is mine to do?

It surprised me that the question came up when I wasn't even trying to think of one. Plus the feel of the question was new. It seemed kinder and that it could lead to the balance I yearned for. The answer might allow me to choose to take care of a project at home, enroll in a class, or take a nap even! I also really liked it because it gave me permission not to feel like everything was my responsibility. With my other life question, no matter how much I did, I was ultimately still aware of an unmet need somewhere else. It was hard for me to ever feel satisfied with myself. But maybe asking, *What is mine to do?* would lead me to that place of knowing, that inner compass, that seemed to be directing me.

I had been looking for a way to use this inner compass without being in crisis. Maybe this question would be a doorway for me.

CHAPTER 31

—⚡︎—

Pondering

What is mine to do? As I turned the question over and over like a puzzle piece, my labyrinth Vision came to mind. Was the Vision holding a clue?

In the year since the compassionate woman emanating her pink light had appeared before me in the labyrinth, I'd searched for explanations. How could this Vision seem more real than my everyday reality? How could someone that I couldn't touch or even see with open eyes be more real to me than the floor beneath me? It wasn't a dream; I was wide-awake. It wasn't "my wild imagination;" any fantasy of mine would have included Jesus and a handful of saints. Plus, I'd always pictured God as a man. At the time, I'd even shaken my head to try and clear the Vision, thinking my mind was playing tricks on me. But in spite of my doubt and disbelief, she remained. She was real.

At times, I could still sense the pink light warming my body. I felt its loving comfort like a soft baby blanket gently placed around me.

I had entered the labyrinth that night mired in self-hate. I never could have forced myself to feel loved, much less experience every cell of my body being washed in some pink light that felt like compassion to me. I felt loved fully, not for anything I'd done. I was just loved. I also felt her deep understanding and concern about my suffering, which eased my pain. Never again could I *not know* or be *unaware* of what compassion felt like. From now on, I would always recognize its presence.

I couldn't explain her away, and my body still knew the sensation of her light. I knew this Vision was real. I could never dismiss it, deny it, forget it, or pretend it didn't happen.

Through the Vision a door to my heart had been opened, reawakening my sense that God was alive in the world. But unlike before, I was newly aware of a feminine expression of divine spirit. I experienced a spiritual presence that cared enough about me to help me to heal, to teach me about compassion, and to comfort me after my surgery. I could have a personal, direct relationship with God again. But this time, it would be different.

As a child, I'd begged and negotiated trades: *Please God, I'll say two rosaries today if you'll just give us a snow day*, I'd pray whenever a history test loomed. This new divine being wasn't one I could bargain with; she didn't control circumstances. On the labyrinth, when I told her about my desire to search for my birth daughter, she said that she would be with me. Even though I had felt comforted and supported by her, the search was still difficult, and in the end, heart breaking. But this feminine spirit had offered me compassion and "to be with me," exactly what I needed to face life as it was.

When I went to Appalachia, left organized religion, and found spirituality in nature, I had kept up these conversations. Only instead of God, I was connecting with Spirit by asking the trees for strength, the sweeping mountaintop views to help me see my way through difficulty, the rocks to help me be steady, and the waterfalls to help me flow with life's challenges. I felt loved just hiking in the mountains.

I knew I could continue my relationship to the natural world, but now I had to reckon with this...Vision. Throughout my search for Lisa and the healing work that followed, I'd felt her loving presence. I continued to thank her and feel tremendous gratitude for her presence. But as I was feeling better, I found that I was assuming she had served her purpose in my life. I thought she was probably busy helping others. I figured I could still talk to her when I needed help.

But I also had this nagging sense that maybe I should *do* something with the Vision. Although, I couldn't imagine what. The only visions I had ever heard about were used to support the faith of whole communities of Catholics, like the children at Lourdes. Mystics like Hildegarde and St. Theresa were led to devote their lives to God and share the messages of love and faith they had received. Some visions had led their seers to become priests, nuns, or church leaders. I had never heard of a person who had a vision and then, like me, went home to fold the laundry.

I wanted someone to tell me what to do with the Vision. But I felt I couldn't tell anyone except my husband, my friend

Mary Meurisse, and my teacher Nancy. The event was too sacred to share. I found there was an intense vulnerability around sharing it. I didn't want anyone to dishonor or dismiss one of the most important moments of my life. Conversely, I didn't want anyone to think I was someone special because this had happened to me. I knew for certain, I was still plain old ordinary me. Stuck in paradox, I was both afraid of people thinking *nothing* of it or *too much* of it. For the time being I wrote a prayer in my journal:

May I one day know how to share that pink light of compassion with others.

Also, the Vision had awakened in me an intense longing for a spiritual community. I wanted to share the search for truth and meaning with others. At times, I had felt that connection at the Unitarian Church, but I knew there was more.

That same fall, the funding was cut from the Women's Resource Center where I had taken the class on Midlife and walked the labyrinth for the first time. When Nancy called to tell me the Center was closing, she added excitedly that she and a few others were creating a new nonprofit called Chrysalis, whose initial purpose was to bridge the connection between psychology and spirituality. Because I had been helping her occasionally with labyrinth walks, she invited me to participate in the programs they were organizing. They had created a retreat day called Ember Day to be held four times a year at the change of the seasons to help people rekindle their inner fires. I loved the idea.

Is this mine to do? Am I to get involved with The Chrysalis Group? I asked myself. For now, the easy answer was *yes.*

CHAPTER 32

—w—

Dreaming

Dreams had been instrumental in changing my life; well, actually nightmares had. So when Nancy told me about a weekly dream group she was starting with her friend Joan, I signed up before I had any idea what a dream group was.

The Talmud has a saying that goes, "Every unexamined dream is like an unopened letter." And I've never been one to leave a personal letter unopened. Nancy suggested I read Jeremy Taylor's book *When People Fly and Water Runs Uphill* in preparation. "All dreams come in the service of health and wholeness," he sums up his philosophy on the first page. He explains how dreams, speaking in the language of symbols and metaphors, generally have multiple layers and meanings. Because dreams can be so complex, he suggests that it is more helpful to do dream work in a group rather than alone or with only one other person. A group is better able to access a full range of possible meanings and find multiple layers of significance.

The dream group format included one dreamer each session. Joan and Nancy had developed questionnaires that were used to help stimulate participant's reflections. There was time allotted for personal reflection and sharing. They also provided opportunities to integrate the meaning of the dreams through artwork and writing.

I'd always had vivid dreams and wondered why I could remember so many each night. I had oftentimes entertained friends with descriptions of my wild nighttime stories. Did they really mean anything?

My last flirtation with dream-study was in college, when I broached the subject with a theology professor, Father Griffin. He told me point-blank that it was a waste of my time, that dreams were silly and meaningless. Analyzing my dreams could ruin my life or make me crazy, he said adding, "Peggy, it would be selfish to pay all that attention to yourself." I believed him. After all, he was a priest.

This opportunity to be in a dream group seemed like a great chance to try something novel and shake off those old ideas. I could be part of a small group of women—including two Jungian trained therapists—who believed that this rich, colorful nightlife of mine had meaning.

By January, I joined five dreamers and two leaders seated in a circle around a small table with a candle in its center. We shared first names and what drew us to dream work. The other women, including the leaders, seemed to be in their fifties. I was forty-one. We were blank slates to each other. Daytime details like jobs, families, neighborhoods were beside the point. One woman had agreed in advance to bring a dream to our first session. She described swimming through a grocery store, and we took time to reflect on the "If It Were *My* Dream…" questionnaires we'd been given. Which image stood out for you? What are your associations with that image? How would you title the dream? What stories, songs, or sayings did it bring to mind?

At first I couldn't imagine what her dream had to do with *my* reality. But I quickly felt like we were solving a riddle. Somehow, even though we had tossed out a hodgepodge of ideas, our dreamer was energized by our insights. And oddly enough, I felt like I'd learned something about myself. My college hunch had proved right. Dreams were meaningful.

The first dream *I* decided to bring to the group recalled the old nightmares where my life was threatened. Only this one had an interesting twist:

I was shot dead in downtown Richmond. But then in the dream I said, "Wait, can I do that over?" Out of the blue the answer came back "yes" and the dream started over. This time, as my attacker approached, I merely lifted off the ground flying, getting out of harm's way quickly. I was so happy to be flying that I headed first to Washington, D.C. then to Disney World. Just as I gently landed in front of Cinderella's Castle, I saw Mary Poppins performing. I joined her on the stage and together we belted out the song "A Spoonful of Sugar," singing:

"In every job that must be done, there is an element of fun.

You find the fun and snap, the job's a game."

As we finished singing, we smiled at everyone. Instead of being shot down, I felt grand, happy, and free.

Telling the dream to this small group of women was as nerve-wracking as giving my first speech in high school. I felt self-conscious and embarrassed, like I wanted everyone to quit looking at me and thinking about my dream. I was tempted to make light of it and say, "Oh it's nothing. Don't bother working on this. It's just a cute, funny little dream." I had plenty of practice dismissing my dreams.

But I stayed quiet, trying to let myself and the other women take my dream into serious consideration. The rest of group settled into the process, which was like holding a container that said: *This dream has meaning. We'd like to help you figure it out.* After some quiet reflection, they shared what stood out for them and also asked me helpful questions. What in this life gives you the same sensation as flying in the dream? What part of yourself guns you down? What have you "risen above" in this life? What are your associations with Washington, D.C.? What about Mary Poppins? What does she mean to you and do you know why the dream-maker picked that particular song for you to sing? In group dream work, although others toss out ideas and questions, only the *dreamer* can say for sure what the dream means.

Mystery novels had been my favorite genre of books, and I began to see that dream work was like piecing together clues. Clarity often showed up as a state of "aha" or "yes, that's it."

This particular dream showed me that I'm in a different place than I was a year ago when I was getting killed over and over. No longer a victim, I was freed up to fly away, to rise above difficulties and live. I didn't have any connection to Washington, D.C., although we enjoyed weekend trips to see museums and shows. Would D.C. figure into my future?

The question, "What part of me guns myself down?" struck a chord. I recognized my inner judge saying things like: *Dreams?* Are you serious? When there are children who need your help? What a waste of time. And you know everyone will think you've lost your mind.

This voice was powerful, spewing old unhelpful attitudes and trying to hold me back. The dream suggested I rise above these old voices and not let them take me down. If I wanted to feel that sense of freedom, I'd have to fly above it.

I smiled remembering that Mary Poppins was one of my favorite movie characters, and I marveled at the fact that when the group asked me the words to this song that I loved at the age of ten, I remembered all of them. The whole song is about work being fun. Although I enjoyed my work over the years, I tended to accept more and more stressful or controversial positions. I had not been on the lookout for work that made me happy for quite some time. My fellow dream group members suggested that I might look for work, volunteering, or a creative endeavor where I experience a sense of freedom like I did flying in the dream or enjoyment like I felt singing on stage with Mary Poppins.

What a great question to ask myself. What kind of work would bring me a sense of freedom and fun?

When I left dream group that day, I felt happy. It had been so interesting to try and figure out what this dream might be about. It touched me the way the group had honored my dream and had been so encouraging. But most of all, I had this great sense of relief. Finally, after all these years, I could connect with my vivid nightlife. It was like I had a group of friends or a guide with me all along and I didn't know it. I had never given myself permission to, nor known that I could, have a meaningful relationship with my dream world. Now I knew that I could. My dream had come to suggest that I look for what would help me feel free. Free enough to fly. For now I felt free to explore the rich symbolic language of my dreams. This was the first of many that would guide me.

—⚍—

CHAPTER 33

Writing

Growing up, I always hated writing. Red ink peppered my school assignments and my masters' thesis inspired my grad-school professor to remark, "It may behoove you to take a writing class." Even after I'd published two books, two curricula, and a handful of magazine articles, I didn't consider myself a writer.

But recently I'd felt compelled to jot down family stories and write about my labyrinth Vision to honor the experience. So when I came across Night Writers, a class on the personal essay led by author Phyllis Theroux, I signed up. A master of the genre, Phyllis' essays had been published in the *New York Times*, *House Beautiful*, and *The Washington Post*, among others. Our class of eight gathered around her dining room table to weave our own stories into personal essays. I was finally "behooving" myself.

Phyllis served homemade apple pie and gave us assignments like "tell me about being alone" or "the dinner table" or "a funny moment." A skilled seer, she could always "shine a light on the gold in the story." I found her guidance magical.

One of my first Night Writer's essays was about the time I spilled the gallon of red paint on my students. Whenever I told this story, my gestures, pauses, and sidelong glances were as vital to the story as the paint itself. How could I possibly write it? The following week, my grand-scale screw-up, and the accompanying humiliation, was a hit with the Night Writers. I learned then that the best personal essays capture universal life experiences. As Phyllis put it, "The more specific to your own life, the more likely a story will resonate with others."

When Phyllis asked us about "being alone" I realized as I wrote that with six brothers and sisters, eighteen aunts and uncles, and forty-two first cousins, I'd rarely spent an hour alone until my two years in Appalachia.

It was through the writing that I began to find my voice. I had never been afraid to speak up for others; now I was writing from my own experience, my point of view, my words, my world. I was learning more than how to relate a funny story in words. I was learning to tell the truth about my life.

After being in the Night Writers group for about a year, Phyllis suggested we write about "valuables." We could interpret the assignment any way we wanted to, but we should notice our very first thought, our strongest association, or what stayed with us about the topic.

For me "valuables" posed a question: What lifelong gifts did I want my children to carry with them? I'd just re-read Victor Frankl's *Man's Search for Meaning,* and his interviews with Holocaust survivors consistently proved that positive memories of loved ones or natural beauty helped them hold onto the belief that there was meaning in life. I decided that I hoped my children would grow up rich in memories. Some, like family traditions, took planning. But lovely moments that quietly whispered, *pay attention,* were everywhere, too.

Around this time Phyllis contacted a woman she knew at WCVE, our public radio station, to ask if local writers could read their stories on the air. Phyllis herself had been an on-camera essayist for McNeil-Lehrer Hour on PBS and she "just happened to know some excellent local writers." The station-manager was thrilled with the idea.

Phyllis chose my story on the topic of valuables to be the first of mine on the radio. The next week, driving to the station I felt stage fright coming on. I was no stranger to public speaking and nothing could be worse than the time I faced two hundred special education directors while holding a life-sized model of a male pelvis, complete with erect penis. (My seventy-four-year-old expert co-facilitator had forgotten to bring the flaccid version!) So why was my throat tight and my stomach churning now? What was I afraid of? I was only putting a personal story out on the airwaves.

Stephanie, the young radio host, met me at the reception desk and invited me back to the studio for the taping. In her smooth FM-radio voice, she assured me that we could fix any and all mistakes. "Just relax and you'll do great," she added. Somehow this wasn't enough. As I began reading I kept losing my breath. Then thoughts began rushing in. "No one will hear this. Right? It's goofy. It's silly. Why am I putting myself out there like this? I'm a terrible writer."

The rushing thoughts competed with the words I was reading, and when Stephanie played back a bit of my first reading, I sounded breathless, like I had run up a flight of stairs and a mad strangler was gripping my neck as I choked out the words.

Stephanie very calmly said, "I loved your story. Let's try it again." Then she hesitated and said, "See if you can relive the moment as you tell the story."

"In the Light of the Moon," I read the title as I settled into that otherworldly night.

Heavy, pounding rain on the roof had been beating a steady bedtime rhythm. As the wind picked up, the electricity went off and the rain stopped. A dark silence permeated the house. I said good night to my ten-year-old son Tommy. "What about the lights?" he asked.

"It's bedtime. We don't need them," I explained. "They'll be back on soon," I added reassuringly.

Then I noticed a bright beam coming through the blinds. Oh no. Maybe we're the only ones without power, I thought as I peeked out to see if any of our neighbor's lights were on. But instead, hanging low above our darkened neighborhood was the brightest, fullest moon I have ever seen.

Tommy ran over to the window, and we stood in awe gazing at this iridescent light. I suggested that he go to bed with the blinds open so that the moon could keep him company in the black darkness of the house. My husband was putting our twelve-year-old daughter Julia to bed as I quietly sneaked past her room and out the front door for a longer look at this extraordinary sight.

Because our house was downhill from the street, with two towering magnolias in front, I had to go up the sidewalk to the street to get a clear view. I looked up and took a deep breath of amazement and immediately went back in and asked my husband and children to come outside. Julia and Tommy jumped out of bed, thrilled to be invited outside in their pajamas at 9:30 on a school night. They burst out the front door, ran past the trees into the street.

It was early October. The air was warm and heavy from the tropical rains, leftover from a distant hurricane that had swept past us during the evening. A hush surrounded us in the blackout. And there in the sky the big moon's white glow was almost too strong to stare at directly. But that is not all I wanted them to see.

A magnificent performance was going on. The moon was decorated by wisps of dancing clouds, thin curtains of changing shapes that were leaping and pirouetting in front of it. The lovely prancing lace was so low that Tommy jumped up imagining that he could catch a ride or touch the hem. Some of the other clouds were running past in a race, only to be held up in a cloud traffic jam we could see in the northeast sky. The silky shapes of the scarves and veils moving quickly in front of the spotlight looked like time-lapse photography. Just watching this fast action made me feel energetic. I wanted to somehow join in.

How could a blackout be so bright? Surely tonight the moon must be giving off some of its own light, we decided.

Turning, we admired our amazingly clear shadows and my husband sang Cat Steven's song about "a leapin' and a hoppin' in the moon shadows."

Then my daughter looked back up into the sky and was so moved by the sight that she began to do what I had only imagined having the freedom to do. She raised her face and hands up and out to the moon and began slowly spinning in circles. Without a word, I followed, and then Tommy and my husband did too. For a brief moment we all spun slowly in circles with hands raised and faces up to the light. I felt the clouds breathing on me, and the moonlight kiss me, and I prayed for this moment to last.

Suddenly, Julia caught herself, looked around at us and said, "Oh no, what if the neighbors see us! They'll think we're crazy."

We giggled imagining all kinds of wild interpretations of our moon dance, but even as we spoke we could not take our eyes off this bright pearl in the sky and the frolicking wisps of clouds that raced across it.

Eventually we went back into the house. The children went to bed with their blinds open, so they could sleep in the light of the moon. Later as I lay in bed, I prayed my children would remember this night and a moon to carry with them forever.

———————

I looked up from my paper and Stephanie was smiling at me. "Perfect," she said, "not one mistake."

"Good advice," I said, "it was nice to be back in that moment."

Driving home, I felt both great relief and a new fear arising. *What had I done?* I worried about what people would think—not just of my writing—but of me and my family doing our moon dance in the street. I reassured myself that it would be played during a mid-day radio show when no one would be listening anyway. When the story finally aired, my phone rang immediately. "How did I miss that moon?" my nature-loving neighbor Sylvia lamented. "What a beautiful story!" Other friends wished they'd been there to join our moon dance in the street.

"Writing is connecting," Phyllis explained later. "The process isn't complete until it connects with an audience." She encouraged me to submit essays to magazines. Putting personal stories out for the public to read was a leap from reading aloud in my writing group. Still, my urge to help people led me to work on a personal essay I had written about the search for my birth daughter.

In all the articles I'd read about adoption searches, I'd never read an account of a birth mother who, after locating her child, was denied a reunion. I wanted to write this story for the other birth mothers who might come up empty-handed like I had. Even without the hoped-for reunion, the search had helped me heal my adoption experience and ease the open-ended worry I'd carried for eighteen years.

In the essay, I admitted, "My greatest fear was that doing the search was a selfish thing to do. In the end the hardest thing for me to admit was that it didn't directly help anyone but me. I had to find that *I* was worth it." As soon as I wrote this I knew how to end the article and I knew why I wanted to publish it: "I want you to know that *you* are worth it too."

The article was published in *People Searching News* magazine, my first essay to appear in print. It had felt very risky, even bold, to share the piece with the Night Writers. Sending it out for publication made me feel vulnerable. But I wanted other birth mothers to hear my story, and I was assured of anonymity only because of the publication's limited readership.

I backed away from submitting essays for publication after that. The heavy-handed editing and rejection that comes with professional writing would only squelch my voice. My task was to cultivate this newfound freedom of speech. I needed a safe place with kind guidance to "behoove" me to keep writing and editing. Night Writers was just the place.

CHAPTER 34

—··—

Finishing

Over the year, my life became full without being too busy. I had settled into my weekly dream group and my biweekly writing group. At Chrysalis, I served as registrar and helped with the labyrinth and retreats. My *Changes in You* books and curriculum were still selling well, so every week, I filled orders and responded to inquiries.

I had begun seeing my therapist, Anne, less regularly. Often, I'd arrive at a session unsure of what I wanted to talk about. Finally I told her I couldn't think of anything more for us to discuss, adding, "Do *you* know of anything I need to deal with?" I had been determined to uncover every wound that needed healing. I wouldn't stop now if we had work left to do.

Anne sat quietly pondering my question and then replied, "No, I don't know of anything right now."

"Well, I want your honest answer. I don't want to quit therapy only to find out two years from now that there was this whole other issue I had missed," I said.

She seemed startled. "Well, I can't promise that you'll never need therapy or to ask for help again." She let me take that in and then added, "I can't even promise that some of these same issues won't ever come up again. But I *can* tell you that I haven't noticed anything that you have avoided or been too afraid to tackle." Then she paused and said very gently, "It's okay to just be in this more settled place and begin to enjoy your life more. You have worked really hard. Maybe you could take it easy on yourself for a while."

We reflected on our work together, and she offered reassurance that it had been just the right time in my life to heal my past. Circumstances had come together to allow me the opportunity. I wasn't ready to ask for help earlier, and my nightmares wouldn't have let me wait any longer. Timing, she observed, sometimes synchronizes with our lives, naturally.

I told her about a recent dream and wondered how it related to my present life. In it, I was standing on the platform at the downtown Richmond train station in the midst of other travelers when a man approached me, dressed in ordinary gray cotton robes with a hood so large his face was in its shadow. He was a gentle presence, so I was not afraid when he approached and stood directly in front of me and said:

"Remember this.
For the soul, three things are necessary:
connection, belonging, and individuation."

I had woken up repeating these three words over and over to myself and immediately wrote them down in my dream journal. Anne, too, wrote them down as I told her the dream. Then she asked, "Do you think it's true? That the soul needs those things?" she asked.

"Well I've been thinking about it a lot since I woke up saying the words, and I can say that 'yes,' it seems true, and I'm also surprised by it."

"What is the surprise for you?"

"Well, if someone had asked me what the soul needed, what is necessary, I probably would have said love, faith, forgiveness—those kinds of qualities."

"So what do these words mean to you?"

"I guess I've been thinking about whether my soul is getting what it needs."

"And?"

"When I think about how I feel in the Dream group, the Writing Group, Chrysalis, and even sometimes at the Unitarian Church, I think I have a sense of belonging. As a matter of fact, I haven't felt belonging and connection this strongly since high school. And having spiritual friends feels really good and right. I can see why the soul needs them."

"What about the individuation?"

"Funny, but I actually had to look up the word. I couldn't remember where I'd heard it before or even what it meant."

Anne nodded and said, "And?"

"Then I saw it was Carl Jung's word. He used it to identify the process through which a person becomes her 'true self,' I was intrigued that the soul needed that."

"What comes up for you about it?"

"Well, I've been puzzled about the separation from my family, but now I think it's related to this notion. I think I needed to individuate from them. I just wish I could do it without the physical separation."

Each time I considered reconnecting with my family, I would panic at the thought, imagining what they'd say about me now. My life had taken a turn that was entirely different from my upbringing. It felt good *not* to worry about what my mother or brothers or sisters would think. My dream artwork covered the laundry room walls. I'd created a class on the Divine Feminine. I'd published the story of the search for my birth daughter. I'd written about my Vision, clearly more Buddhist than Catholic. I assumed my family would disapprove, but joining the Unitarian Church? To the Catholic Church, Unitarians were pagans. Hadn't I spent years of elementary school raising money to save the world's pagans?

I didn't believe my family could accept me, or the changes I'd made in my life. I wasn't willing to stop my spiritual journey, yet I wasn't ready to explain it or defend it either. The changes in me were new, so I still felt plenty of doubt and vulnerability. I wasn't ready to stand up for myself or face their possible judgment.

Besides that, my dreams relating to reconnecting with my family consistently sent a pretty clear message: *Not yet.* In the most recent one, I had gone to see my family. As I approached the house, someone walked up and pulled my plug. I "deflated," becoming just a pile of skin in a puddle on the ground. Apparently I needed some further work to hold my own.

Anne suggested that I pay attention to my individuation. "You'll begin to have a clearer sense of yourself." She also encouraged me to listen to my inner guidance and my dreams. And she assured me that I could come back anytime.

I thought I would feel uneasy letting go of this lifeline I'd had for two years, but instead, I walked out of her office and into the daylight filled with gratitude.

CHAPTER 35

—⚡︎—

Longing

And, just like that, I had reinvented myself. Chrysalis, dream group, and the writing workshop now filled my days. Each was interesting. I was even having fun. But a key ingredient was missing from the mix. I couldn't put my finger on this particular longing. I just sensed an absence. Undefined.

Whatever-it-was had fueled my years in the classroom. In my twenties, it gave me the courage to fight the sixty-year-old speech therapist who insisted twelve-year-old Heath, a deaf boy with Down Syndrome, shouldn't be taught sign language. Six weeks later, Heath proudly translated sixty flash cards into sign language for his mother, concluding with three words she'd never heard him say: I. Love. You. I felt it again as I diagnosed fifteen-year-old, Jay, who'd been marooned in eighth-grade with a form of dyslexia so severe that educators had nicknamed it "word blindness." As I explained his test scores, Jay looked up at me and said, "You're the first teacher who didn't think I was stupid." We spent the rest of that semester decoding road signs, so Jay could earn his learner's permit, transfer to vocational school, and realize his dream of becoming a mechanic.

And when the girls in my fifth-grade sex-ed class took turns dipping a tampon into a glass of red-tinted water, delight came over me. "Cool!" they said, as the tight white bullets expanded into soft pillows and turned red. An ordinary day at school, another teacher might say. But, for me, the knowledge that these girls would move into puberty free from the bodily shame and disconnect that had marked my own childhood brought a satisfaction like no other.

I had always cared deeply about almost everything. This was both a curse and a blessing.

Passion had fueled my efforts. It was a self-sustaining cycle that worked like this. Because I cared deeply, passion arose along with the energy to "do." Then, being involved in work that I cared deeply about further energized me and led me to continue caring and feeling like my work made a difference. It mattered. Passion was a compass for me. It directed me toward meaningful work and gave me the energy to do it.

But where was my true north now? Yes, I had this new inner awareness. I was asking: *What is mine to do?* and *What would be fun or freeing?* These questions had ready answers in the mom department. But it was not pointing toward any particular kind of paid work or profession. I longed for my old experience of passion. Could I will myself to be passionate? No. It needed to arise. Some days I wondered if it would ever arise again.

Around the time this deep longing gnawed at me, I happened to go to a Bruce Hornsby concert. His rippling piano riffs and laid-back vocals were all over the radio waves those days. But in concert, the man was on fire. As he sang and played, Hornsby and his grand piano became one. I watched from my third-row center seat while he sweated, knees up, seat bouncing, rocking, pedaling, pounding, straining, grimacing, and grinning for two and a half hours. His passion was palpable. The music and the musician merged, stirring the deep longing I'd felt for those transcendent moments when my own gifts had found their purest form of expression in my work. William Butler Yeats had once asked, "How do you tell the dancer from the dance?"

After the concert I wrote an essay about the transcendence I'd witnessed in Hornsby on stage. I longed for work with the power to consume me as Bruce's music consumed him. It wasn't dissatisfaction I felt. I enjoyed my groups and classes; each day was interesting. But I had known the deep joy of losing myself in meaningful work, and as I sought to reclaim it, imagined several work scenarios. I would teach, maybe. Or consult. Now that I knew the question, I was impatient for an answer to emerge. I scanned the want ads to see what piqued my interest. Nothing did. Why, I wondered? Why couldn't I know?

Dreams Overnight, May 1995

Two weeks after the Hornsby concert, I attended a Chrysalis-sponsored "Women's Dream Overnight," organized by our dream group leaders, Nancy and Joan. "So let me get this straight," Dan asked, looking over his newspaper at breakfast. "You're going to a slumber party for grownups?"

Twelve-year-old Julia's eyes widened, and she set down her spoon in her cereal bowl: "Want to borrow my sleeping bag, Mommy?" Spiritual growth wasn't always solemn, I conceded. I hadn't had a sleepover with women-friends since college. I was looking forward to it.

The Overnight was held in a large downtown liberal Episcopal Church. About twenty of us arrived with our sleeping bags, pillows, and dream journals. The canvas labyrinth was laid in the church's carpeted community room about fifty feet square, and we rolled out sleeping bags in the adjacent formal library. We met in small groups for some preliminary dream work, then gathered on the labyrinth to invite and honor the night's dreams. At ten o'clock we entered into a silence that would last until the next morning at eight. Some of us wrote in our journals or did artwork. Occasionally someone stood and tiptoed toward the labyrinth, which was available to walk all night.

I laid my sleeping bag in the corner to the right of the labyrinth opening. Since I'd had my Vision while walking this labyrinth, I felt a warm connection to the space. I had walked it several times since my initial time and hadn't "seen" anything or anyone. But the labyrinth still brought a quiet peace. When I entered with a question in mind, I'd usually receive a gentle piece of guidance by the time I finished walking. Sometimes I'd get a symbol. Other times, I'd hear words to a song.

By eleven o'clock, everyone began getting ready for bed. The room was quiet, lit only by the soft glow from a handful of votives flickering around the labyrinth's edge. I was keyed up, filled with gratitude for my fellow dreamers and my proximity to the forty-foot labyrinth, which was rarely unfurled.

I decided to walk it. I slowly followed the painted lines on the canvas, the back-and-forth path weaving me around the center. My mind quieted. When I arrived at the rose-petaled center I sat and prayed. Just content to sit, the time passed. I was the only one awake in the room, just me sitting cross-legged in the middle of the labyrinth. I was in heaven. There was nowhere to go and nothing to do but just be there. I began feeling sleepy, and since I knew I wasn't in anyone's way, I laid on my stomach with my head resting on my forearms in the center of the soft canvas labyrinth and soon fell into a deeply restful sleep. I had no idea how long I slept.

At some point, I was awakened by—a poem! I could both see the words and hear their rhythm. I knew I needed to write it down quickly before it got away. I tiptoed out of the center of the labyrinth, making a beeline for my journal and pen. Quickly I wrote:

"COME PASSION!"
Where are you?

"Come Passion!"
I need you.

"Come Passion!"
I am you.

"ComePassion,"
You are me.

Compassion.

I had never noticed a relationship between the words "come" and "passion." All these months I'd been asking, *Where is my passion?* I had been shouting to the universe, *Come Passion!*

Now there was this poem though. Maybe I wasn't to look for "passion" to lead me but rather "compassion." Where would compassion lead me? How would compassion lead me?

A few days later I reflected on my Vision and the poem. The poem repeated the lines I had used to invoke God the evening I had the Vision. "Where are you?" and "I need you." And the poem contained the same words spoken by the woman in my Vision, which were, "I am you and you are me." If she was right, was *come passion* the same as compassion? I thought about how I'd felt washed in her light of compassion. I wondered if someone like me could possibly offer compassion in this, its purest form. Could I access compassion that healed? I had no idea how to do such a thing. But I had to admit, *that* would stir my passion.

—⁓—

CHAPTER 36

Trusting

Work, I knew, would figure into my future. And I would either be passionate about that work, or I would experience compassion. Still, I had no idea what that work would be. My inner world seemed like a busy intersection, gridlocked as the unanswered questions piled up. Luckily I seemed to be surrounded with people who didn't know the answers. The Unitarian Church, in fact, was just the place to embrace questioning. Whenever an evening program piqued my interest, I'd attend.

That's how I encountered the Humanist Group.

One Sunday, the church bulletin announced that the Humanists would meet to discuss the question "What is the Meaning of Life?" on Wednesday. I was thrilled at the prospect of discussing this among intellectual and open-minded Unitarians, especially humanitarians.

That Wednesday, I was surprised to be joining a group of men, all ten to twenty years older than me. I was curious about discussing such a profound topic with a group of men. Where in the world were the women?

Dispensing with introductions, the group leader presented facts about the size and advent of our solar system. Human life was comparatively recent, he noted, and reeled off an impressive list of books he'd been studying. Finally, he asked: "What is the purpose of the universe?" He wasn't asking about the meaning of life, as I'd expected. The men batted around ideas about the origins and the evolution of the universe, in highly scientific terms. After about twenty minutes of banter, one man said, "What about psychology?" His tone was derogatory. "They make such a big deal over emotions. Why have human beings evolved with feelings? Why do we all dream at night?"

My cue to speak. Here was something I understood, something personal. I loved dreams. Plus, I was still focused on the meaning of life itself. I wanted to explore that question. So I spoke up: "I've been in a weekly dream group for a year now, and I find that my dreams are full of information about the meaning in my life."

The men turned and glared at me. Granted, I was trying to nudge the subject a bit. But the men seemed upset. One by one, they fired responses at me.

"All scientists I've ever read say that dreams are merely the random misfiring of neurons." His body was coiled tight, jaw clenched. I saw his anger, and felt a stillness come over me.

The next one spoke, "All psychologists and scientists I know think that looking at dreams is as helpful as staring at your navel."

Another, "How can you prove that dreams are any different than throwing a pile of random objects on the table and reading meaning into where they land?"

Interesting, I thought. The priest at Notre Dame had used these arguments to dissuade me from studying Carl Jung. I sat quietly, while another continued the attack.

"A dream is nothing but a rehash of the day before."

The man sitting next to me chimed in: "I'm diabetic and I have nightmares when my glucose level is high, and I need to give myself a shot. Nightmares are just chemical reactions in the brain." Arms folded across their chests, heads nodding, the men reached a consensus: Dreams were meaningless. They seemed intent on proving me wrong and changing my mind.

Another time in my life, I might have burst into tears and bolted from the room. I surely would have backed down. But that evening, under the glare of the Humanists, a perfect clarity settled over me. It was unwavering truth. I, for one, had received healing and insight from my dreams. I didn't need to prove it to anyone. It was just true.

Very calmly I looked around the room, into the eyes of each of the men. "I *said*," pausing, "*my* dreams are meaningful. I never said *yours* were."

I surprised even myself. I didn't care what these men believed. I felt no judgment about their dismissal of dreams and no desire to convince them about my own experiences. I was completely calm. We sat in awkward silence until someone returned to the comfortable topic of science.

But as their discussion faded, I knew I'd tipped the balance on some inner scale. This was a turning point. For the first time, I'd withstood the negative judgment of others, and I hadn't cared one iota.

I didn't try to win them over.

I didn't need to be liked.

I hadn't wanted to appease them.

Somehow, I'd risen above their judgments. I'd been impervious to their hurt.

I had trusted my inner experience.

I knew my own truth. I had trusted it over theirs.

I spoke it.

Declared it. To men, even. Men who held stubbornly to their beliefs.

I didn't know how clear I had become until this moment. For a whole year, I'd written down my dreams every morning and delved into their meaning with a like-minded group. The guidance and support I'd received from dreams left me certain that they were leading me toward a life filled with mystery and purpose. If I hadn't understood this before, I knew it now.

That was my first and last meeting with the Humanists. How could I have confused them with Human*itarians*. When I got home from the meeting, my husband kindly reminded me that Humanism is a coldly rational way of looking at the world. "Um, and Peggy?" Dan added, "Humanists generally don't believe in God." I had faced down a roomful of atheists— not philanthropists. And I was stronger for the experience.

—m—

Belonging

Speaking up to the Humanists felt so good that, soon after, I took a bold action on a dream.

In the dream, I'd been entrusted with a chest of precious gems and artifacts. My mission was to protect the chest until I could put it in good hands. Night after night, I guarded these treasures until, in a new dream, I met a group of students who understood the value of my treasure. They knew how to care for the carved wooden icons I'd found, and I trusted them to keep my cache safe.

When I jotted the dream in my journal, I sensed a message about permission. *You're safe now*, my dream was saying. *It's okay to share your valuables; you've found the right people.*

The dream message encouraged me to share the story I had written about my Vision with my dream group. I reworked the essay over and over, hoping to capture my labyrinth Vision in language vivid enough to convey the presence of her compassionate spirit. The week before Christmas, I offered the story to the women in my dream group as a gift.

Before reading it, I recalled my recent treasure-guarding dreams. I wanted to give them a gem I had been safeguarding. I hoped my Vision experience might hold meaning for their life as it had in mine. After I read it, I gave them each an envelope with a copy of the story folded around a small oval piece of violet velvet that had pink glitter, scattered like stars, across it, a small symbol of her robes and light.

This was a huge leap of faith for me. And the women honored my gift. No one tried to interpret the story. They simply received it respectfully. The words "I am you and you are me" seemed meant for *all* women, not just me. And that morning, I knew I'd put them in safe hands.

In the New Year, I formed a women's spirituality book group. Seven of us gathered to explore the idea of the Divine Feminine and discuss *The Feminine Face of God* by Sherry Anderson and Patricia Hopkins; *Crossing to Avalon* by Jean Bolen; and *A God Who Looks Like Me—Discovering a Woman Affirming Spirituality* by Patricia Lynn Reilly.

I immersed myself in a photography class, which brought the natural world into focus. By that spring, another dream changed my relationship with the Chrysalis Group: In the dream I was in the hardware store, paying for the key to my new office. I was excited about finally having this job, the one I had searched for in my waking life. I looked down at the key and recognized the pink plastic tag on it. It was the Chrysalis office key. When I woke up, this seemed odd. Chrysalis didn't have any jobs.

That week in dream group, I described the key image during our brief check-in. A month later, Nancy called and asked if we could meet. She was writing a book about midlife, she explained, and she needed help running Chrysalis so she could focus on the book. "Your dream about the key felt like a message for *me*," she said. She wondered if I would consider serving as Chrysalis' *President*, while she served as CEO. I was shocked, but the answer was a clear "yes." *Yes*, this is mine to do. The work even met Mary Poppins' requirement for "an element of fun." I loved the people who served on the Chrysalis board. And I could take classes for free. I loved the programs Chrysalis offered, so I considered this tuition perk a form of pay.

I'd been worried that the "new work" I was anxiously awaiting would consume more hours than I could spare. But this job was perfect. I'd be immersed in an organization dedicated to change and growth, spirituality, and psychology—my interests, exactly.

Nancy was a mentor to me. I admired her integrity, and I'd sought her wise counsel more than once. I was flattered that she'd chosen me to step into her shoes and thrilled to work closely with a woman I wanted to emulate.

Was this the "new work" I'd sought? It felt right, but my hunch that something else would arise never left me. I just didn't need to know that particular answer right now. I could wait.

I was no longer who I was, and not yet who I was to become. I pictured myself somewhere between the caterpillar and the butterfly. What better time to be president of a group called Chrysalis!

I settled into my new role aware that Chrysalis was guided by thoughtful people of integrity who had come together to create a safe space for people to explore their inner landscape and consider how it's connected to Spirit, to themselves, and to the world at large. Chrysalis offered practice groups like the dreams group and Ember Days (quarterly silent retreats); spiritual tools like the labyrinth; and classes and speaker programs designed to stimulate and inspire.

Nancy vetted all speakers carefully. She knew their books well; often she'd studied with them. Under her discerning eye and leadership, Chrysalis attracted nationally known speakers. Jeremy Taylor, cofounder of the International Association for the Study of Dreams and author of *Where People Fly and Water Runs Uphill,* shared his dream expertise. Jean Bolen, author of *Goddesses in Everywoman* and *Crossing to Avalon,* discussed the gifts and challenges of midlife. The Rev. Lauren Artress, the Episcopal priest from San Francisco who introduced the labyrinth to the United States, led several workshops on how to use this spiritual tool. And Marcus Borg, author of *Meeting Jesus Again for the First Time,* led a lively program on the historical Jesus.

Nancy looked for thoughtfulness and depth. She was adamant that Chrysalis would *not* offer superficial psychology, quick fixes to complex emotional or spiritual issues. She hated the term "New Age" and dismissed psychics, astrologers, and channelers as ungrounded charlatans lacking in spiritual and psychological depth. Chrysalis, she made it clear, would never support New Age programs.

Through her work at the Women's Resource Center, as a therapist, and teacher herself, Nancy knew a lot of people. When she thought someone would enjoy an upcoming program, she'd call to invite them personally. It was Nancy's invitation, in fact, that first drew me to a Chrysalis event. These well-tended connections and the carefully chosen programming earned Chrysalis its reputation as a safe space to explore spirituality and psychology.

That fall, my friend Barbara and I formed our own weekly dream group. The ongoing groups were full and more women were expressing an interest. Barbara and I had become close through our work on the Chrysalis board. We both had education backgrounds, experience in group-facilitation, and combined, we'd logged five years in dream group. Barbara also had a Master's in Religious Education. Nancy and Joan gave us their blessing.

The teacher in me was overjoyed. I'd found a place where I could soak up the knowledge and insights I'd been craving then turn around and share them with like-minded people. When Kay, a psychologist with an expertise in Himalayan art, joined the board, we connected immediately, and within months, we were collaborating on a new class, "Women in Myth and Folktale—Forwarding Our Journey Through Story." Kay brought her love of stories and her expertise in psychology and art. I devised the lesson plans using my teaching and facilitating skills. Together we decided that our class would explore the question: What guidance could these stories hold for us as women today?

Mythology was new for me, but its similarity to dream work was uncanny. "Myths and dreams speak the same language," Joseph Campbell once wrote. Both read like puzzles filled with symbols. At school, the nuns had considered mythology, with its gods and goddesses, heresy. It defied the Church's core belief in one God. No Goddesses.

Through Chrysalis, I had uncovered a deep network of interesting thoughtful people of all different faith backgrounds. I felt rich in friendship and connection. For the first time in a long while, I felt at home with myself. At home in my life. Chrysalis was providing what the dream said my soul needed: connection, belonging, and individuation. And I was serving a non-profit whose mission was to provide a safe haven for personal and spiritual growth. Exactly what *I* needed.

—⁓—

CHAPTER 38

Becoming

Just after Julia's twelfth birthday, Dan asked her if she would like to become a Bat Mitzvah when she turned thirteen. Through the Bat Mitzvah ceremony, she would affirm her faith and be embraced as a member of the Jewish Community. Preparation required intensive study of Hebrew so she could recite prayers and read aloud from the special Torah kept in the Ark at the synagogue. She thought it over and said "yes" she would like that.

When we met with the Rabbi, he assigned her Torah and Haftarah portions, based on her Bat Mitzvah date and the Jewish Calendar. Some students liked to choose a theme, based on the readings. Julia could select poetry or music that fit the theme and include it in her service.

"You like mystery stories Julia?" the Rabbi asked.

"Yes," she said.

"Think of this as a mystery. Read the English translations of your Hebrew Torah portions and ask yourself: What do these readings mean? How do they relate to each other and to you? If you can answer that, you'll know the theme."

Julia's Torah portion was about what God required of Moses as a spiritual leader of his people. The Haftarah, seemingly unrelated, inferred that when we do a good deed called a mitzvah, because we want to not because we have to, we can become a light for one another. Julia puzzled over these notions for the next few weeks until, finally, she told us she had an idea about the theme.

"What about courage?" she asked. "For Moses to lead his people and for us to do good deeds, I think both take courage."

We thought that sounded just right, perfect for Julia who was very outgoing and had shown some early signs of leadership in school and on her soccer team. Although Dan had carefully and thoughtfully taken responsibility for Julia's religious education up to that point, I loved the concept of a Bat Mitzvah and was very interested in helping Julia prepare for hers. There were afternoon Hebrew lessons and meetings with the Rabbi. For my own Confirmation, at age eight, I memorized and recited one hundred catechism questions. The Bishop confirmed over one hundred of us all in one ceremony. I loved helping Julia create a Bat Mitzvah service that joyfully reflected a more individual and personal connection to her religion.

For her twelfth birthday, I had given her a simplified story of my Vision. Although I agreed with Reform Judaism's basic teachings, I wanted Julia to know that God encompassed both masculine *and feminine*. If she could understand the creator's feminine nature, she could access her own divine connection. I was only beginning to become aware of it myself.

I wondered about the notion of courage from a feminine perspective. What could Julia and I find out about courageous women? She changed her theme to "*women* and courage" and we looked for readings about courage that were written specifically by women.

I asked my friends for ideas, curious to see if women defined courage differently then men. They did. The masculine notion of courage emphasized fearlessly marching into battle. Men used words like bravery and heroism. Even the Thesaurus, compiled by men, lists "fearless" as the primary synonym for courageous.

Instead, women defined courage as the capacity to face something, even when you're afraid. Women talked less about battles and more about everyday courage—the courage to speak up for others, the courage to honor your beliefs. Julia found a piece by Helen Keller about the courage to do what is right even though it is "discomforting to the last degree." We found authors who described the courage to live and love fully, moving beyond all fears. Women often referred to a spiritual center that reinforced their inner courage. A couple of weeks before her Bat Mitzvah, Julia chose a perfect quote to print on the service program. It read:

"When we face our fears and let ourselves know our connection to the power that is in us and beyond us, we learn courage." Anne Wilson Schaef.

I enjoyed researching Julia's Bat Mitzvah theme, but the planning left me tangled in the details of the luncheon after the ceremony and kids' party that evening. There were invitations to order, catering menus to choose, and games to plan for the kids' party at our house. It seemed as complicated as a wedding. Should we invite this person or that person? Serve chicken satay or tuna salad? What should Julia wear? What do I wear? Who should do the readings? I wanted to give a speech during the service. What did I want to say?

In the last two weeks I began obsessing, sure that we had chosen the wrong menu. I rearranged the luncheon and fretted about how we'd keep thirty-five middle schoolers entertained for two hours at our house. In fact, my stress had nothing to do with party details. I was imagining Dan's Jewish family and friends judging me, a former Catholic Unitarian Non-Jew, hosting and organizing my first Bat Mitzvah. I lost all perspective.

Finally, ten days before Julia's service, I had a dream. In it, a gathering of small cloudlike tornadoes entered my bedroom, surrounding me in my bed tenderly offering the message, "All will be well." I woke up grateful for this comforting dream. I felt calm, and as I wrote it down, I remembered another message the white tornadoes had shared. It was something like, "The meaning is in the effort and the purpose."

I needed to remember the purpose of Julia's Bat Mitzvah and why I'd become so involved. I knew it wasn't about what we served for lunch or what other people thought of us. It was about Julia becoming a Bat Mitzvah, someone who is expected to follow the commandments and is now thought to be adult enough to make her own choices. It marked her commitment to the Jewish faith. She'd chosen to become a full member of

Dan's synagogue, Congregation Or Ami. For me, it was about helping Julia get started on her spiritual path.

With my perspective firmly in place, I could finalize the details without obsessing.

A week before the Bat Mitzvah, the Rabbi told Julia that she was doing such a good job with her Hebrew and speeches that she could lead the entire service if she wanted. He would sit on the side of the bema, coming up to join her only three times briefly: first to stand beside her when she read from the Torah, later to offer a few words and lead the Kaddish after the parent speeches, and finally to bless her at the end. She liked the idea of leading the service.

When the big day arrived, we left early for the synagogue to be ready before our guests arrived for the morning service. At ten thirty, Julia stepped up to the podium on the bema. She wore her beautiful new ivory dress and her white-blond hair fell to her waist. She drew her 4'10" frame up tall, looked into the audience with her bright blue eyes, and welcomed us in a strong clear voice. Without missing a beat, she read her prayers, told us when to stand or sit, and invited the readers up to the podium. Even the hardest part of the ceremony—reading Hebrew directly from the formal Torah, which has no vowels—she managed with calm assuredness. She shared, in her own words, what she thought each of her Hebrew readings were about. And then she gave her speech.

In recent weeks, I had helped Julia with her speech on Women and Courage. I guided her in noticing small ways that she had found her own courage. She wrote about standing up for a girl who was teased in fifth grade. And when the "cool" kids at her new school snubbed her, how she'd made lasting friendships with the "uncool" kids. She cited women in history, like Eleanor Roosevelt and the courage she summoned to bring about important social change.

So as Julia read her speech, I thought I knew it by heart. Still, she surprised me. She'd added a paragraph at the end: "There are many people in my life I look up to," she said. "One of them is my mom." I was stunned.

She continued, "My mom had the courage to go to the Appalachian Mountains of Georgia by herself to teach and to start two special education programs. Later in Virginia when Family Life Education was being introduced in schools, my mother trained the teachers and wrote the first Family Life curriculum for children with special needs. I am very proud to have her as my mom."

My heart fluttered and my eyes welled up. She ended by saying, "I hope that I will have the courage, not only to speak up for what I believe to be true but, to live a life that is full of courageous actions and ideas." Julia came down from the bema and walked over to where Dan and I sat in the front row and we hugged. I wondered how I would ever give my speech I was so choked up. Throughout the months of preparation, what I'd hoped most for her was that she could know the power that resided in her and beyond her, that could serve as a well of strength. She'd barely entered adolescence, but already Julia was on her way to knowing this about herself.

Next, Dan gave his speech telling Julia, who now sat in the front row before him, that when she had decided to become a Bat Mitzvah she was "taking part in a process that has occurred for over three thousand years—the study of Torah, prayer, and their meaning and purpose." He continued, "You have connected yourself with the Jewish people and over four thousand years of Jewish history, saying prayers which have been said for millennia, connecting with a long unbroken line of faith and community." And then he acknowledged her ability to recognize the right thing to do, even when it's difficult. He shared a story about her generosity and invited her to live the words inscribed on an award she'd received in fifth grade.

"What we keep we lose, and only what we give remains our own."

Now it was my turn. I first explained that when Julia was a baby, we had chosen her Hebrew name "Hannah" at her Naming Ceremony because it meant "courageous one." I then cited Mary Pipher's book, *Reviving Ophelia*, which identifies the difficulties adolescent girls face today. In it, Pipher describes four qualities shared by girls who thrive in adolescence and in turn tend to become strong, courageous young women. I wanted Julia to know she could find them all in the coming years.

The first was a sense of belonging. For girls, it's important to have roots and be a contributing member of a community. The second was self-acceptance. The third was finding ways to be helpful and discovering something they feel passionate about; something bigger than their own lives. Finally, strong girls had at least one person they could love, trust, and keep faith with.

In closing, I offered a prayer that she would find community, self-acceptance, passion, and love in the coming years and said, "I believe you will live the courageous life of one named Hannah." I walked toward Julia and gave her a big hug, finally letting the tears come. We looked up and realized everyone was crying and we laughed. Then Julia continued with the final portions of the service. As it ended, I knew the service had marked this changing time for Julia in a wonderful, beautiful way. The rest of the day was pure joy and celebration, the details falling into place.

It wasn't until later, as I reflected on the service, that I realized the four qualities I had listed in my speech were exactly the traits I'd found only recently myself: self-acceptance, a community of belonging, meaningful work, and most importantly, friends I could trust and keep faith with.

I suppose it's never too late to get adolescence right. The eight-year-old girl who had memorized one hundred catechism questions wouldn't recognize Mary Pipher's four strong-girl traits for many years to come. Like Julia, I was finding the courage to become myself.

CHAPTER 39

—◊◊◊—

Healing

One Tuesday morning after our dream group, Barbara asked, "Peggy are you familiar with cellular memory?"

"Yeah, I've heard the term, but I don't know much, why?"

"There's a man named Dick Overly coming to Richmond who heals cellular memory through something called Butterfly Touch Massage. I wondered if you might be interested."

She shared an article she had read. Even after healing following psychotherapy, clients oftentimes reported re-experiencing trauma, residual anxiety, or depression that was unrelated to anything in their present life. The article raised the possibility that the memory or trauma was lodged in the cells of the body. Through experimenting with gentle touch, some therapists were finding they could release the old trauma. I was intrigued.

I didn't have any present issues to talk to my therapist Anne about, but I felt discouraged that I still had nighttime episodes of sudden fear, imagining a burglar in the house or the nearby South Anna nuclear power plant having a sudden meltdown in the night. In daylight I still occasionally re-experienced nervous stomach, suddenly becoming hyper-vigilant checking out my surroundings, concerned about my safety for no apparent reason. Too often I found myself asking my husband, "Do you think everything will be okay?" or "Am I safe?" And in reply Dan would gather me into his arms and very patiently say, "Yes Peggy, everything is okay. You are safe." I wondered how he knew but I didn't.

Now that my psyche was healed, why was my *body* afraid?

Barbara had made an appointment with Dick Overly. "You want to give it a try?" she asked. Normally I would have easily said "no." I'd never even had a massage. My old childhood belief that linked massages with prostitutes and paid escorts was hard to shake. Plus, I was leery of having a stranger touch me.

But I trusted Barbara. In her fifties, after years serving as the Associate Director of the Women's Resource Center, she had enrolled in massage school and was about to begin her practice in therapeutic massage. I admired the way she was connected and in touch with her body and seemed comfortable in her skin. Now she was trying this new type of massage, which supposedly healed cellular memories. I decided to give it a try too.

How ironic that I was comfortable enough to talk and teach about sexuality and health issues, yet I was uncomfortable with the idea of any kind of bodywork like massage. Why didn't I feel at home in my skin, comfortable in my body? I wanted to find out.

When I showed up for my appointment, Dick explained that with Butterfly Massage, I would stay fully clothed, lying flat on my back, and he would use two fingers and gently tap on my joints like ankle and knee, shoulder and elbow. He would be inviting healing. Seriously? I was going to pay him to do this? How could a gentle touch with two fingers possibly have any effect on me?

I laid down and within minutes of him gently touching me, so lightly it literally felt like butterfly wings, my body responded. My legs jerked. He reassured me in a calm voice, "Just let your body move the way it wants to move. This twitching is a kind of release." As he continued, my body shook and shuddered, all completely involuntary. My mind, in its usual running commentary, thought this was one of the strangest things I could ever remember happening to me. Yet, I felt compelled to keep going, to let this man continue "healing" me. When it was finally over after forty minutes, I felt exhausted.

"What do I do now?" I asked after I got up.

"Take it easy the rest of today. But otherwise nothing in particular."

I left wondering what in the world had just happened. Had I been healed or just shaken up? He only tapped me. How could that make my body release something? Plus what was I releasing?

I drove home and called Barbara. I was dying to hear about her appointment and to tell her about mine. Hers had been interesting but hadn't involved so much body shaking. She felt good after her appointment but couldn't really tell if anything had changed for her. I told her about my session, and that rather than healed, I felt cooked and exhausted. What a weird day, I thought as I waited for my kids to get home from school. I felt embarrassed to have tried this crazy massage, so I didn't mention it to anyone, not even Dan. I went on with life and forgot about it.

But two months later, while routinely making the bed one morning, it hit me. I had not had a single episode of fear since that session. I sat down on the bed. Two whole months. In the absence of fear, I had a greater sense of safety and well being. How had he done that? Was it really because of that session that I felt safe?

When I heard he was coming back in town soon, I scheduled another appointment. This session would be completely different. Once again, he touched me gently with his fingertips, but instead of twitching and shaking, my body became still and quiet. I felt like I was floating in a black void. My heart was beating very slowly, and I could hardly tell I was breathing. Then I began dreaming, only I was *awake* and dreaming.

A young woman with long blond hair beckoned me to join her. She was lovely, smiling at me and inviting me to stop breathing. I wanted to go with her, to this other place that seemed easier. I let myself stop breathing and my heart got very still. Suddenly I realized that to stop breathing was death. I opened my eyes and pulled in a full, deep, lungful of air. I wanted life!

He said, "Yes, take some nice deep breaths. When you are ready, get up slowly and we'll talk for a few minutes."

I was disturbed and frightened. He apologized for not having more time to process my experience but noted that his next client was waiting.

Thank goodness for Barbara. She immediately suggested I call Joan, our dream group leader who was also a therapist. Luckily Joan was happy to fit me in.

During my session, I realized that the young woman in the dream-like event was *me* at twenty-two. When I stopped breathing after I gave birth to Lisa, my body was collapsed on the hospital floor unable to breathe. This other part of me had floated up and out of my body, around the hospital corridors, peaceful and happy.

Over the years whenever I had felt unloved or heart broken, or berated myself for mistakes, I would wish I was dead. I had wondered why I would become suicidal so easily and so often. There was always this underlying belief that it was okay to die. There was no evil in the invitation of this youthful me, she was simply calling me to a place of love where all was well.

During my session with Joan I realized that this part of me—that had split off and had taken refuge deep in my unconscious—had resurfaced simply to offer me loving kindness, compassion, and ease from suffering. However, this younger self also believed that the only way to find these qualities was to leave this body, this life.

I needed to heal this part of me. I had to bring her into my consciousness showing her what I knew now that I was forty-three, no longer twenty-two—that kindness, love, and compassion were available here and now. And I could face life's challenges with inner strength and courage.

Death was no longer a helpful or comforting solution for my troubles.

Although I could understand that healing cellular memory had merit, for now, I'd had enough.

CHAPTER 40

—⚬—

Flying

Our dream group had been meeting for two years and we'd noticed an interesting pattern. Birthdays often bring important dreams. My forty-fourth birthday was coming up in February, and I was hoping a vivid dream-message would come with it. It did. My birthday dream was one of the best presents I'd ever been given.

In it, I was standing on a catwalk inside a huge cavern in the side of a mountain in South America. Like a large ship-building station, there were scaffolds and platforms buzzing with workers putting the final touches on a round flat silver hovercraft designed to travel beyond the known universe. The astronauts were already aboard. Standing nearby, the creator of the spacecraft anxiously awaited the test flight's liftoff. I peered over at him and recognized the white bushy hair and mustache. *Albert Einstein*! My jaw dropped in surprise. He'd been holed up in this mountain for years, secretly creating this spaceship for the United States government.

As I stood staring in awe, I heard a whirring sound and turned to see the hovercraft lift off the ground and exit the large opening in the side of the mountain. I held my breath. But as the space ship flew out of the mountain, it tipped to one side, then the other, lost power and gently crash-landed. I glanced over at Einstein. He was distraught. Clearly he'd invested years in this project. My heart ached for him and I went over to offer some comfort. Albert's head was down, but as I approached, he looked up at me.

"You know, you don't actually need a vehicle to fly," I said.

He looked perplexed. "What do you mean?"

"Well, I can fly."

His bushy brows knitted. "How?" he asked.

I looked directly into his eyes and said definitively, "Flying comes from focused intention within."

To demonstrate, I silently floated up off the ground and flew around the cave using slight movements of my arms and body to turn myself or to ascend or descend. Finally, I lowered myself to a standing position beside an astonished Mr. Einstein.

"You can do it, too," I said.

I waited while he thought about this. Then I said, "Here, I'll show you."

I took his hand in mine and together we lifted off the ground and flew around. This was Albert's first flight. He loved it. With a feeling of freedom and ecstasy, we flew out of the cave and high into the sky. Soon after, we landed on a deserted white sandy beach on a Caribbean Island. Albert was so happy. We sat together on the beach, enjoying the sunset like old familiar lovers. Albert pulled me close and wrapped me in his arms; I rested my head on his shoulder and sighed contentedly. Together, we watched as sea turtles mated before us and the late day sky splashed bright orange and pink above the azure sea. I could tell Albert deeply admired me and appreciated my teaching him to fly. Inside, I knew *everyone* could learn to fly. I was no different from anyone else. On the other hand, I was thinking about Einstein's brilliant mind and how the whole world valued his genius.

As I lay in his arms on the beautiful beach, I knew that I had always loved him. But now I wondered, where was our relationship going?

The alarm went off and Albert disappeared. Stirring in my bed, I wanted desperately to return to the peace and love I'd felt in those fleeting moments I'd spent in his embrace. His loving comfort called up an intense physical longing in me. Our separation was heartbreaking. How would I live without him?

As I awoke gradually, I giggled to myself. In my dream, Albert Einstein was an old man—hardly sexy. In real life, Einstein had died forty years ago. The dream romance between us was absurd—but as I lay in bed staring at the ceiling, my heart still ached for him.

I rolled over. My husband who was just beginning to awaken asked quite innocently, "You have any good dreams last night?" He often asked me this because I usually began my day writing down my dreams.

"Tell you later," I answered as I sat up, opened my dream journal and began writing, hoping to capture every detail I could remember. I wasn't ready to tell Dan that I had woken up thinking about having sex with Albert Einstein!

This dream was so vivid. I'd felt Albert's arms around me as the sunset lit the sky. I couldn't wait until Wednesday when my dream group met. They would laugh, sure. But they could help me dig for its meaning—and I was deeply curious.

It was my turn to share that week. And I was right, they loved my Einstein dream, and they had lots of questions: What did I associate with Albert Einstein? What was my relationship to physics and mathematics? What does flying mean to me? What is my association with energy?

To me Albert Einstein had meant genius, expert rational thinker, physicist, and mathematician. Math had always been my favorite subject and the one I was best at, even winning awards, and I also loved physics in high school. My association with energy was that many people throughout my entire life had remarked on my high level of energy. But these answers didn't seem significant or meaningful.

I wondered how I'd known that "flying comes from focused intention within," when he'd asked how I did it. Focused intention within? I had never heard those words before. What in the world was I talking about? I remembered paying attention inside myself; I could recall the feeling from the dream. And after wishing very hard that I could fly, I would lift off. I'd had many flying dreams before, but usually I hid the fact that I could fly. Here Einstein had admired me for it. Before, the gift seemed too weird, I'd hidden it. If people knew I could fly, they'd be scared of me. Still, I'd admired Einstein's mental genius. Why, then, had I downplayed my own capacity to fly?

Following the session I read White and Gribbin's *Einstein—A Life in Science,* and discovered that we had an unusual circumstance in common: Both of us had given up our first baby for adoption when we were twenty-two. Like mine, the baby of Einstein's and Mileva Maric's had been a girl. The pair met as students at the Federal Institute of Technology in Zurich. Einstein was teaching at a small private school and working on his PhD thesis, when his fiancée Mileva, who was finishing up her studies, became pregnant. In a letter, Einstein promised to marry Mileva. But his parents forbade the marriage, believing the couple wasn't prepared to raise a child. Mileva went home to Hungary and gave birth to their daughter, Lieserl, in January of 1901. It is not known what happened to her. One year later, when Einstein had a job, his family consented to their marriage. The biographers weren't clear how the adoption affected Einstein, his wife, or their subsequent marriage. And I didn't know what this situation had to do with the dream, but it was certainly my first unexpected connection to Einstein.

Einstein's ideas about energy fascinated me, but nothing seemed to fit. Dreams don't always give up their secrets when we'd like. We have to wait for that confirming "aha" moment when a piece falls into place and it suddenly makes sense, when we suddenly *know*. In the meantime, we have to get comfortable with *not knowing*. I was convinced this dream was speaking to me, but I couldn't decipher the message. For now, all I could do was trust in the mystery and wait.

In three months, the answer would land on my doorstep.

CHAPTER 41

—⚭—

Reconnecting

When I'd asked my family for a separation, I thought it might last the summer. Instead, three years had passed. I felt ready to end the separation. My mother's seventieth birthday was coming up, and I knew there would be a gathering. I thought it might be a good time to visit everyone.

I wrote letters and made some phone calls in hopes of reconnecting. It was not easy.

When I decided to do the separation, I only knew that I needed to free myself from feeling judged and ashamed. I needed to silence the inner voice that railed against me. The voice that insisted the world would be a better place without me. Any negative remark seemed to take me to an emotional ledge where all I wanted to do was jump. My family's attitudes and opinions had triggered my feelings of shame and self-hate. I had needed help climbing down from that ledge.

Looking back, I still believed that this separation truly had never been about any one person in my family. And yet the paradox was that it was about my relationship with them collectively.

Together they represented the Catholic dogma, the rigidity, the narrow-mindedness, and the black-and-white thinking of my youth. I had a lifelong pattern of looking to this "family" to see who I was, to know right from wrong, and to see how I should live my life. I liked to please others and get along. I wanted to be loved and accepted. I was sensitive to their thoughts and opinions and oftentimes imagined or assumed they would judge me negatively for my choices. They were literally the external reference point for my life.

Also, for eighteen years I had assumed I was lovable *only as long as I kept my secret.* I had always assumed the worst—that they wouldn't love me if they knew the truth. When I found out my birth daughter didn't want me in her life, I couldn't risk their rejection, too.

The separation had been a necessary time for me to shift these lifelong patterns of looking outside myself to find truth and acceptance. It had been the only way I could disentangle myself from old ideas and attitudes. Dismantling my old relationship with my family had to occur before I could create a new connection with them.

Although I had made the choice to separate from my family, the process that followed had not been in my control. I had merely allowed it. If I had been in charge, I would have completed the task within that summer as planned. But there hadn't been a task to complete. Instead, a change in me had to occur over time. Here I was three years later, a member of a Unitarian Church and president of a nonreligious spiritual group who did dream work on a daily basis, led labyrinth walks and silent retreats, and read voraciously about the feminine nature of the divine. Not one of these would have passed my old, "Would my family think this was a good idea?" test. Yet here I was, living a life I loved. Free to be me. I was happy.

After three long years, I no longer needed their approval. I hoped that, with my newfound self-acceptance, I'd be better able to accept their attitudes and opinions without taking them personally. During the separation I realized that my family knew each other as a whole, but not as the individual adults we'd become. I hoped each of those relationships would shift as I attempted to create a new connection with my family.

It was going to be hard though. They were upset with me. They had been hurt by my separation.

I needed to remember that the question for me during the upcoming visit was not, could my family love me and accept me? It was simply this: Could I accept *myself* in their presence?

We drove to Atlanta for my mother's seventieth birthday party. Everyone had gathered at my brother Kevin's house, which was on a small lake. The party was difficult for me; everyone seemed uncomfortable in my presence. But Julia and Tommy enjoyed playing with all their cousins, and Dan went around interviewing everyone, catching up on family news. I gravitated toward the nieces and nephews, the ones too young to know about the separation. They simply enjoyed this Aunt who was happily giving them rides on the pontoon boat and playing on the hammock.

I couldn't control what lay ahead. I'd begun a new connection with my family, and for now, that was all I could know. The rest would take time. Time for them to feel comfortable with the new me. Time for them to forgive me. I knew that I loved them, and I needed to reconnect. I was willing to wait.

CHAPTER 42

—m—

Believing

Three months had passed since the Albert Einstein dream, but I was still turning this vivid mystery over in my mind looking for the solution that would illuminate my next step.

I'd returned home to Virginia grateful that I could finally hold a place of self-acceptance, even with my family. I understood what it meant to be true to myself. I could tell I'd come a long way. If a change was coming, I was ready. Still, my waking life looked the same.

Or was it? Ever since the Einstein dream, I had been noticing odd coincidences. Had I crossed the room and reached for the phone before it rang? Twice? Not possible, I thought. I hated to acknowledge these strange happenings, even to myself.

But they did remind me of a Chrysalis retreat I'd taken a year and a half before.

Our facilitator had emphasized the need to take care of ourselves as part of our spiritual path. On Saturday, right before the afternoon break which would be in silence, she asked us to think about one new way we could begin to take care of ourselves. I was already eating better, exercising, sleeping well, and for the first time, I was even attending a weekend retreat. What more could I possibly do? I abandoned the question and went for a quiet walk along the lake, instead.

About an hour had passed when an idea crept in.

You could believe yourself.

I stopped short. It was a subtle thought. But it got my attention. I knew exactly what it was referring to. I argued with myself. I do believe myself. I believe my dreams. Look at the way I held my own with the Humanists. I believe my Vision. I know it was a spiritual experience. Spiritual leaders and even saints have reported visions. That other stuff is just crazy. Leave me alone.

You could believe yourself.

One little sentence. And it had such power to annoy me. I had been so peaceful walking along the lake. Now I was irritated. Memories were coming in, memories of unusual experiences that I had dismissed, not believed. The word paranormal came to mind. I'd stuffed these experiences in a little closet I had created in my mind. I didn't want anyone to know. They'd think I was crazy. And if I believed them myself, then what? Would I be considered mentally ill? What good would it do?

When the group reconvened, we broke into small groups and discussed what had come up. Everyone else had practical, lovely, normal suggestions: Getting more rest. Cutting back on volunteer work. Setting aside time to paint. When my turn came, I thought I might get away with just saying the sentence, "I could believe myself." But the group wanted to know what "believe myself" meant.

"I've had some out of the ordinary experiences that I don't really believe."

"Like what?" They wanted to know.

"Well sometimes," I hesitated, then quickly blurted out, "I know in advance when something is going to happen."

A woman in the group, in a very matter of fact way, said, "Oh, that's just intuition or psychic ability."

"What else?" someone asked.

When I described a weird light I once saw around a person, the same lady said, "I take Tai Chi. It sounds like you saw energy," as if that should soothe me.

Seeing energy? Isn't that impossible? But she believed me. So did the others. In minutes, the group came to a consensus— I should believe in my own experiences. Believing myself was a perfectly legitimate way to take care of myself.

The phrase stuck with me for weeks, but still, I thought it best to forget my weird happenings. Luckily they didn't happen often, and I was pretty good at covering up the fact that I could see things, feel things, or know things that no one else seemed to notice.

Only now, ever since the Albert Einstein dream, the episodes were more frequent and more peculiar. Lately, I had started feeling other people's aches, pains, and emotions in my body.

"Are you okay?" I asked my friend Marcia one day.

"Oh I threw my back out yesterday playing tennis," she said. Then she described the sharp shooting pain in the lower right side of her back, exactly what I noticed feeling as soon as I walked up to her. This pain left me immediately after we parted.

During dream group, a woman who was relatively new to the group, took a seat beside me. Inexplicably, I felt a wave of sadness wash over me. Where had that come from? I was fine just a moment ago. I sat there wondering why I was sad when suddenly, I "knew" this woman was leaving her husband and she was distraught. I'd never heard her say a word about her marriage. But a few weeks later, when we were about to work on her dream, she shared her separation story with the group.

Feeling other people's ailments or emotions was confusing. The natural boundaries between my world and others' had softened. I couldn't tell which feelings were mine and which belonged to someone else. Usually the only cue that I was picking up outside feelings was the suddenness with which a new emotion or body sensation arose in me.

In the past, I'd sometimes dream about events before they happened. Now I *knew* things before they happened. It was creepy.

I was a practical, logical person. Psychics, I believed, made lucky guesses or they made vague predictions that could mean almost anything. I scrambled to apply logical explanations to my growing list of odd experiences. Maybe I just saw the pain on Marcia's face and empathized. And the woman whose marriage crumbled, had she dropped hints about it in dream group? Each time I received "psychic" information, I'd dismiss it saying, "This is simply not possible. It's just a coincidence."

Then I'd stuff the experience into that little closet, which by now was full of the other "paranormal" experiences I'd been denying—like the green light that shot out of my father's chest when he was dying, the dreams that predicted events before they happened, and every time I'd walked toward the phone before it rang. The closet was full and the door was refusing to close. I was finding it harder and harder to dismiss or deny my experiences. You could believe yourself. Ugh, that sentence.

You could believe yourself.

What for? I wanted to yell back. How would it help *anyone* if I believed these crazy events were real?

CHAPTER 43

—⚏—

Reading

Focused intention within. It was June and the words I'd spoken in the Einstein dream still puzzled me. I trusted the dream's mystery, but as spiritual practices go, *not knowing* is the most annoying one I know. I was feeling frustrated and impatient.

Then one afternoon in June, the key to unlock my dream came by way of the U.S. postal service. A glossy book catalogue in the stack of mail caught my eye. I started browsing, flipping the pages absently, when three words jumped off the page: "focused intention within." My head jerked in surprise, and I blinked to make sure I'd read them correctly. There they were. My words to Einstein were nestled in a publicity blurb for *Your Sixth Sense,* a book about intuition by a woman named

Belleruth Naparstek. I went straight to the bookstore, bought it, and started reading.

"Although psychic ability has been variously mystified, glorified, obfuscated, demonized, and reviled," the book began, "when all is said and done, it's nothing more than a basic human capacity, a skill of great practical value, that can be further developed by just about anyone."

Really? Did other people believe this? Was intuition a normal part of myself? Could I learn not to fear it? What made me think it would get me locked up in a mental hospital? She went on to compare intuition to other gifts, like playing the piano. Most of us can learn to play, but some people possess a natural talent for it. My favorite quote from chapter two read, "We are all hardwired for this, but some people come installed with some truly great software."

Was it that simple? I was born with great software? The book was filled with case studies of people whose paranormal experiences had led them to develop their intuition. I read on, nodding in recognition. I'd been pushing the same odd experiences into my overstuffed closet for years.

"So this is intuition:" Naparstek writes, "when, through our own sensory apparatus, we pick up feelings, sensations, perceptions, and emotions that are not ours but belong to someone or something else or that are just plain hanging in the air. Our boundaries are extended to include more than just us." Exactly! This was what had been happening to me.

She considered intuition a mere expansion of our sense perceptions. Her matter-of-fact tone made intuition seem so "normal." When she described what she calls psychic knowing (which I did *not* want to believe), I got goose bumps. Her definition of psychic was "a sudden, cognitive pop, an instantaneous awareness of a whole idea, sometimes a whole set of ideas or a complete conceptual system, that bypasses anything we would consider to be the normal process of thinking." I had definitely experienced that before.

Once during my first month at college I woke up knowing that someone's father had died. Although I dismissed the feeling and tried to stuff it away, I felt edgy all day. Late in the afternoon I returned to my dorm room, and as I went to unlock my door, I could hear someone crying in the room next door. It turned out that the girl whose bed was literally on the other side of the wall from mine had just learned that her father died suddenly. She was packing to go home. This frightened me.

As I continued to read *Your Sixth Sense* with these very sensible, down to earth descriptions of this supposed "natural" human capacity, it occurred to me that I wanted to learn more so that I would no longer fear my intuition. I began taking notes. The book was organized like a course and included explanations of terms, how intuition works, and lists of specific things one could do to cultivate and maintain intuitive ability. It even covered the *ethical* implications of intuition: No eavesdropping on other people's lives. No showing off, even if you *do* know your niece got the scholarship before she does. Handle all psychic information with care; confidentiality is critical.

I could not put this book down. I'd been dismissing these experiences all my life. For every example she described in the book, I could name my own corresponding experience. One woman "saw" her lost wallet in a dream; then found it. Check. Another felt an urgent need to call a childhood friend—the day she'd been diagnosed with cancer. I nodded. Still another couldn't walk through a crowded room without picking up everybody's aches and pains. Been there, done that.

Even as a child, I'd been unbeatable at hide-and-go-seek and guessing games. I *always* seemed to know how many jelly beans were in the jar. And in seventh grade, when my friend Peggy asked the Ouji board where she'd live when she grew up, I closed my eyes, placed my fingertips over the pointer and spelled out the letters T E X A S. At the time, neither one of us had ever traveled much further than New Jersey. But by the time we were thirty-five, Peggy and I had *both* lived in Dallas.

The book seemed written just for me; as if Naparstek herself knew I'd been studiously ignoring my own intuition. She was reassuring me, inviting me to welcome and enjoy these experiences. They can be helpful, she wrote, they're a beautiful part of you. I couldn't get over how excited I was about this book. I felt like I was waking up to a new world.

You could believe yourself. I recalled the words I'd found so annoying as I walked around the lake at the retreat. Yes, I could. Finally, I could believe myself.

Naparstek had interviewed forty highly intuitive people to write the book. They were all apparently "regular people" with jobs, houses, and insurance policies. Most of the forty worked in healing fields. There were psychologists, acupuncturists, nurses, and spiritual counselors. One was a corporate consultant. Artists and writers rounded out the mix. None of them sounded even slightly crazy. Each used their intuition in practical ways and described their experiences in calm, rational terms. Why had I never met anyone like this?

The names and contact information of her forty subjects were listed in the back of the book. Three lived in the

Mid-Atlantic area. I desperately needed to talk to someone, so I called all three of them.

Two never returned my calls. The third was David Davis, Ph.D., from Northern Virginia, described as "an intuitive trainer, corporate consultant, and individual counselor with in-depth knowledge of energy and healing which he integrates successfully into his corporate work." It said that he saw individual clients and worked with business leaders and government agencies on how to use their intuition. I was really curious about how employees of the United States government and large corporations were using intuition.

During our introductory phone conversation, David asked what led me to call him. I gave him some examples of things in my "closet." He was not at all surprised and said those experiences were just what he works with. We scheduled a two-hour appointment because of my long drive and equally long list of questions for him. Before hanging up he said, "Now let me tell you that in my experience the work we are going to be doing together begins now, so watch your life and see what comes up. I'll see you in a month."

With that, my closet door burst open, and I began to take a look at all these episodes of intuition. Only this time, instead of dismissing them or trying to explain them away, I practiced believing myself.

CHAPTER 44

—m—

Sensing

It was a long month waiting for my appointment. A dream I'd had in March was now leading me to an "intuitive trainer" in Reston, Virginia. How weird. I reconsidered the comments and questions I'd gotten from my dream group to see how the mystery was playing itself out.

The dream said that flying comes from "focused intention within," and *Your Sixth Sense* described intuition as arising from "focused intention within." Did this mean that intuition could feel free and joyful like flying did in the dream?

Also, maybe Einstein represented the rational masculine mind, and my flying symbolized feminine intuition. This would mean that Albert was admiring my intuition while I was holding his intellect in high regard. The dream ended with me wondering where this relationship was going. Would we have sex or be married? Would the union of the intellect and intuition happen? Only time would tell, but the relationship of these two qualities within me was certainly going somewhere.

During the month awaiting my appointment with David Davis, I read several more books on intuition and was particularly fascinated with *Second Sight* written by Judith Orloff, M.D. a psychiatrist who is also psychic. In the prologue she says, "The only mention of premonitions or other psychic abilities I ever found during my medical education was in textbooks labeling such claims as a sign of profound psychological dysfunction." This explained my fears. This had very clearly been the message I was given growing up. Little did I know that the message arose, not only from family or Catholic attitudes, but from what the medical community believed at the time.

Judith Orloff's story was about shutting down the strong natural psychic ability she demonstrated as a child, because it was disturbing to her parents. She told about her first experiences "knowing" things before they occurred, like "knowing" exactly when her grandfather, who lived in another state, had died. In the book she finds that later, in order to grow into adulthood, she had to allow the reawakening of this core part of herself. And finally as a physician she told stories demonstrating how she used her psychic ability in her psychiatric practice to help her clients. Her stories were very compelling. I was touched by how her intuition seemed to arise from caring deeply about her patients.

My experiences seemed insignificant compared to hers. I was not nearly as psychic as she was, I told myself. But I did wonder if I could somehow learn to use my intuition in a helpful way. I had just received a mailing about a Mind, Body, Spirit

Conference in Boston in September where Dr. Judith Orloff was billed as a keynote speaker and was also leading a one-day post-conference workshop on intuition. I was so intrigued by her book that I registered for both the conference and her workshop.

As the time approached for my first appointment with David Davis, Ph.D., I began having second thoughts. It was one thing to attend a workshop where I could mix in with the crowd and be invisible and take in what I thought was important. But a one-on-one session with an "intuitive" was scary. What if he wore robes or had crystals in his office? What if he made psychic predictions about my future and he was wrong? Or worse, what if he saw all these bad events that were about to happen to me and they were true? I reminded myself that during our phone conversation David told me he was a former engineer and that he taught business executives and government employees how to use their intuition. How weird could he be?

On the appointment day, I woke up nervous. Even though Julia and Tommy were away at overnight camps, I worried about the long drive, the cost of the session, and the possibility of disappointment. On top of that, a delivery truck carrying the four thousand copies of the long-awaited third printing of my *Changes in You* books was scheduled to pull into my driveway at seven a.m. Six years after I published my sex-education book, I was still filling orders from distributors, non-profits, and individuals. Every reprint was a nerve-wracking process. This particular shipment was late and backorders were piling up.

I heard the truck, right on time, and quickly tried to finish breakfast, taking the last bite of my English muffin. Just as I bit down, I heard a loud crack and felt crunching. What was a rock doing in a piece of bread? I spit the rock onto to my napkin only to realize that it was one of my molars, confirmed by the sudden shooting pain in my jaw.

The delivery driver pounded on the garage door. I ran down the stairs, cradling my jaw in my hand. As the two men began unloading the boxes onto a dolly and wheeling them into my storage room, I decided to check the order. I opened a box of books. Right paper, good color tone on the front, illustrations clear and dark enough, the changes I'd made were correct. I was relieved. Then I turned the book over. Blank. The text on the back of the book was completely missing. I was mortified. When I showed it to the head deliveryman, he leaned his elbow on the dolly and said, "Well Ma'am, what do you want us to do?"

"I can't sell it this way," I said, as if he cared.

"We'll just take them back to the warehouse then."

As they wheeled the boxes back to the truck, I felt sick thinking about delayed back orders and four thousand books hitting a landfill. I should have been calling the printer to straighten out this mess. Instead, I was leaving for Washington to talk to an intuitive therapist. Had I lost my mind?

I found a piece of gum, chewed it up a bit and covered my aching broken tooth. On the drive, I practiced talking pleasantly with my temporary chewing-gum tooth. "Everyshing will be otay," I reassured myself.

Two hours later, I pulled into an office park in a D.C. suburb. As I walked into the building I passed doorplates for insurance agents, accountants, and therapists. Then I entered Dr. David Davis' suite and sat quietly in the waiting room. When he stepped out to greet me, I shook hands with a very short, dark-haired, straight-faced man dressed in black. He invited me into his office, a sparse room with a few black leather swivel chairs, a desk, and a sliding glass door leading out to a small wooded area. We sat facing each other in his comfortable swivel chairs.

He began by asking me about the dreams and experiences that led me to call him. Each time I described what I considered to be a paranormal experience, he named it for me. I told him about holding my father's hand as he was dying, praying that he would feel better, and seeing the green light shoot out of his chest, through my hand, up my arm and out my elbow. David told me that the green light was energy, and that I had probably pulled pain energy out from around my father's heart. The fact that I could *see* the energy meant I'd had a *clairvoyant experience*. Clairvoyance, he added, was the ability to see beyond the range of normal vision. The dreams that had given me direct information were called *precognitive dreams*, ones which inform us of an event in advance. He suggested I continue to pay attention to my dreams. When I explained that I could sometimes feel other people's physical pain, he said that was called *empathic intuition*. He said I'd need to learn to distinguish my own pain from what I sensed in others in order to stay healthy. With his direct ability to both name and normalize everything, I thought, "Maybe in some circles I'm ordinary."

Following this, he asked about my past, especially related to the healing work I had done in therapy. By the time I had disclosed much of my story, I felt shaken. Between my botched book order, my broken molar, and these personal revelations, I felt so vulnerable that my eyes welled with tears. I had not wanted to cry in front of him. But David sat with me very calmly and patiently. After a short time he said that we were now ready to begin.

"Actually," he said, "we're more open when we are a bit shook up."

"If that's true, then I'm definitely ready."

David said, "Intuition is about expanding sense perception. Let's try some practices. I'm going to do something with energy and see if you can sense it." I was sitting about eight feet away from him. "So, I'd like you to sit comfortably, relax, and notice what you feel." Then he added, "You may want to close your eyes, if you feel safe, so that you can focus your attention inside your body."

I didn't know what to expect, but I decided to try it. Feet flat on the floor, hands on my knees, I sat up straight. I took a few deep breaths and closed my eyes. Almost immediately I felt it. My thoughts raced. Oh my God this is weird. Maybe I should leave. But this is kind of cool. Wow, this feels good. What is he doing? I opened my eyes and there he was, across from me, eyes closed, sitting quietly as if in meditation. Doing nothing. I closed my eyes again and returned to these unusual, yet pleasant sensations.

After a time he interrupted the silence, "Are you feeling anything?"

"Yes, what are you doing? Are you doing something? How are you doing that?" I blurted out.

He smiled and calmly requested, "Let's just start with you telling me what you experienced."

"I can't do that," I answered with resignation. "I don't know how to explain it. It was just all body sensations."

"That's right," he confirmed, "all body sensations. That's exactly what I want you to describe. Just try. Articulating energy sensations will be part of your work with me."

"Okay. I'll try." I hesitated, looking away, searching for the right words. "It was like softly, a cloud of gentle air came out from you and surrounded me. Then my body calmed down. My body felt reassured like everything was going to be okay. The distress I had been experiencing lifted up and off me. I feel very peaceful and accepting of myself right now."

He nodded in affirmation. "Now let's try something else."

"Wait, was I right? Is that what happened? Did you do that on purpose? How did you do that?"

"This work is about experience. Let's do some more, and then I'll try to answer your questions."

I agreed to try some more.

"Just notice what you feel," he said.

Once again, I sat up straight, rested my hands on my legs, and closed my eyes.

This time, my pelvic area got very warm. A stream of heat moved down my legs. Then it flowed up my body. A glowing electric heater centered in my abdomen was radiating warmth through my bloodstream. My intellect took over, my eyes popped open, and I demanded, "What is going on here? I'm getting heat…"

"Where?" he interrupted.

I pointed to my abdomen.

"Yes, I'm offering your lower energy centers more energy," he said.

"But you're across the room just sitting there. How are you doing this?" I needed to know.

"Intention," he said.

Oh no, my Einstein word again.

He continued to explain, "I'm intending to offer you energy where you seem to have less. You need more energy in your first and second chakras. Do you know what chakras are?

"No, not really. I've heard the word."

"They are energy centers. For now just know that the first one is between the legs and the second is just below the navel."

"So offering energy where I need it feels like heat?" I asked.

"Sometimes to some people," he answered. "It's possible to have other body feelings as well."

He continued to offer me energy from across the room and I could feel warm flowing sensations in different parts of my body. My mind didn't know what to do with this. My body on the other hand was feeling quite good!

After about twenty minutes of these energy type practices he said, "Let's talk for a bit. Do you have some questions for me?"

"Yes," I said as I picked up my journal and opened it to a list of questions I had written.

"Good," he replied, "let's hear them."

"If receiving more intuition is a gift, how am I to use it?" I asked pen in hand ready to write out his authoritative answer.

He responded immediately as if he was expecting the question. "Use your intuition to figure out the answer to this. There are many possibilities. You are the only one who will know the answer."

Quietly, I sat there taking in his response feeling a bit disappointed. I had hoped he would know *for* me. Although it wasn't the answer I had hoped for, it did make sense. I read out my next question. "How do I separate intuition from fear?"

"Great question," he said, "Fear can appear to be intuition. Someone is fearful about something and then it happens. Some people actually intuit everything through a lens of fear. It's very important that intuitives are aware of, and work through, their fears. Otherwise they tend to only sense things like illness, loss, or accidents. You can learn how to discern the difference between fear and intuition. But generally, when intuition comes in, it is neutral, not emotion packed like fear."

"How do I keep fear of intuition from blocking reception of information?" I asked.

"That is a matter of practice. The more you practice, the more comfortable you will become. This will lead to more trust and less blocking."

That was helpful for me. I definitely associated receiving intuitive and psychic information with being judged as crazy—a behavior that could potentially get me locked up. This old mindset needed adjusting.

I took a deep breath and referred to my list again. "How can I activate intuition by choice instead of things just popping in?"

"That's also an example of something to practice. If you'd like I can teach you specific practices that will help you learn to open up to your sensitivity and also close it down. Actually the energy exercises we did today were practices."

"You can just turn it on and off?" I asked.

"Yes and so can you. It's a process of integrating your intuition. At first it takes lots of work and attention but then you'll settle into a flow that feels more gentle and natural."

"That sounds a lot better than where I am now with it. I would like you to help me learn how to move in and out of it comfortably."

"Good, we'll start there next time."

"For now, how can I practice believing my intuition?"

"I want you to start documenting your practices. You can use your notebook. Any time you intuit something write it down. Anything and everything that you get. Then see what happens. When you get a 'hit' notice how the information came in. Was it a body feeling? A voice? A dream? An image? Write down anything you notice. And we'll take it from there."

"Sounds good," I said closing my notebook. That seemed like enough questions. Except then I realized I hadn't asked my most personal question. "Before I go, could you tell anything about me from reading my energy?"

He said I really needed more first and second chakra energy for my physical health, which I had already picked up from the earlier exercise he had done. But next time I'd have to ask him how one goes about getting more energy, especially for a certain part of the body.

Then he paused and looked around me and remarked in a dreamy voice, "But I'm most intrigued by this pink field of light around you. It's like you are energetically pregnant."

As he said this, I began to sense the field of light and felt myself becoming absolutely certain of its presence. What is this? I wondered.

Still looking around me and not at me he asked, "What do you think this light is about?"

"That's my question," I said, expecting him to explain the light.

"Yes, it is. Isn't it," he said with a knowing glance.

CHAPTER 45

Waiting

I liked David. He seemed trustworthy. Like me, he'd faced his own difficulties around opening up to his intuitive abilities, and he spoke openly about them. Although he could apparently do some pretty cool things with energy, he hadn't shown any ego around it. He took his gift in stride. It was simply a natural part of his world, integrated seamlessly into his life.

I always noticed how other people taught concepts. David had combined talking with practicing expanded sense perception. He was the right teacher for me, I decided, and I'd found him at the perfect time. I was also fascinated with five dreams I'd had recently that all seemed to be about the notion of freedom. The past years had been liberating, yet in these dreams, I wanted freedom. Since I hardly thought of myself as imprisoned, I wondered what freedom I wanted right now?

Immediately, I knew. I wanted the freedom to believe myself, to acknowledge the truth of my own intuition.

In my Einstein dream, flying seemed like the ultimate expression of freedom. If flying represents both intuition and freedom then maybe in my waking life, if I was free to believe my intuition, I would feel free. Then besides genius, Einstein might represent an exceptional understanding of energy. Let's see, if I represent the freedom to use my intuition, and we're thinking about having sex in the dream, then what follows? Energy and intuition. Yikes. That thought was a little too close for comfort. I turned on the radio to the pulsing beat of Steppenwolf's *Born to Be Wild* and listened to music the rest of the way home.

That week, my excitement turned to anxiety. I didn't know how to "practice." Psychic events had always occurred randomly. I couldn't *make* them happen. To make matters worse, nothing out of the ordinary showed up that week.

David reassured me that my intuitive experiences wouldn't necessarily change; I'd just be more aware of them. This seemed less frightening than sensing energy fields or being clairvoyant. For now, I should focus on opening my first chakra, he said. Not only did I need to love my life; I needed to love *my body* in this life. He talked about tuning into my body by paying attention to subtle sensations. He suggested seeing what my emotions could tell me and especially to notice what made me feel excited. Connecting to the body was a vital step toward developing my intuition.

I felt relieved. He suggested I read Barbara Brennan's book *Hands of Light* to better understand the chakra system and the human energy field. I bought the book and tried her exercises, like rubbing my hands together and holding them in front of me to feel or see the energy between them. I was surprised by how much I could feel.

I played intuitive guessing games. Before I entered my house, I'd guess whether there was a message waiting on the answering machine. When the phone rang, I would guess who was calling before I answered it. I was an incredibly good guesser. I also started noticing when I felt comfortable and uncomfortable with other people. I noticed who energized me and who drained me. There, too, I always seemed to know.

But, excited as I was about my discoveries, my children were now twelve and thirteen, and that summer they were my main focus. I enjoyed "holding home base" as I called it. Our house was a good place to hang out. I was available. I was intrigued by intuition, but my job as a mom came first.

In September, after the kids started back in school, I went back to see David at his office.

"What happens when intuition and the rational mind disagree?" I asked him. In the past, my logic ruled.

But David had suggested letting my intuition make some decisions. "See what happens," he offered.

We talked about the role the body plays in picking up intuitive information and processing it for us. "Some people who are intuitive focus their awareness outside themselves," he explained. "But if I stay grounded in my own body, I usually get more accurate and useful information for my clients."

I needed to continue working on grounding my own body, so I could pay attention to the messages it was receiving.

But nearing the end of this session, David and I hit an impasse. Yes, I was developing my intuition, but ultimately, what was the purpose? How was I going to use it? It was fun being a great "guesser." And feeling energy between my hands was kind of cool. But David used his intuition in his work. I still didn't know why I was developing my intuition, and I wanted him to tell me. This so-called energetic pregnancy he had noticed during my first session was growing increasingly uncomfortable and had lasted too long. I worried that I was wasting my time and money on these sessions.

He sensed my impatience and said, "I still believe you'll know how you are to use it. Maybe I can help though. I remember you mentioning a list of hints you've received from dreams and intuition about what comes next. Would you share them with me?" he asked.

"Sure." I opened the back of my journal where I was collecting this list of intuitive hints and began my review.

"Number 1. It will have something to do with my Albert Einstein dream." I looked at him and added, "I already see how the dream is related to intuition but not to how I could use it. So the dream could also be a hint about physics, math, energy, or perhaps flying?"

He looked out the window with a serious look on his face. "Okay. Go on."

"Let's see," I said as I looked down at my notes. "Number 2. It will be more controversial than sex education." I crossed my arms. "I'm sorry, but that seems impossible." I had even perused the want ads with this in mind. I couldn't imagine a more controversial job than launching sex education classes in Jerry Falwell's backyard.

He just smiled. "What else?"

"Teaching and writing will be part of it. At least this is familiar turf." I looked up but he just nodded for me to continue.

"This new work will somehow tie in all the pieces of my life. Good luck there. My life story feels like a crazy jigsaw puzzle."

"And fifth, it will not require another college degree. Thank goodness."

"Is that it?" my psychic detective asked, making sure he had all the known clues to solve the mystery of my pink energetic pregnancy.

"No there's one more," I said. "This one's my favorite: It will be hard to explain. Isn't that just great? I don't know what job I'll be doing, but once I find out, I won't be able to explain it to anyone else either. Now *that's* reassuring."

We laughed, but I felt so frustrated I wanted to cry. He took a deep breath and sat in silence for a few minutes. "How about if I offer some different possibilities based on your list of hints? You see if anything resonates with you."

"That sounds okay."

"You could study Polarity. It's a hands-on healing practice that balances a person's energy. Some massage therapists use it."

Even though I was practicing feeling energy, I couldn't make the leap that it could heal. Plus, I had no interest in being a massage therapist.

"No, I don't think so," I said.

"You're a teacher. What about teaching workplace groups how to use their intuition."

Oh my, I couldn't imagine getting that comfortable and skilled that I'd even begin to know how to do that. "No I don't think so." I said.

"What about becoming an acupuncturist?"

"Yikes, no thank you. The idea of all those needles terrifies me."

He paused and thought some more. "Well, you've written some books. Would you like to write a book for me or about me? I've studied many different healing modalities that have not been written about in the west." He went on a bit about how much he knew.

"No, I don't think so," I said. This was starting to feel weird.

"Okay, how about this. I've just heard about a program for newborns, born to coke-addicted mothers. People who have studied energy healing go in and hold the babies in a certain vibration to help them cope during their first few weeks of life."

I shook my head. I couldn't imagine learning how to do that or how I'd ever convince anyone in Richmond, such a conservative town, to allow an alternative therapy like that.

Finally he said, "Maybe your recent dream that took place in Africa means that you are to channel ancient healing information from Africa?"

With this last suggestion he'd crossed my "woo-woo" line. Channeling?

"Okay we should stop," I said. I was one far-fetched suggestion away from walking out of his office and never coming back. "Clearly I just don't know yet. I'm tired of waiting, not knowing, but I'm not going to figure it out today." I felt a strong urge to steer the conversation to a subject we both had in common like, "What did you think of engineering calculus in college?"

As we parted, I was obviously still frustrated, but David Davis, Ph.D. held his ground. "You will know," he reaffirmed.

—◦◦◦—

CHAPTER 46

Birthing

Two weeks later, I flew to Boston for the National Mind, Body, Spirit Conference. The speaker lineup read like a Who's Who in this emerging field—Jon Kabat-Zinn was presenting on mindfulness meditation, Brian Weiss, author of *Many Lives, Many Masters,* would speak on past life regression, and theologian Matthew Fox would expound on spiritual liberation. Maya Angelou would cap off the weekend with a poetry reading. I was a mom and "good-guesser," traveling alone to join the nation's leading-edge thinkers and participate in a workshop on intuition with Judith Orloff, M.D, the psychic psychiatrist.

I arrived at a fancy downtown Boston hotel, wary of New Age people in flowing robes and sandals, wearing crystals, and relating to me by my astrological sign. Instead, the lobby bustled with medical professionals, psychologists, and social-worker types, all excited about the speaker and workshop lineup.

The conference was exhilarating. For the first time in my life, I found myself among literally hundreds of people who shared my interest in intuition, healing, spirituality, conscious-ness, and mindfulness. With each speaker and workshop, my perspective expanded.

On Sunday night, before Judith Orloff's post-conference workshop, I had a vivid dream of giving birth to a baby. Finally, my baby. The energetic pregnancy that David Davis had noticed had finally ended—my "baby" was here. At last, I would know how to use my intuition.

I sat quietly with my journal and asked, *What does this dream mean?* The baby is here. What does it represent? I waited. Nothing came to me. Maybe my dream-birth was just wishful thinking. I'd wanted a connection so badly, and for so long. I let the dream go, disappointed.

In her eight-hour intuition workshop, Judith Orloff encour-aged us to consciously challenge our psychic abilities through deliberate practice. She led us into a state of readiness to receive psychic information, first by entering a quiet mental state, and then by focusing our attention inward and tuning into a silent blank space. In this state of receptivity, we held the intention to keep a sense of innocence and awe while we were tuning in and waiting for information. She helped us differentiate between psychic information and ordinary thoughts. Like David, she agreed that intuition generally arrives as neutral information with no emotional charge attached to it. I was stunned when she added, "Psychic messages give me strength." I had always considered them a weakness or a liability. "They remind me I'm not alone—that time and space don't really exist in the linear way we know them," she said, adding, "Timeless help is available to all of us."

She talked about gathering information about a person's energy, health, or whatever they need help with. We practiced "reading" people's energy fields and noticing its size, feel, or color. She taught us how different sensory input impacted a person's well being. I had never practiced accessing information about people's health or energy. It was so much fun trying out these new techniques. They left me feeling wide open to new possibilities.

During the afternoon break, Judith offered to sign books if anyone wanted. I ran up front, practically knocking people over, gripping my copy of *Second Sight*. This wasn't like me. I wasn't the "groupie" type. Why was I so intent on getting her autograph? I stood waiting my turn, fascinated as I watched this psychic psychiatrist read each person's energy field before writing something personal based on what she saw. When it was my turn, she gave me a puzzled look, tipped her head to the side and said, "What do you do?"

Why do you ask, I wanted to say, but instead I answered, "I'm an educator and the president of a small nonprofit group similar to the one that organized this conference."

She looked puzzled.

"But I sense a shift coming," I added. Her eyes got soft as she looked back at me. "Do you plan to help people?" she asked.

"Yes, definitely," I said.

"Good," she said as she smiled, quickly wrote a note in my book, closed it and passed it back to me, then turned to the

next person. Threading my way back through the crowd that
had formed around her, both hands held tight to the book as if
I had just been presented with the Holy Grail.

Slowly I opened *Second Sight* and turned to the title page.
She had written:

> "To Peggy,
>   A Healer,
>   Love, Judith Orloff"

My eyes filled with tears, and I ducked into the restroom
to take a few moments alone. Why was I so moved by these
words? They'd been written by someone who didn't even know
me. What were these tears about anyway? I was not sad or hurt;
I was deeply touched. I had never allowed myself to consider
being a healer. Yet it felt true, like a part of me that I'd known
long ago, was finally coming home.

Mysteriously, I even knew exactly which of David's suggestions was right for me. It wasn't anything he'd listed during
my previous session. Weeks ago, in August, he'd given me a
brochure for a three-year program called The Art of Healing.
At the time, I had ignored it. But now, The Art of Healing
was calling my name. I even recalled flying up to D.C. in my
Mary Poppins dream. I had always sensed something significant would happen there.

That evening, as I sat in the Boston airport waiting for my
delayed flight to Richmond, I wrote in my journal:

"Today I have given birth to a newborn baby healer, who,
the dream tells me, is very fragile, beautiful, healthy, and a
great responsibility for me to care for. Life will never be the
same again. I feel so lonely."

Tomorrow, my friends will ask, "How was the conference?" I must decide what I'm ready to share.

Then I will tackle the laundry, drive carpool, make dinner. So soon after I've given birth. So soon...

CHAPTER 47

—m—

Beginning

"Guess what!?" I was so excited as I arrived at my next appointment with David Davis that I started right in. "I know what I'm supposed to do!"

We hadn't talked for two weeks, but he picked up the thread immediately, "How interesting. Well what is it?" he asked.

"I'm supposed to enroll in the Art of Healing Program you told me about in August."

"Oh? Oh! That started last month. I know they have a large class. Let's see," he said, thinking out loud.

How could it have started? I was confused. "David, I *know* I'm supposed to do this. Did you tell me the teachers are friends of yours?"

"Yes, Hmmm." I could tell he was trying to figure out what to do.

"Do you think you could call them and see if they'd take me even though I've missed the first month?"

"Yes, I can do that for you. Did I mention that I'm actually one of the four people who designed the program?" he asked.

"No, you didn't." I said calmly. Inside I was cheering, "Yes!" Surely, he could get me in.

"Could you help me catch up on anything I missed last month?" I asked, wondering about the pushy woman who seemed to have taken up residence in my body. I actually knew very little about the program, but it lasted three years.

He agreed to call his friends on my behalf and promised to give me an answer by the end of the week.

A few days later, I was relieved and excited when he called to say I'd been admitted to the program. The first year of the Art of Healing involved driving to D.C. from Richmond three times a month. I absolutely hate long drives, and I-95 was always congested. But, for once, my usual commuter-resistance was mysteriously absent.

My first full-day workshop was scheduled for the next Sunday.

I spent the two-hour drive to my first class rehashing my usual doubts about the time and money I was spending. What if the other students were fakes or flakes? Was I really intuitive? What if I couldn't feel energy with my hands? What if everyone else was better at sensing and seeing energy? What if I couldn't move energy like David?

I reminded myself that I was following dream-guidance and synchronicities. For the better part of three years, I'd wanted to know what my next work would be. I felt sure that I'd been led here. In spite of my reservations, I stayed grounded in my desire to help others heal, and my hope that I could do it through intuition and energy.

I also thought about David's description of the two teachers leading the program. Mary Branch Grove had a grounded, no-nonsense approach to healing. She possessed a wealth of technical information gleaned from her training and practice in energy work and clinical social work, along with healing practices like Craniosacral Therapy, Esoteric Healing, and Shamanism, which I knew nothing about. She was only in her early forties, but already she had fifteen years of healing arts experience.

The other teacher, Helen Yamada, specialized in intuition and dealing with very subtle energies. To me, all energy seemed subtle, so I couldn't imagine achieving her skill level. She and David had both studied with nationally-recognized teacher Rosalyn Bruyere, who wrote *Wheels of Light*. David thought I'd probably find a natural connection with Helen, given her focus on intuition and her deeply spiritual nature. Their background and experience reassured me a bit.

When I arrived, I was surprised to find the Art of Healing was held in Mary Branch's office suite, located in a business park. In addition to a classroom space, the suite had four private offices and a kitchenette.

The class consisted of nineteen women ranging from early twenties to mid-fifties. I wondered about them. Did these women work? Have families? I couldn't tell. The first classmate I met told me she worked for the National Security Agency. Her job was classified "top secret"—her *husband* didn't even know what she did. We were two accountants, a lawyer (on disability from chemical poisoning), a hypnotherapist, two massage therapists, an emergency room nurse, a couple of government-administrative types, and a woman who insisted she was a witch, active in a large Wiccan community. A few of us were married. Only two had children at home. How would I ever feel at home with this group?

Since classes started a month ago, Helen jumped right in. "Today we're focusing on energetic anatomy," she said, launching into a basic review of the stomach, liver, pancreas, and gall bladder—complete with anatomical illustrations of the internal organs. "Now we're going to feel the energy of each organ and compare and contrast them."

Is she crazy? I thought. How can I do that? It's not even possible.

Helen stepped in to reassure the other panicked students.

"Remember, just notice," she said. "See if you feel anything. See if the liver feels different from the stomach. Just try it."

"But how do I even know I'm on the liver?" Janet asked.

"That's the point. Today you will begin to know the liver so that later you'll recognize it when you work on someone else's." Helen said.

"But how do I get to the liver?" I asked.

"You are going to lay your hand over it and hold focused intention to feel the liver."

Oh my gosh, those words again! "Focused intention." My dream, Belleruth Naparstek's description of intuition, David Davis's instruction, and now my new teacher were all talking about "focused intention?" What *was* it exactly?

An apprehensive "help" was bubbling up in my throat. Did I really want to sense a stranger's gall bladder? Wouldn't we just be pretending anyway? There was no way to prove what we were feeling. Would I be the only one to admit I don't feel anything?

Then out of the blue, I got a message. *Suspend disbelief*. But how could I? This was ridiculous. Wasn't it? I'd never heard of feeling organs with my hands. Still, the thought remained, holding my inner rant at bay.

Suspend disbelief.

Then, suddenly remembering a prayer I had written recently, I laughed to myself. Maybe it was pertinent to this situation. The prayer was:

> *Dear God, please help me to remember*
> *that if I can teach Albert Einstein to fly,*
> *I can do this!*

Yeah, sure, I can do this. Give me a liver! If nothing else, this would certainly be a different way to spend a Sunday.

Everyone began moving chairs and setting up the five massage tables, which had been folded and stacked in a corner. In groups of four, we had one person lie on the table while the other three took turns feeling for the liver and the stomach. At first, I watched. When my turn arrived, I was shocked to find that I could, in fact, feel Jen's liver and stomach. They had distinct vibrations and completely different attitudes. I saw a bit of color for each.

Tentatively, we each reported what we were "getting." And remarkably, we were "getting" something similar. When it was my turn on the table, Lisa put her hand over my liver, and immediately, it felt like a vibrating laser light was heating it up. I'd never thought much about my liver, but right now it was lit up and hot. I could have traced an outline on my skin.

"What are you doing?" I asked fearfully.

She quickly pulled her hand back, "I'm sorry. I can't tell when energy is coming out. I was just trying to sense in."

Lisa was a beautiful woman over six feet tall and full-bodied, more than twice my weight. She'd had mysterious episodes where massive amounts of energy flowed from her hands. It kept her awake at night sometimes.

"How do you deal with it?" I asked.

"David Davis is helping me. Do you know him?" she asked.

"Yes," I said, "I've seen him too." Interesting coincidence.

"Well, he's helped me a lot with my energy, and he's the one that said I needed to do this program," she explained.

I looked around the room at my classmates and wondered why the others had enrolled. Did they all have big energy experiences?

Still lying on the massage table, I looked back at Lisa. Had she accidentally cooked my liver? Would I be okay? We called Helen over. Lisa and I explained the situation and she taught Lisa to hold her hand above, instead of on, my body and how to sense in without running energy. This felt safer to me.

After we'd each taken turns, Helen asked for feedback. There were comments about color and vibration and sensations. Helen's tone was respectful of each student's experience. I got up the nerve to ask my question.

"Do organs have personalities?"

Helen laughed, "What did you notice?"

"The pancreas is rather cranky in some people. The stomach is active and busy. And the liver seems serious about its work like a director might be."

A few others in the group nodded as if they knew what I meant.

"Keep this in mind when you work on people. It may be helpful." Helen told me.

"Is that right though?" I asked.

"There isn't any specific right or wrong here. The point is to notice and compare. If that's the information you're getting then it will probably be useful to you. Someone else may specifically get color, and they'll use that to do healing with those organs."

No right or wrong? How can I learn to do something that doesn't have a *right* way? I couldn't wrap my brain around that kind of teaching. She wanted me to learn directly through my experience. Then how did I get personalities? Would I be psychologically evaluating organs while others shifted their colors? We spent the rest of the day sensing into other organs, and I came to know the difference between a stomach and a pancreas the same way you can reach for a blanket in the dark of night and know whether it's wool or cotton.

We learned how to use a pendulum to check the body's chakras. As the class ended, I noticed a camaraderie growing within the group. We were exhausted, but along the way, we'd become intimates. Was our connection specific to those who'd felt the subtle vibrations of each other's internal organs? Our teacher had asked us to practice on friends. Would mine let me sense their organs? My rational side wanted to laugh the whole crazy day off and never go back. But I couldn't get over this newfound capacity to sense energy in each organ of the body. It was one of the coolest things I'd ever done: like walking my whole life, and just today, discovering that I could also hop, skip, and jump. I couldn't wait for the next class.

CHAPTER 48

—ɯ—

Practicing

"…and I'm in charge of decorating for the dance, so I need to stay after on Thursday and Friday. Can you pick me up?" Julia asked.

I'd just arrived home from my first day of class, and we were finishing dinner. My mind lingered on the metaphysical plane where livers have personalities, energy radiates color, and intention, when focused, can move mountains. Just then, our worlds couldn't have been any more different.

How was this little girl of mine decorating a gymnasium? "Dance?" I said backpedaling. "When is the dance, Julia?" I was struggling to reenter the here and now.

"Friday. Remember?" Julia looked at me. Could she see that I wasn't quite with it?

"Can you drive me?"

"Sure," I said, "that sounds like fun, decorating."

Julia's and Tommy's task these days, as they were entering adolescence, was to fit in and begin to find their way in the culture. Their world revolved around friends, school, teachers, and sports. Cool clothes, stylish haircuts, and blemish free skin became their focus. And, right now, the self-centered worldview that defines adolescence was working to my advantage. My "sex teacher" job, once a source of pride, now mortified my middle-schoolers. They seemed relieved when I'd left the field. They wouldn't have cared if I was studying Aztek VooDoo Bellydancing in D.C. The point, for them, was: Can I have a friend over? How do I look?

"So what did you learn about in class?" Julia asked, surprising me by showing a glimpse of her thoughtful preadolescent self. On the drive home, I'd decided not to say much at first.

"I learned a whole new way of looking at the body as energy."

Julia looked at me perplexed and Tommy sat up tall and said, "Cool." I had their attention.

"Did you know that people in China, India, and Tibet have been aware of human energy for thousands of years? Native Americans, too."

"No," said Julia. "But why are *you* studying it?"

"I just find it really fascinating," I said.

"Sounds a lot better than finding least common denominators," said Tommy.

"Want to see something cool?" I asked.

"Yeah," they both said.

I reached into my pocket and pulled out the acorn I'd been given that day in class, letting it swing from its chain. "This is a pendulum. You can use it to get information about a person's chakras or energy centers. They're like little tornadoes that come off the body in the front and back. If you hold the pendulum over the tornado or chakra it spins to show how open it is."

"You mean you just hold that over someone and it spins?" asked Julia, eyes wide.

"Yes. Do you want to try it?" I asked.

"Yeah!" they said in unison.

I ushered them into the living room, and Julia sprawled out on the green rug while I knelt beside her.

"There are seven main chakras along the center of the body," I said as I waved my hand from the top of her head down the midline of her body. As I pointed to each, I explained, "The first is between the legs, second just below the belly button, third right below the ribcage, fourth is the heart chakra right in the center of the chest, fifth is the throat chakra, sixth right between the eyes and seventh on top of the head." I paused. "Okay, Julia, let's see, why don't we read your heart chakra first."

I held the end of the chain allowing the acorn to dangle over her chest. The pendulum was momentarily still and then began a clockwise spin. The size and speed increased until it was spinning in a six-inch diameter. I was impressed. When I practiced at school I had a much harder time picking up the spin, and no one's heart looked like this.

"Cool," she said as she checked out the spin. "Try my other chakras," she said. We tried a few more and then Tommy was chomping at the bit.

"Do me, do me," he pressed.

"Okay, Tommy, so which one do you think is your biggest?" I asked.

He thought about it for a moment and then answered, "My stomach, because I love to eat."

Lifting the pendulum over his solar plexus, I could feel his third chakra energy just tug on the pendulum and begin a huge spin. He was twelve and I remembered my teacher explaining how the third chakra related to ages seven to twelve developmentally. I read his other energy centers, but Tommy's third was the most open. Interesting.

"So how am I?" he asked.

"You're great! You were absolutely right about that hungry third chakra," I said.

My husband had been quietly standing by, arms folded, leaning on the doorway, observing this odd parlor game.

They turned to him and said, "Do Daddy. Read his."

I looked at him questioning, do you want to do this?

He said, "Okay, I'll try it."

Dan lay down on the living room rug with the three of us kneeling around him. I held the pendulum over his first chakra. At first it was still. Then it started a spin. Uh oh.

"Isn't that spinning backwards?" Julia asked.

"Well it's spinning counterclockwise which has a different meaning than clockwise," I explained trying to avoid saying anything negative. "Let's see about the other chakras." I moved on to the second.

"Hey that one is backwards too!" said Tommy.

"What's the different meaning?" asked Julia.

My mind raced. The basic interpretation I had learned that day was that a counterclockwise spin meant the chakra was closed in a very serious way and needed immediate attention. Of course, I hadn't learned what kind of attention Dan's chakra needed or how to give *any* chakra the attention it needs.

What's an energy-worker wife to do? I thought. I continued to read Dan's other energy centers. They were all spinning counterclockwise.

Finally I announced, "Okay according to what I know so far, your chakras are closed and therefore, Dan, you are dead." We laughed.

"Obviously I have more to learn. I'll ask my teachers next time. Maybe spouses show up counterclockwise?" I said, hoping my husband would feel better.

He shook his head and smiled, clearly wondering what I had gotten myself into. I puzzled over my new path too, but I couldn't get over how much fun I'd had playing with the pendulum and sensing organs. Would I find all of my classes this compelling?

The next afternoon, I drove back up to D.C. for the first of my Monday evening classes. The focus was on releasing blocked energy. We practiced assisting each other in opening places that felt "tight" or "closed." It was fascinating. The work involved very gentle touch, holding intention, and waiting very patiently until the healer or client could feel the release. It seemed like we were doing nothing, yet we could feel when a release had occurred. In the midst of practicing on my partner, I realized that this was similar to the Butterfly Touch Massage treatment I'd had with Dick Overly. He was doing energy work not massage, I bet. I wasn't sure what I released that night in class, I only knew that I felt better. I hoped that I could become more aware of what was happening during the work and learn how to talk about it. Words failed this subtle and mysterious process.

I arrived home after midnight and found Dan reading in bed, waiting up for me.

"You shouldn't have waited up," I said not wanting my new schedule to ruin his sleep.

"That's all right. I wanted to make sure you got home safely."

"Thanks, but really, next time please don't wait up."

I got ready for bed and he kept the light on, reading. When I slipped under the covers, exhausted, he said, "So how was it?"

"Very interesting," I said, reaching for my bedside light. "It was good. Good night."

Dan sat up with his light on. "Peggy, come on. I sat up waiting. I want to know what your class was like."

"I'm really tired. I don't even know how to talk about this stuff yet." I couldn't think of anything that I could tell him that he would understand or accept. I couldn't make the leap from pure, weird experience to logical, rational explanation.

"Just tell me a little bit then," he said.

"Not now. I'm too tired."

"Peggy, this isn't going to work."

"What's not going to work?"

"You've been seeing that intuition guy in D.C. You went up to that conference in Boston. Now you've suddenly enrolled in this three-year program, and you've hardly told me anything about it."

"I just don't know if you'll understand. It all seems crazy, so I'd rather not talk about it."

"That's not really fair. You aren't even giving me a chance. All this new stuff you are studying is creating a distance between us."

Dan was right. I'd felt it too. I thought maybe it was inevitable. We were too different. I didn't see how we could bridge the gap widening between us. I felt sad and I stayed silent.

"Either you start telling me what you are learning or our marriage will never survive this."

My husband never talked this way. Was this really true?

"I may not understand, but I'll at least have some idea," he added.

I looked at him and wondered if it would work, imagining him laughing at what we did tonight in class or dismissing it as crazy.

He read my mind. "I'll try to be respectful," he promised.

I sat up and said a little about what we'd practiced that evening in class. I watched his eyes glaze over as he tried to make sense of my experiences. As he listened respectfully and asked questions, I remembered that he had loved me enough to let me change and grow in the past. He always had, why not now, too.

A short while later I came across a Chinese proverb that I put on my desk at home. It read, "Some things cannot be explained, only experienced."

I couldn't necessarily explain *why* these techniques worked—but I could tell Dan *about* my experiences and *what I was learning* from them.

CHAPTER 49

—⁓—

Learning

By November, five friends had offered to be my guinea pigs as I stepped tentatively into my role as…as what? I settled on the term energy worker. I had only been to three classes, but my teachers were encouraging us to practice. I took a leap of faith and ordered a massage table.

I was still president of Chrysalis, and Barbara and I still led our Tuesday dream group. But I decided to bow out of the group led by Nancy, my teacher and mentor of five years. She wasn't happy about it. My energy work crossed her New Age woo-woo line. Mine too, for that matter. And I could tell she felt betrayed as my path veered from hers. David had become a valuable mentor, and I had new teachers. Why was this so hard for us, I wondered? Hadn't

Nancy been telling me all along to follow my heart and my dreams?

Dan and I rearranged the guest room, and set up my new massage table in an alcove where I could see my first "clients." I felt like I had a cool new toy, and I was inviting all my friends over to play with it.

During those early sessions, we had great fun. No one, including me, knew what to expect so our appointments went something like this:

"Can you feel that?"

"Is that *ice* in your hands?"

"I'm seeing lots of red; what about you?"

"Wait, is that a *vibrator* on my knee?

"That's so cool!"

"What's so cool?"

"My *feet* are hot. And you're touching my shoulders?"

Everyone experienced energy work differently. Some would feel heat or cold, pressure or a vibration. Some felt it in one part of the body, but other times they'd feel it all over. Sometimes, a person had no sensations until they got off the table at the end and noticed they felt more relaxed or happier.

Over time, the results went deeper. My friends would feel better, or get insights into troubling situations.

"*Ohmygosh,* my headache's gone…!"

"I feel so much more *awake*."

"I think I know what to say to my husband…"

"I feel tingly all over, like I'm swimming in champagne."

My friends would report pain ending. They'd get intuitive information about their body—or their life. My practice "clients" consistently felt better, or happier, more peaceful or more energized. They loved it! Through word of mouth, others I knew began calling to ask if I would practice on them.

My "clients" weren't the only ones benefitting. I was more aware of where the energy was going, and how to focus it on specific areas where they needed help. I was becoming very intuitive.

Back in D.C., my class continued to both delight and frustrate me. We had no course outline, no textbook, and Helen and Mary Branch continued to emphasize that there was no right or wrong. We never knew what we would learn next, and once we did, we couldn't look up the material in a book. As an educator and teacher trainer, I couldn't help wondering about the lack of organization and planning.

But I had to admit, we were all learning a lot. And I discovered that I'm more open to what is new, when I have no idea what to expect. I consistently arrived at class curious, open, wondering what we'd learn that day.

Still, I took detailed notes and drew diagrams. After class, I synthesized all the information and typed up my notes. Seeing it in writing made it concrete and somehow this helped me believe that it was legitimate. These typed notes became my own energy work handbook, which was very useful as I practiced on more and more friends at home.

During that first year, we learned the difference between running energy and allowing it. We got to release emotions and clear blocks from the body. We learned to balance energy between chakras, organs, and glands. We opened chakras, repaired chakras, or tuned them to a higher vibration. We worked right on the body and in the energy field. I felt the difference between blood and bone energy. I learned to run different types of energy for different body systems. We learned about color healing, harmonics, and polarity. And I was learning how to do all of this by quieting my mind, being open and expanding my sense perception, bit by bit, each class, and every time I practiced on someone.

In February, Mary Branch focused the class on perception. Our task was to articulate how we received each piece of intuitive information. I was now getting various sensations in my hands like vibration, heat, cold, buoyancy, texture, and dense versus thin. I was also seeing a lot with my inner eye like colors, images, and different lights. *Knowings* came in as a word, a sentence, or a fully formed idea. I still used the pendulum to read the chakras, but I also listened carefully for information from my clients. I noticed that the client gave me information when they reported a sensation or an image or when I observed a difference in their breathing, skin tone, or facial expression.

I still experienced other people's physical issues in my body. This often helped me to locate an energy block or know where releasing might be helpful. Unlike before, this no longer scared me. I knew how to notice it and let it go while I continued to work on the person. I also momentarily experienced the other person's emotions when that information was helpful for the healing work.

Writing this list helped me acknowledge how far I'd come in a year. I listened as each classmate described her intuition. Receiving confirmation for the ways we each found guidance was very encouraging. At the end of the day, I noticed that I no longer feared my intuition.

Still, I had my doubts. It seemed like I was constantly asking myself: Is this real? Did that really happen? Did I really sense that? If I'd needed proof, I was getting plenty of it from the electrical gadgets in my life.

My car kept blowing fuses. Craig, my mechanic, looked at the fuse panel inside the driver's door, took off his baseball hat, and scratched his head. "I'll tell ya, I don't really know what's making it cut off like that." By my fifth visit, I wondered if I should tell Craig that my energy was probably blowing the fuses. I imagined his sweetly puzzled expression shifting to deep suspicion. My energy? I might as well apologize for being a witch.

At home, my clock batteries failed constantly. My watch stopped. And every time I sat at the dining room table to pay bills or fill a book order, one of the chandelier bulbs would blow.

"Anybody have any questions from last session?" Mary Branch asked.

I tentatively raised my hand, "Um, I seem to be blowing light bulbs and fuses and draining watch batteries. Do you know why?"

"Oh that's normal," she said.

Normal? Normal to whom? I wondered. I'd never known anybody who could blow a light bulb just by walking into a room. But suddenly classmates were blurting out their own fiascos with lights and electronic devices.

Mary Branch went on to explain, "Don't worry, in time, your appliances, lights and wristwatches will get used to your new vibrations. Either that or you'll modulate your energy, to make it more compatible with your electrical gadgets."

I imagined walking into the house and warning the refrigerator and living room lights, "I'm home. Ready? Can I come in now?" Or talking to the family computer, which Mary Branch had gently teased I might crash next. "Hi Computer. How are you today? How does my energy feel? Can I turn you on?" Was it really possible for me to lead a normal home life *and* befriend my appliances? Mary Branch suggested I check out *Wheels of Light* by noted energy healer, Rosalyn Bruyere.

The book cited research completed at UCLA by Dr. Valerie Hunt in 1974, which measured the frequencies of the human energy field. This study confirmed where the human energy frequencies fall on the electromagnetic spectrum. Interestingly they were within the range of electrical and phone current, rather than say microwaves, infrared, x-rays, or visible light. This might explain what happened next.

By May, my energy sessions were humming along. After a practice session with my Night Writers teacher, Phyllis, I happened to notice that our phones were dead. I checked the outside box and found the phone line was active coming into the house. Dan and I checked every phone jack inside the house. Baffled, we called a technician. After checking the whole house, he announced that he'd found the problem in the guest room.

"But we've never used that phone jack," I explained. "There's not even a phone in there."

"Well you don't need a phone for this problem," he said. "It's been struck by lightening."

"Really?" My mind raced. "We haven't had an electrical storm lately, have we?"

The phones had gone out on a sunny day. This didn't make sense.

Still, he looked at me and said slowly, "Yeah I know. Seems unlikely, but I'm just telling you what I see. This phone jack's been hit by some power surge like lightning."

Power surge like lightning? I noticed my massage table folded up and off to the side. My eyes got big and I wondered how Phyllis was doing.

"The good news is I can fix it. No big problem."

"Great. Thank you," I said, relieved that he hadn't turned to me and said: Yeah lady. Just what are you doing down here to blow out the phone system in your house?

My husband and kids had taken my first year of monthly absences in stride. I told Dan what I was learning in class. He was supportive of my fledgling practice and intrigued by my propensity for blowing light bulbs and watch batteries.

The kids rarely asked me about my program. I was glad. As the practices got more complex, it was harder for me to explain them. When they did ask, I gave simple answers like, "Today I learned about the energy of each of the organs of the body." They were satisfied with short, simple explanations. And I shifted from energy worker to mom by the time they came home from school.

At the Middle School that spring, my husband and I attended a parenting class. The presenter showed us how to create a home environment and develop a relationship with our children that could help prevent alcohol and drug use during the teen years.

Near the end of the session the speaker explained that developmentally it is normal for children to begin to separate from their parents at this age. "The trouble comes when a teenager relies on drugs or alcohol to assert their independence," he said. "Parents can take the pressure off by doing a bit of separation themselves. Surprise them. Do something different. Take a tango dancing class or go midnight bowling. A child is less likely to do something risky to prove their independence when they have less to prove."

I looked at Dan, nodding at this logic. But he was just smirking at me with a twinkle in his eye, smiling. What was so funny?

"Blowing up light bulbs?" he whispered, and I got it, holding back a giggle. I was doing *plenty* to support my children's individuation.

CHAPTER 50

—∾—

Opening

As my second year of classes began, I was eager to start working out of my own office. I had logged over two hundred hours of training including sessions with Judith Orloff, Belleruth Naparstek, David Davis, and a weeklong intensive with noted healer and author, Rosalyn Bruyere. People were calling to make appointments, asking for help with life questions or wanting to heal physical issues. With the kids back in school, I now saw five or six people a week.

"How do we know we're ready to start our own practice?" I asked as we met that first weekend.

"How many clients are you seeing a week, Peggy?"

"I average five to six, but I've seen as many as nine."

She said, "In that case, start your practice now."

She explained that most energy work programs required far fewer hours of instruction. I had more than enough hours of training.

I was excited and soon talked to Barbara, who was looking for an office for her massage practice. She was focused on March. "But if we started now," she said, "we might find something by January." We both assumed an office search would take a few months.

Instead, I dreamed we found the perfect office space. The dream prompted me to check that Sunday's classifieds. And there it was: two offices in a perfect location. We went to see it. The small house was owned by a couple of therapists whose offices were on the first floor. They were renting the two offices upstairs. This was the place.

For two years, the therapists had pressed to get their building zoned for massage therapy. They were hoping to find another massage therapist to occupy the upstairs office. Only recently, Richmond had stopped requiring massage therapists to submit medical documentation that they were free of sexually transmitted diseases when applying for a business license. The zoning change meant Barbara sailed through the licensing process for her certificate of occupancy.

I was another story. In 1998, I didn't know a soul in Richmond doing energy work in an office. But the city-issued application asked me to describe my business. How would I explain this to the folks in City Hall? At home, I wrote up a very direct, clear, two-paragraph description of my work and handed it to my husband for review. He took a look and shook his head.

"Chakras? Energy? Healing? Peggy, this will never do. It raises way too many questions."

An expert in local government law, Dan explained that the city wanted enough information for tax and zoning purposes only. I didn't need to teach them about energy work.

"You just don't want to raise any red flags," he said.

We worked on it together, each time I said less and less, until it sounded *normal*. Dan suggested I keep the term "educational consultant" since I was already under that category. Together, we whittled my job down to this:

"Peggy Siegel is an educational consultant. She will be educating individual clients about the energy field of the body and how it relates to physical, emotional and spiritual well being."

Later that week the city issued my business license. I was relieved. By the first week of November, Barbara and I had each set up our offices, months earlier than we had originally thought we would.

After the busyness of the move, in came the doubt. Would anyone pay for a service I'd been offering for free? I decided to charge a discounted rate since I was still in school, and I offered a free session so people could see if energy work was helpful.

My office was a small, bright, cozy upstairs space with two large windows which looked out into treetops. I had arranged a desk, two chairs and a massage table. A corner shelf held my sacred objects, including my favorite statue of Kuan Yin, the Buddhist Goddess of Compassion, my pink glass rosary beads from childhood, and a red Tibetan prayer flag from my teacher Mary Branch.

As I sat quietly in preparation, I thought, if anyone had told me at any point in my life that when I was forty-five, I would be opening a practice doing hands on healing using the energy field of the body, I never would have believed them. How had I ended up here? I thought over the incredible combination of dreams and synchronicities that had led me here.

All that time, as I'd wondered what new "job" would be next, I had no idea that something this unusual would come up for me. No wonder I couldn't find the job in the classifieds!

The hints I'd shared with David Davis were all true: This work absolutely combined intuition and energy, just like my Albert Einstein dream had suggested. I had doubted any job could be more controversial than sex education, but energy work certainly was. I hadn't needed another college degree, as predicted. The last hint was that the work would involve teaching and writing. Friends were already asking me to teach an intuition practice group, and I could imagine myself teaching energy healing at some point. As for writing, for now, taking notes and writing about client sessions gave me a deeper understanding of this form of healing.

I was on the right track. I was touched as I considered the sheer number of details, all falling into place, to help me find my way. I felt supported by some mysterious force in the universe.

Finally, I also understood why I'd needed three years between completing the adoption search and beginning the Art of Healing. It had taken that long for me to let go of old patterns. I no longer looked outside of myself to see who I was. I had learned to connect *within*, to find my own inner truth. It was essential that I explore dreams and write and talk about my life. It took time to believe my intuition, not fear it, so that I could receive and accept the guidance available to me.

Guidance that would lead me to this new office ready to see my first client.

Energy healing answered a deep unformed longing. I hadn't even known exactly what I was yearning for. I thought I had wanted passion back, and a way to express my gifts. It never occurred to me that I might have another gift, one that I didn't even know about yet, one that had never been cultivated or expressed. The longing was not simply for the qualities of passion and focus, but rather, it was arising from this strong inner pull to become more of myself.

Is that all there is of me? I had asked.

No there is more.

I had discovered I was a dreamer, a writer, and now a healer.

—∭—

Part III

1998-2004

—∭—

"Everyone who is seriously involved
in the pursuit of science
becomes convinced that a spirit is manifest
in the laws of the universe —
a spirit vastly superior to that of man."

Albert Einstein to student Phyllis Wright in
1936 when she asked if scientists pray

> "Everything should be made as simple as
> possible, but not simpler."
>
> Albert Einstein

CHAPTER 51

—⟶⟵—

Explaining

As I began seeing clients, I found a kind of relief in finally
arriving where it seemed I had been heading for several years.
It wasn't simply the practical issues falling into place—the sign
on my door, the fresh stack of business cards, or client intake
forms—that gave me the sense of relief. Rather, the feeling
was internal. I had moved into a life that answered both of the
questions I had been asking—Who am I? and What is mine
to do? It turned out that I was a healer, and it was clear to me
that seeing clients in a professional space, was mine to do at
that time.

I found it interesting that my new work focused on helping people, but I hadn't returned to my original life question,
Who needs my help? I wasn't scanning my world for people who

needed energy work. I could have, but I didn't. My sense of always wanting to help others, even rescue them, had left me. I could see that now. I was ready to *be* of help. But I would wait until I was asked.

This healing work was an expression of my true nature. And I felt a sense of peace in knowing that I could help people without compromising this truth.

I was also "coming out." I'd felt I needed to conceal what I'd been learning and studying in the Art of Healing. But, with the opening of my practice, it was time for me to share what I'd found to be true about energy work.

Now my concern was getting the word out. I believed in the value of energy work, and I wanted others to learn about it. How could I convey this? I decided to create an information sheet.

I had produced hundreds of handouts over the years as a teacher. I would do some research, organize my thoughts, get clear on the key facts, and write them up. But, in three years, I never saw a single handout in the Art of Healing Program. We didn't use a textbook. In fact, the teachers encouraged us *not* to read the few books available on the subject. They wanted us to learn from hands-on experience without being influenced by what we read. How would I articulate over a year's worth of practices and insight? I laughed as I remembered telling David Davis that my next profession "will be hard to explain." I thought that was the funniest hint ever. But it was true! How was I going to write up an explanation of energy work when all I really wanted to do was read them the Chinese proverb on my desk, "Some things cannot be explained, only experienced."

I had talked about energy work with the friends I had practiced on, but I never figured out a clear way to describe it.

Instead, I'd try to intuit what kind of information each person was ready to understand. How could I create a handout meant for *anyone* to read—men, women, old, young, open-minded, closed, spiritual or not?

I decided to begin by explaining energy work as a healing modality emphasizing that although it seemed new, it was ancient in origin. After playing around with a half-dozen descriptions, I settled on this one.

For thousands of years, the healing systems of Eastern cultures have recognized and worked with the flow of a vital life energy (or energy field) in and around each person. It is believed that physical, emotional, and psychological illness is the result of an improper balance or an interruption of this vital energy flow. If this delicate natural balance is restored, the person once again becomes a unified center of well-being, health, harmony, and wholeness.

Energy Work is a healing-arts practice based on this ancient Eastern understanding of the human energy system. This practice deals with the electromagnetic field around the human body (the aura), which is generated by the spinning of smaller vortices of energy called chakras. Chakra is a Sanskrit (Ancient Indian) word meaning "wheel of light." In Energy Work the intention is to restore the body to its natural balance, which includes a sense of vitality, appropriate feelings, clear thinking and reasoning, willingness to embrace change, responsible and creative self expression, intuitive understanding, and a vital spiritual life.

Yes, I liked it. I felt better, clearer. I thought it sounded legitimate. Next I noticed that with many people there was usually some fear about trying something new, and this was definitely new in Richmond. I wondered how to reassure someone through written words that energy work was safe and not scary. Maybe it would help a prospective client to know in advance what the actual session would be like, I thought.

I wrote that my sessions always begin with a conversation about what the person wants to work on. When we move to the massage table, the client remains fully clothed and lies on her back. Most energy work is done in silence, though the person can speak up any time if he or she has a question or comment. In addition, I wrote that sometimes I ask questions for feedback or share my impressions. I close each session with a conversation to allow time for processing the experience, asking questions and discussing possible follow up.

But the handout still didn't explain why anyone would seek out energy healing. I needed to articulate the possible benefits of energy work, based on my own experience. This is where I felt excitement and enthusiasm. To me, energy work held infinite possibilities for healing and changing lives for the better. I had seen it myself.

My own sessions with David Davis, and the practice exercises we'd done in class, had released the anxiety I'd held in my body, and I couldn't believe how much my chronic stomachaches had eased. But the most dramatic result had occurred just recently in class. We were learning how to run energy to promote deep muscle relaxation. When I told Sharon, my partner for the exercise, that I had TMJ, chronic inflammation of the temporomandibular joint, and that I'd worn a mouth guard every night for the past seven years to fend off the headaches and earaches associated with TMJ, she decided to practice on my jaw.

My expectations were low. My nighttime jaw clenching was unconscious and my dentist had already told me I couldn't do much to prevent the TMJ that resulted from it. Sharon worked very slowly, sending energy deep into the muscles. It felt warm and relaxing on my jaw. She then directed the deep relaxation energy to other muscles that were connected to these jaw muscles. The results seemed miraculous to me. After this hour-long healing session, I'd never needed my mouth guard again.

Energy work had also helped heal my chronic lower backaches, which an orthopedist attributed to a misshapen sacrum and osteoarthritis in my hip and back. The sessions had also helped me with emotional issues. I'd learned how to hold onto my own energy in the presence of people who drained me, or who made me feel anxious. But perhaps most importantly, I'd formed a new, positive relationship with my body. Energy work was directly responsible for this remarkable change.

The classmates and friends I practiced on also seemed to have transformative sessions. Some people had said they experienced relief from anxiety, depression, or chronic pain. My clients who were seeing psychotherapists said they felt our sessions had given them the strength to work through painful emotional issues and made their therapy more productive. For some, energy had brought clarity. Others told me they had received the strength to stand up for themselves in difficult relationships or at work. Two friends of mine who were undergoing cancer treatments said the energy work seemed to lessen the stressful side effects of chemotherapy and radiation. With their discomfort relieved, they felt calmer. I hoped my words would convey how much I loved receiving energy healing and offering it to others.

The final section of the handout needed to be about me. So far I had only worked on people who knew me. It seemed like new clients would find it easier to trust me, not only if they knew about my training in energy work, but that I'd also been a classroom teacher, had taught at a university, written books, and been president of a few organizations. I even decided to mention that I was married and had two teenagers. I wanted to convey that I was a family person, active in the community— that I was a regular person who just happened to be trained in energy work. I re-read the paragraph and thought I sounded like a very normal professional person.

In the end, I came up with what seemed to be a straightforward and simply-worded handout. I was amazed how difficult it had been to figure out what I wanted to say and how I wanted to say it. But afterwards I found that I had clear words to use to describe the work and to answer people's questions about it. I hadn't realized how much I needed to do this for myself. Seeing it in writing made it all more real, believable, and clear to *me*.

Paradoxically, while I was busy spreading the word about energy work, I also avoided mentioning it to others. I knew plenty of people who would think it was bogus or crazy. It reminded me of the Humanists at the Unitarian Church. Dream work had been invaluable to me, but I didn't need to prove it to the men who disputed it. Once again, I was clear about what I knew. I had no need to convince anyone. It was easy for me to accept that others were uninterested or not ready to try energy work. After all, that had been me not long ago.

"The most beautiful experience we can have is the mysterious. It is the fundamental emotion which stands at the cradle of true art and true science."

Albert Einstein

CHAPTER 52

—∞—

Preparing

Although I was pleased with the clarity of my new handout, how legitimate the work sounded, how *normal* I appeared, I knew in my heart that energy work, at its core, was inexplicable and deeply mysterious.

Clients would ask where the energy came from, "Is it your energy? Don't you feel drained?" But I was certain it wasn't my energy. I felt great, not one bit tired. On occasion I even got a dose of the energy I ran on clients. "No," I would tell them, "it's definitely not my energy."

The question that inevitably followed was, "If it's not your energy, where is it coming from?" Sometimes I responded that many people believe in a universal life energy field and that energy work taps into that. But even so, the question then became, how did I tap into it and run it into another person? I used extra sensory perception and intention, I could've said. But still, when I really thought about that, I could only ask myself, how did simple intention direct the flow? And how did a client's body know what to do with the energy I was running? In the end, I always came back to accepting the fact that this work was pretty darn mysterious. "That is the mystery of the work," I would say to clients.

I discovered a quote by St. Augustine that I found intriguing.

"Miracles do not happen in contradiction to nature, but only in contradiction to that which is known to us of nature."

Yes that was it. I believed that energy work was a part of the natural world but that we just didn't know very much about that world. I put the quote on my desk at work. Beneath it, I added:

Dear Creator, may I accept all miracles
so that I may come to know more about
your gifts of creation.

I wanted to remain open to the mystery. It was the open door behind which all possibility resides. And inside that possibility, lay the essence of healing. An essence that, on many levels, was unknowable. I could not dissect it. Or explain it. Or categorize it. The best I could hope to do, was to be with it, in a state of presence. Because in the presence of this, healing happened. With this intention, I hoped to learn something new with each and every client.

I was grateful that the Art of Healing program lasted three years because both teachers still had new techniques to teach us. We learned more about Esoteric Healing, especially effective for endocrine issues and long distance healing. We practiced using intuition to employ dreams or the energy of possibility to shift someone's energy. We learned how to redistribute energy that seemed to have converged in one part of the body. With its balance restored, the body's energy was smoother and could flow freely to promote healing.

We learned how to prepare patients for surgery and which energy frequencies would help speed their recovery. Another set of practices returned balance to emotions, body systems, or wherever it was needed. We learned to create energetic holding centers, called "eggs" which worked like time-release capsules in the body supplying ongoing energy which seemed to improve immune function, or increase a person's vitality. We also learned the tender work of assisting a person at the end of life.

But the three-year program brought other benefits. Besides giving me ample time to heal some of my own physical and emotional issues, it offered me enough practice to understand my healing abilities and my relationship to intuition. I learned that the energy came *through me* and *to me*, but was not really *from me*. Even so, each day of practice taught me that *who I was* and *how I was* mattered. My own physical, emotional, and spiritual well-being affected the energy and intuition that came to me and through me. So it mattered how I prepared for the work, I discovered.

After much trial and error, I developed strategies and practices to support my own wellness. I had to be in good shape, for instance. Although I wasn't giving my own energy to others, running energy was physically demanding work. I needed to exercise regularly, eat well, and be feeling well. Any ailment could distract me from the intense focus that was necessary. If I was tired or feeling run down, I had trouble accessing intuition and the energy flow was usually diminished.

From the start, I had several clients who were undergoing harsh cancer treatments that compromised their immune systems. I became very proactive about my own health, so I wouldn't risk passing them a cold germ or bug. I was careful to eat well and get enough rest. I washed my hands more often and avoided anyone with a cold or other virus. If I thought I was coming down with something, even as minor as a cold, I was careful not to see clients. I would stop and check in with myself to see if *I* needed care or healing.

In the past, I'd work through exhaustion and illness, ignoring my body and bragging about it. Now that I depended on it, I valued my body in a new way. I owed it my attention and appreciation.

I had to be well emotionally too. If I was distressed about an issue, angry, or triggered into an old unhelpful pattern, I would find myself distracted, without the necessary focused attention. I learned to work through relationship issues sooner rather than later, and I practiced letting go of home and personal issues so that I could bring my full attention to the present moment and the client.

Over time, with suggestions from my teachers, I developed a set of morning practices that helped prepare me physically, energetically, and spiritually for my workday. I started waking up half an hour earlier than Dan and the kids, and going downstairs to the guest room where I had created what I called "sacred space." I had a basket that contained a statue of Quan Yin, a small replica of the labyrinth, and a book of intentions

I had written—each reminders of the transcendent. I began by placing my objects on a cloth in front of me on the floor and lighting a candle. I sat quietly for a few moments and then read some of the prayers and intentions from my book. Sometimes I wrote down an intention for the day.

After reading the prayers, I did a series of yoga postures and breathing practices followed by chakra-opening exercises to increase my energy. I ended each morning practice by listing the first names of the clients I had scheduled for the day. With the intention of openheartedness, I said each name aloud and asked intuitively if there was anything I could know that might be helpful for their sessions. After each name, I sat in silence and waited for a moment. In my mind, I might see a symbol, or become aware of a question to ask them or get specific information about their energy. No matter what came to me, I held it lightly knowing that it may or may not hold meaning. This was a simple practice to open my intuition and my heart.

There were mornings when I resisted, but this early set of practices made me feel more connected to my body, my intuition, and my spirituality which was a good way to start the day.

I'd never had a job where my own well-being was so necessary. Never before had a large part of my work been to keep *myself* in shape. It carried over into how I scheduled my clients. It took several months to discover that I felt best when I scheduled two clients in the morning and two or three in the afternoon. Each session ran ninety minutes or, for new clients, two hours. I usually finished by four or five o'clock, so I could be home when my kids finished after-school sports.

Besides caring for myself, I was surprised to discover I also needed to care for my *office* space. The energy of my office seemed to matter. I learned how to clear it of unhelpful energies and to fill it with healing energy. I once had a young man say, "I think it would be healing for me to just sit in your office." He was onto something. I sometimes got the impression that healing happened as I merely sat with a person—that the space itself could be healing.

Even my time between clients seemed to matter. To close each session, I developed a practice of silently offering a blessing. I would express gratitude for any intuition and healing that came through me for my client's benefit. This seemed to clear the office and prepare the space for the next client. I also discovered that I couldn't run an errand or make unnecessary phone calls during the day. It would shift my attention and energy in an unhelpful way. So when I was at work, I was at work.

I felt clear that it wasn't just me doing this work, yet all the inner work I had done, the preparation I did each day, the ways I took care of myself and my office space, all seemed to make a noticeable difference.

It was both me and more than me.

And the more I learned about what I brought to the work, the clearer I was of what was *more* than me.

And during these years of my full-time practice, I experienced a lot that was *more than me*. Often, it caught me unaware.

"Coincidence is God's way of remaining anonymous."

Albert Einstein

CHAPTER 53

—⟋⟍—

Being "In the Pink"

Once during my first year of practice as my schedule had become more full, three of my clients in one day each reported a similar phenomena. It took me until the third one to *get it*.

The first client, Jennifer, was suffering from a condition for which doctors had no known diagnosis or cure. Debilitating pain inexplicably traveled through her body. Energy work relieved the pain for hours or sometimes days, so she was coming on a regular basis.

I always began the bodywork part of my sessions by feeling the energy field. I did this by raising my hands above the body and slowly bringing them in closer to find the edge of the field. When I came to it, I felt a very slight resistance almost like the feel of like-poles of two magnets coming closer to one another, a slight pushing back as if I was in contact with something that I couldn't see but could feel. It was like I was sensing into a cloud around the body. Sometimes it felt full and puffy, while other times it was thin and close to the body. It could be very dense with a clear edge, or with a person who was very ill, I could barely find it.

Jennifer's was once again thin and close to her body. I could see why she felt so weary. Her intention was to receive energy for increased vitality and energy to relieve her pain. As I gently began, I also held an intention to bring loving kindness to the session, honoring the way she was living with her circumstances. As I was offering this loving energy, she suddenly said, "I'm seeing all this pink." Her eyes were closed. Oftentimes clients reported seeing colors, which was fascinating to me because it often related to the color or vibration of energy I was running. But I wasn't intentionally running pink energy.

"That's interesting," I said.

"No, I mean I've never experienced this. Even after I open my eyes and close them again this pink light is there."

"What do you make of it?"

"I don't know. I just know it's here."

I told her about other people seeing colors, but I was pretty certain her experience was different in some way.

During my second client's session, she too started talking about this beautiful pink light. Afterwards she said she felt wonderful. I was grateful that she felt better but curious about two clients in a row seeing pink.

My last client of the day was Sandy, a middle-aged woman, who had grown up with a neglectful and abusive mother who was still a very difficult person to contend with. Having never known a real mother's love, Sandy was often triggered into old patterns, feeling unlovable, even though her husband and close friends clearly loved her. After years of psychotherapy, she still struggled with feelings of worthlessness. Her intention was to move toward greater self-acceptance so that she could receive all the love coming her way. When she laid down on the massage table ready for the energy work, and I raised my hands above her field in order to connect, she stated her intention, "May I accept myself and know that I am loved."

After the opening, I began by putting my hands on her feet to run energy in a process called chelation, which fills and balances the field. Running energy felt like offering a flow of energy that was directed. When I did this, I usually felt it moving through me. It might flow into my back and circulate through my arms and hands or other times it seemed to enter in the top of my head and glide to my arms. Slower vibration energies sometimes came in my feet and up my legs, into my abdomen, through my heart to my shoulders, arms, and hands. The flow could feel like a hot or cold fluid running through my veins. Or I might sense a moving vibration or tingling sensation. At times I didn't have a specific body feeling with it, I seemed to just know where it was located or where it was heading. But no matter how it entered me or flowed, it left me through my hands. Clients seemed to have a wide range of experiences, which differed from session to session.

But something was different here. Instead of feeling a flow of energy into her, I felt what seemed like a big ball of loving energy around us. It was like being in a sea of love. I couldn't feel where I ended and she began. I was enjoying these sensations when suddenly I noticed her eyes pop open.

I calmly asked, "What are you noticing?"

"You are pink. We are in this big bubble of pink," she said as tears came to her eyes.

"How does it feel?" I asked, wondering about her tears.

"I've never felt so loved in my whole life. I can feel this pink light loving every cell in my body."

Those were my words. She had said the same words I had used to describe the pink light I had experienced on the labyrinth, "feeling love in every cell of my body." Was I doing what I had hoped I could one day do? Offer that same pink light of compassion to another person? Would it help her like it helped me?

Silence settled upon us. She continued to feel this sense of being loved with complete self-acceptance. I felt adrift in a cloud of loving.

Afterwards she said, "Now I know what self-acceptance feels like."

"What is it like?"

"Well, I can't really describe it. I know it in my body though. I didn't know what to aim for before. In the past I would hear all my inner judgments and my mother's voice that I had internalized. I tried to *think* my way into accepting myself for who I am. I thought about what I did that made me lovable. I'd have all these arguments in my head. But this was different. I just felt loved, even for laying there on the table doing nothing. All of me was loved. It was quiet. Now I have a body feeling to aim for."

"Maybe stay with this sensation a bit longer, so you'll be able to remember the feel of it."

She sat quietly for a bit and then asked, "Why was it pink?"

"I don't know," I said, "but, in my own life, I think of pink as the color of compassion."

"Yes," she said, "that's it, compassion."

When Sandy left I had all kinds of questions. Was I channeling the same light I had experienced on the labyrinth? When people saw pink, did that mean the woman I had seen on the labyrinth was there? Even though I couldn't see the pink light now, I sat quietly and noticed that I could still feel the energy of loving-kindness.

Was she here with me? There was no image, no way to prove it to myself. It just seemed clear that something very important had just happened. Perhaps it was possible for me to hold the intention to offer this pink light of compassion. But today the pink light had shown up by surprise. Could holding the intention to offer compassion and loving-kindness call it up for future clients? I hoped so.

The words of the woman on the labyrinth came back to me: "I am you and you are me." Every time I considered this notion my head hurt. I could not figure out what she meant.

For the time being I decided that I could accept my relationship with mystery, doing my part and allowing an opening for *other* healing to come through. But I would definitely remember to try this: When someone needs love or acceptance, silently invite pink healing light.

"It is not that I'm so smart. But I stay with the questions much longer."

Albert Einstein

CHAPTER 54

—⚭—

Questioning

I was excited to have come so far. After two years of classes, I could feel energy, "read" people's energy fields, and access a dozen or more energetic healing techniques. I could connect with my intuition. And sometimes, I even knew about things before they happened. I'd started using my intuition both at work and at home and I was leading an intuition practice group on Friday mornings. My practice had grown quickly through word of mouth, and I was becoming more confident about my capabilities.

But each monthly weekend class invariably left me feeling humbled. There was so much I didn't know.

One month, as Mary Branch was guiding us through an Esoteric Healing exercise, I became discouraged. Instead of running subtle energies into the body through our hands, we were instructed to hold our hands above the body and allow it. We had to hold specific points in the field based on the principles of Sacred Geometry. I could *not* seem to feel these energies or tell what was happening. The long periods of silence, stillness, and waiting had left me feeling bored and frustrated.

Mary Branch also expected us to track the healing energy that our classmates were offering when they practiced. But I was third-eye blind, unable to see or feel anything, and I became convinced that everyone else could sense more than I could. I was the only student in our class doing energy work full-time, and I wondered what made me think I was qualified. I pulled Mary Branch aside when we broke for lunch.

"I can't do this," I said. "If I can't even tell what is happening when I'm doing the work, how can I possibly sense into what another healer is doing?" I was thinking that maybe I should take what I've learned so far and quit the program.

"Peggy, it's good to have your confidence shaken."

That seemed ridiculous. I couldn't imagine how losing confidence would help me in any way.

"But don't you see," I told her, "I'm in Richmond, alone. I need to be confident in the work. I have no one to ask for help if I get stuck like this. How can I go back and offer energy work when I feel like I've just been shown how much I don't know and can't do."

She smiled at me knowingly, which I found annoying. "This will make you look at things more closely and ask new questions."

By the end of the weekend, I knew she was right, of course. I realized that whenever I was satisfied with what I got intuitively, I would become less curious. This new process required my ongoing curiosity to see further. It kept me looking and digging for information and wondering, always, how I might access the next piece of helpful intuition. I needed to stay with the questions much longer.

That year, over and over, I was shown how much I didn't know. We'd learn something new, and I would lose all confidence, questioning why I was even doing this when I knew so little. When I hit upon this issue yet again, my teacher Helen shared a statement that healer Rosalyn Bruyere stressed:

"We cannot learn *that* which we think we already know."

My confidence was interfering with my ability to learn. I had to be shaken up to remember to be open and curious. I had to become skilled at "not knowing."

I did pretty well with this notion as long as I would eventually get guidance and the person benefited in some way from the work. But as it turned out, I had even more to learn about "not knowing." I wanted to approach my work each day with a sense of confidence. But how could I do that and still be aware of all that I didn't know? Didn't confidence itself arise from a sense of self-assurance about what I knew?

The answer arrived soon after, during a client session. One day I watched from the second floor landing as Elizabeth, who was in her seventies, dragged herself up the stairs and into my office. For the past two months, she had been struggling with severe sudden-onset migraines of unknown cause. She had dark circles under her eyes and could hardly hold her head up. The daughter of a minister, Elizabeth had prayed for relief, and she wondered why God hadn't answered her. The year before, when Elizabeth had first come to see me, the months of energy work we did together had helped her overcome her lifelong battle with depression. She felt lighter and happier than ever. I loved seeing Elizabeth; she had a lively spirit and lived her life with integrity.

But in the past two months, her painful migraines had left her feeling discouraged, and once again depressed. She was traveling to Duke University's Headache Clinic but even they hadn't figured out the source of the headaches nor settled on a treatment plan yet. At least the energy work had been relieving her pain temporarily. I only hoped that it would this time as well.

That particular day I'd already seen three clients who were all suffering from serious physical illnesses. When Elizabeth came in, we talked momentarily but she was anxious to get started. She set the intention to receive healing energy to relieve her pain. I used a specific technique we had learned for headaches. It was one of the processes that had been so hard for me to learn since it involved "allowing" energy instead of running it and my hands were to be in a specific location in the energy field rather than on the body. Allowing energy felt like offering a puff of energy. It was more like holding a certain vibration of energy and waiting until the client took it in, or directed it themselves. It almost felt like I was sending a message to the person's body saying, "This is possible. Harmony and balance are possible. Do you want it?" Or it sometimes felt like the puff of energy was calling to the person, "Come be like this vibration," or "Here is your natural vibration; this is how you come back to balance." Allowing energy was more passive than running energy. I was offering the energy without directing it.

During the session, Elizabeth's body appeared quiet and calm, so I assumed it was helpful. At the end she slowly sat up on the massage table. I asked, "How are you feeling?"

She moved her shoulders, stretched her neck and then put her head in her hands. "Oh no," she moaned, "I think it's actually worse."

When I saw her pain and thought I had made it worse, I felt terrible.

"Why don't you have a seat and I'll get you some more water," I said, buying myself some time. I felt choked up, like I wanted to cry. On the way downstairs to the water cooler, I thought about these four difficult clients I had seen in a row. Why am I doing this work? It's too hard. I'm not helping anyone. I can't stand to witness so much pain every day. I can't face her again. What am I going to say to her? I'm embarrassed and sorry that I didn't help her. How can I charge money for this session? All these thoughts arose as I walked down thirteen steps to our waiting room, filled two cups at the water cooler, and trudged back up the stairs again.

As I reached the landing, I stood outside my office door, took a long deep breath, and tried to collect myself. And in that moment, a crystal clear notion quite suddenly came to me in these words,

> "The ego needs confidence.
> The soul *only* needs trust."

What? The message repeated. "The ego needs confidence. The soul only needs trust." I could feel in my gut that it was true. This work wasn't about how great I am or curing people, it was based on some bigger picture that I oftentimes can't see. I stood there momentarily feeling a shift as I prayed silently,

Then may I be blessed with trust in this moment.

The heaviness that I had felt, lightened up as I stepped back into my office, still clueless about what I would say to Elizabeth.

I handed her a glass of water and took a sip of mine. We were quiet together. She hung her head and looked down at her hands. I prayed for trust. I waited.

Then suddenly she looked up surprised, and said, "Oh I get it now," as if I had just explained something to her in the silence.

"What?" I asked.

"I've been absolutely certain the migraines were a punishment from God for something I did or didn't do. I've been spending all my time, for weeks, doing life reviews to figure out what I did wrong. But suddenly I can see. It's a headache, just a headache." She paused. "Okay so it's a bad headache going on for weeks. But still, it's a headache."

"Yes, just a very bad headache."

"Yeah, God's not punishing me."

"No," I said, surprised she had been thinking that. "I don't think it works that way."

"You know what else I've been thinking?"

"What's that?"

She shook her head like she was trying to wave away an idea. "This seems kind of crazy. I'm a little embarrassed to even admit it. I've been noticing every mean person around who seemed to be in good health and asking, 'Why is that bad guy feeling so good? Why do *good* things happen to *bad* people?' I guess that was a pretty unhelpful thing to focus on."

"Yeah, I'd say so. Glad you can see that now."

As we parted she smiled and said she was better. She was leaving with some headache pain, but she had handed over and put down the suffering.

It had come to her in flash. The headaches were causing physical pain. These *thoughts* were causing emotional suffering. After she had gone, I sat for a while amazed at the way the session turned out. When I had trusted that there was a bigger picture I couldn't see, I had re-entered my office still not knowing what to do or say. And in that space of trust, she got clarity. Clarity of mind came even in the midst of a painful headache. I could see how her mind—her thoughts—had caused emotional suffering, thinking she had done something she was being punished for.

Then I realized I was doing the same thing to myself. I'd gone downstairs for water, a very neutral task, but my thoughts in those brief moments caused my discouragement. If I'd stayed with "what was," that her headache was still painful, I probably would have naturally felt compassion for her. And if I'd stayed with my own experience, I might've felt compassion for myself. It had been a hard day for me seeing four clients whom I liked and cared about all facing very challenging health issues. I was used to days where, one after the other, clients would feel better, get well, or tell me that they'd taken a small but significant step toward their healing. It was hard to have a day like this where the benefit of energy work was unclear.

With other jobs I'd had over the years, when I hit difficult circumstances and felt discouraged, I reminded myself of successes and accomplishments and even asked others for verification and encouragement. Eventually this feeling of self-assurance would arise and I convinced myself to have confidence.

This was not going to be effective any longer. This new work was not about ego or confidence. Apparently it was about soul and trust. I had to trust in the mystery. I had to trust in what I knew *and* in what I didn't know.

Doing work that involved interplay between me and some mysterious forces in the universe required a whole new level of trust. I had to trust that I was supposed to be doing this work and that I was skilled, clear, strong and intuitive enough. But I also had to trust in the work itself and all the mystery behind the work. This was easier when my clients were doing well or when the work was clearly beneficial.

Trust was taking on some new dimensions.

The soul *only* needs trust.

"Not everything that counts can be counted,
and not everything that can be counted, counts."

Sign hanging on Albert Einstein's office at Princeton

CHAPTER 55

—ᴍ—

Arising

One morning while waiting for my next client, I found myself just staring at that quote and prayer on my desk.

"Miracles do not happen in contradiction to nature,
but only in contradiction to that which is known
to us of nature."

St. Augustine

*Dear Creator, may I accept all miracles
so that I may come to know more about your gifts of creation.*
Me

The more energy work I did, the more aware I became of the unexplored gifts of creation present in the natural world.

In school I had learned about gravity and centrifugal force, for instance. Even though they were invisible, these forces had been scientifically proven. But I wanted to know this: Would a scientist someday confirm the invisible forces or energies I was coming to know? Would someone invent a device that could measure the stream of energy coming out of my hands or quantify the field of pink light that had surrounded both me and my client.

Would there ever be a way to calculate what seemed like natural driving forces I had noticed arising *within* my clients?

It wasn't just their chakras or their energy field I was curious about. I had observed two other forces or powers that arose *within clients* to help with their healing. The first and most obvious was this: The body wants to be well and at ease. Just as gravity pulls us to the earth, the body naturally gravitates toward well-being. When we get cut and bleed, platelets immediately form a plug at the site and proteins in the blood plasma form strands that strengthen the plug creating a scab. Our complex immune system works away without our awareness, sending white blood cells to attack invading unhelpful bacteria or heating the body with fevers to attempt to kill unhealthy viruses. We don't have to think about any of this. It just happens.

Was it this same driving force within ourselves that also knows where the body needs *energy* for its healing or well-being? For example, my client Sarah held the intention to experience peace in her body. She was feeling stressed due to radiation treatments for lung cancer. I didn't know exactly where her stress was because she could only describe her sensations as generalized discomfort and unease. As I ran the energy into each of the major joints and chakras I held the intention for the energy to help her feel more calm and peaceful. Afterwards she reported that she could breathe easier, her shoulders had relaxed, her face no longer felt tight, and her jaw stopped hurting. The body somehow knew where relaxation was needed and how to use the energy to promote this shift. This was consistently true.

Although I began every session with an intention and some idea of how I would offer the energy, the person's body also seemed to play a role in receiving and directing it wherever it would help meet the intention. How did the body know how to do this without her awareness or mine? And what drove this response?

Observing where the energy went, how the body used it, and what the client reported afterwards always mystified and intrigued me.

I noticed a second, equally strong innate energy pulling each person toward *wholeness*. Time after time, I witnessed a client's internal push to wake up and live with full expression and to keep becoming whoever they were meant to become. When this natural force was stifled, messages arrived through vague symptoms like having no energy or feeling stuck. Sometimes a client felt a general heaviness or dread each day upon awakening. Some had insomnia. Most had already been to a doctor and told that nothing was wrong, or they knew intuitively that it wasn't a medical issue. Some came with dreams or an interesting set of synchronicities that they wanted to figure out. Usually these experiences were messages. Just like *my* body had sent nightmares and malaise to wake me up, so too others were finding their own wake up calls, which led them in turn to call me. Together we worked to listen to the wisdom of the body. And usually, the body led us to explore their life more deeply.

Allison was referred to me by her family doctor. She kept getting sick and the doctor, who happened to be a very intuitive client of mine, sensed that she was in some way making herself sick. About forty years old, a large sturdy woman with a gentle countenance, Allison was an assistant manager in a hardware store that was located in a neighborhood with many older homes that people were restoring. She became familiar with the regular customers while talking to them about their plumbing and electrical needs. During the past five years, she also found herself knowing detailed information about their physical or emotional health. She saw cancers before diagnoses. She knew a woman's grief the day before her mother suddenly died. She was remarkably psychic. "What do you do with these knowings?" I asked.

She put her head down and said, "I feel sick."

I waited.

Finally she looked up at me forlorn. "I try to push them away," she said shamefully.

"How does that feel?"

"Sick. This is what has been making me sick I bet." She paused. "I want to do something with this," she said.

I explained to her how it was possible to integrate her intuitive abilities. I told her my story. Even after the very first session, she began practicing writing down and believing the messages that seemed to come to her. She didn't do anything with the information except practice accepting it. Within the week she began to feel better. During her next session she said, "I feel like I'll be who I'm meant to be when I integrate this."

Within two months, Allison's anxiety was gone, her health improved, and she began studying energy healing.

The client's body played a role in the healing process, always reaching for a state of wellness and wholeness. I could trust the body's wisdom to guide my work. I couldn't know how stress was affecting Sarah, but I could trust that her body would direct the flow of healing energy to relieve her stress. With Allison, I only knew initially that the body had messages. She had to accept herself and her gifts in order to become more true to herself. We were both surprised to find that she had natural healing capacities.

Confidence wouldn't have helped me in either of these two circumstances. I didn't know where the healing would happen or where it would lead the person. I had to trust that the work would be guided by these natural beautiful internal powers that want each of us to be *well* and *whole*.

"Our separation from each other is an optical illusion."

Albert Einstein

CHAPTER 56

—ɯ—

Seeing

I took detailed notes after each energy work session to keep track of a client's chakras, energy flow, and issues they were addressing. I wrote down what they noticed and experienced. But I rarely wrote about *my* experiences. They were easy to dismiss if I didn't take the time to ask myself, "What just happened to *me* here?" There were two types of experiences that I was very curious about.

One, I thought of as "the seeing thing." I became aware of it happening the first time I saw my client Sally. But I remembered that this kind of shift in "seeing" had first occurred when I was fifteen when my friend Roxanne invited me over to her house for supper. When I arrived, Roxanne opened the kitchen door welcoming me and introduced me to her mother who was cooking. Just then I heard a funny animal type noise.

"Oh, that's Robbie, let me go get him," her mother said as she hurried down the hallway.

Roxanne had never mentioned a brother.

"He's thirteen," she said her eyes following her mother, not looking at me. "But he's mentally retarded, so he's more like a baby."

Then zooming into the living room in a baby walker came a creature with a large head, long broomstick-width arms and legs, and tennis-ball size joints. In the first split second I was shocked and distressed. But almost immediately, I felt a shift as I began looking into his big brown eyes. There, I saw a beautiful child inside this most unusual body. We smiled broadly at each other, and I got down on my hands and knees and started talking to him as I did all toddlers. We played peek-a-boo and made sounds back and forth to each other. I crawled around chasing him as he scooted in his walker giggling.

Roxanne and her mother had never seen Robbie so lively and happy with anyone outside the family. At that time, most severely handicapped children were institutionalized from birth. So on the rare occasions that they took Robbie out in public, people either stared or deliberately turned away. This was the first time I had ever seen a severely handicapped child. They wondered why I wasn't afraid or how I knew exactly how to play with him. I didn't know, it had just happened naturally.

Later as I became interested in special education and worked in institutions and schools, I found that initially I might be distracted by a child's physical differences, but almost inevitably, as I looked into the child's eyes, I would suddenly "see" him or her. And when that happened, I could feel myself looking past any physical or developmental disability and a deep caring would well up in me. This was usually accompanied by a real sense of ease in being with them. Playing with them or teaching them naturally flowed from "the seeing thing."

I hadn't thought about the "seeing thing" in many years until Sally showed up.

Sally was suicidal. She was referred by her therapist, who had tried every approach imaginable. Sally's psychiatrist had also prescribed various combinations of antidepressants. Nothing was working. "I'm going out on a limb here," the therapist said to me. "But I've tried everything."

During our first session, Sally revealed only a small part of her difficult past, one filled with violence and abuse.

Her story was troubling and appalling. But as I listened to her tell me about her life, I simply felt calm. Instead of seeing the brokenness she was describing, I could only see her, who she really was, beyond the trauma she had experienced. Deep caring came up in me and with it arose ease in knowing how to be with her and how to offer the energy healing.

After the energy work session, when she got off the table, she said, "How did you do that?"

"What?" I asked her.

"I feel different."

"How so?"

"My body feels lighter. Everything doesn't seem so dark and heavy around me. I feel safe. I can't remember ever feeling this way."

With this new experience she was able, for the time being, to step away from the dark ledge she had been standing near.

This kind of seeing allowed me to hear a client's story—whether it was about tragedy, life threatening illness, or terrible mistakes—and still see the person's true nature. I couldn't make myself see this way. It seemed like it would come upon me, oftentimes by surprise. When it did occur during a session though, the energy work was usually very helpful, as if being seen this way was healing in itself.

But another aspect of "the seeing thing" had me curious. It happened the first time I saw my client Candace. She had been in therapy for many years, but she felt stuck. As I sat across from this gentle, soft-spoken woman in her mid-forties, she told me about her abusive and controlling ex-husband, and how she'd lost custody of her children. As her stories unfolded, I became very present, listening intently to what she was saying and noticing my intuition. My full attention was on her, and in this moment, "the seeing thing" came over me. No matter what she said, I could "see" that she was going to be okay. I sensed her integrity, her desire to heal, and how well she would be once she got beyond the depression.

The mysterious piece arrived during the sense of deep caring. My heart felt wide open and then it was almost as if I lost myself. Not in a bad or crazy way. I lost *who* I was. I just was. There was no ego, no saying I'm the healer, you are the client. No self-consciousness. Whatever usually separates me from others dropped away. I only felt our shared humanity. There were no thoughts like, "Oh how sad, poor thing," or "How did she make that decision?" I wasn't feeling love for her because she was brave or gentle, even though she was. No judgments, positive or negative. Compassion felt easy. There was nothing at all in the way. I wasn't touching Candace or running energy, but without any effort, it felt like I was creating space through simply being. And in quietly holding this space for Candace, in simply "being" compassion as she told her stories, it seemed like a healing process, that was there all along within her, was set in motion.

These remarkable episodes of love and compassion made it difficult to face my all too human imperfections.

I would leave work aware of this capacity to see people and love them unconditionally, and of course, my deepest desire was to carry it over at home. I loved my husband and children. But they could be so annoying at times. They could get on my nerves in a split second. I wondered how I could feel this deep unconditional caring and love for my clients and then at home be furious at my husband for burning his toast every morning, smoking up the house, or giving him the cold shoulder for arriving ten minutes late for dinner, yet again. How could I face the fiery anger I experienced when my teenagers didn't come home on time or lied to me?

But maybe that was the point. I am all of this. I'm human. Like everyone, I have a great capacity to love and I can also be judgmental. I can be present and patient, or rushed and impatient. I may be able to see at times, but of course, I have plenty of blind spots.

I found these truths to be very irritating.

"The only real valuable thing is intuition."

Albert Einstein

CHAPTER 57

—ɯ—

Playing

The shift from work to home wasn't easy. Not only did work set the bar pretty high for offering love with every move I made, I ended my work day buzzed energetically and my third eye, home of my intuition, wide open. In other words, after practicing running energy and being in touch with my intuition for five or six hours, I was tired but also very sensitive. I tried to allow myself some time to get grounded and in touch with my surroundings after work. David Davis had told me I'd learn to modulate my energy and my intuition, and he was right. Luckily, I rarely received information out of the blue like I had before. And just as Mary Branch had predicted, I was blowing fewer light bulbs.

Even though I turned my intuition down after work I still had fun playing with it at home. I could practice without anyone knowing. I got a lighthearted feeling whenever I practiced and it tickled me each time I was correct. I'd try to guess what was inside the mailbox. Or anticipate who was on the phone when it rang. I sensed into the best time for phone calls and I was often right. I'd ask myself, "Is this a good time to catch my sister?" or "Is now the right moment to call the doctor?" And when I just wanted to leave a phone message, I would "check in" and see if I could intuit when that person would be out. Most of the time, I was correct.

The guessing games reminded me of singing in my Mary Poppins dream: "You find the fun and snap the job's a game." Now I understood the dream's message. When I practiced my intuition at home, *snap,* it added an element of play to ordinary chores.

The intuitive skill that came in most handy at home was remote viewing—the ability to correctly produce information about a person, place, object, or event that is located somewhere else in time or space, completely out of sight to the viewer. In class, we practiced this skill to help find lost items. I wasn't very good at finding *things* because I didn't feel a connection to objects. But I discovered I was pretty good at finding *people* remotely, in a different time or place.

One night in particular, I had awesome results with Julia, who had just started high school. She was required to attend an evening science lecture at a very large high school. Because she needed a ride home only an hour after she was dropped off, I decided to attend the lecture with her. We were running late, so I sent her into the auditorium ahead of me and went to find parking. Five minutes later, I entered the cavernous pitch-black space. Down in front, the speaker was showing slides; the only light in an auditorium packed with over eight hundred students. I couldn't see anything, and I had no idea where Julia might be sitting. I stood in the back of the left hand aisle, closed my eyes, and asked to connect with Julia. Within moments I "felt" that she was on the far right side of the theatre about two thirds of the way back. I crossed over to the right-hand aisle, walked one third of the way down, and there she was!

"Oh my gosh, how did you find me?" she whispered.

I just smiled, "Lucky guess."

I also used this skill once my children learned to drive. When they took the car out, I could check to see if they were okay. And if they weren't home on time, I used remote viewing to locate them. I usually got an image—similar to a photograph—that gave me a hint about where they were. Once, while I waited for Julia to arrive home from a track meet, I got an image of a particular highway overpass. I knew the overpass was near Exit 183, so I figured I could expect her home in about eight minutes. Right on cue, eight minutes later, Julia pulled our blue station wagon into the driveway.

Remote viewing saved me a lot of worry, but I didn't tell anyone except Dan that I had this capability. I figured my children would think it was creepy. But I set clear boundaries. I would never use intuition to invade their privacy, just like I never went through their rooms once they got to high school. When it came to my kids, remote viewing was mainly for safety purposes.

Both Julia and Tommy ran on the cross-country team. I quickly discovered that I could practice remote viewing to find them on the 3.1 mile course, or afterwards when they disappeared among hundreds of runners cooling down, or in the vast crowds that gathered for the awards. My cross-country version of remote viewing worked like this: I stood very still, got centered, and quieted my mind. Then I closed my eyes, said the child's name to myself, and waited in a silent inner space that looked empty. Within moments usually, I could feel their location or see it in my mind's eye. The only catch was I needed to wear sunglasses and step away from the other parents. I didn't want anyone to interrupt my silent waiting or—more importantly— to notice that I was watching the race with my eyes closed!

Cross-country and track turned out to be great practice grounds for different ways to access intuition. Julia was a very serious varsity runner. Occasionally, in a dream the night before, I would get her race time or her place at the finish. I told Dan about it sometimes but swore him to secrecy. I didn't want my predictions to affect her race outcomes. Still, whenever I was right, Dan and I would share a knowing glance. Before long he started waking up with his own intuitive information about Julia and Tommy's races. Sometimes he was even right.

Intuition brought me some other odd gifts, too, like traffic prediction! If highway traffic slowed to a crawl, for instance, I immediately asked, "When will this clear?" The answer usually came in the image of a digital clock—the time showing me when the traffic would clear. Sometimes I got a visual of what-ever was causing the jam. Once I got my answer, I could relax and wait patiently to see if I would be right. About ninety-nine percent of the time I was.

My husband grew to trust my traffic prediction skills. One Saturday as we started off for Virginia Beach, we hit stopped traffic on the highway before we had even gotten past down-town Richmond.

"What do I do?" he asked.

Right away, I saw in my mind's eye that the traffic jam continued onto the ramp leading to the beach highway.

"Exit here, now," I told him, as he quickly exited and encountered yet another bottleneck.

"Wait, what happened to your intuition?" he said, annoyed as he scanned for a way around this unusually heavy traffic. At first, I couldn't figure out what had gone wrong. Then I realized I'd only viewed the highway. I hadn't zeroed in on what was causing the traffic jam or checked on the downtown roads. It turned out there was a big event at the coliseum and the highway exit was clogged when beach traffic converged on coliseum traffic. "We should have stayed where we were!" he said.

He was right. "Whoops, sorry," I said. It struck me as funny that my lawyer husband and I, who'd both dismissed psychic ability as a woo-woo hoax, were now using it to predict traffic snarls. Even funnier, he was annoyed when my psychic prediction proved wrong!

To my delight, I also sometimes used intuition for shopping. Once I needed a nice dress for an upcoming fundraiser. I hated clothes shopping, plus I didn't have the time or energy to run to every store in town trying on dresses. I wondered if remote viewing could help. I started by creating a clear intention to find a classic black or navy blue dress, but I had to be even more specific. The dress needed to be in Richmond and within my budget. Then I sat still and closed my eyes, quietly holding my intention. I cleared my mind and waited. I didn't think about stores or picture the dress. I was sitting in the middle of open, empty black space where anything was possible. Several minutes went by. Then I saw it—an image of a large nearby department store that usually felt overwhelming. I asked internally, "Where is the dress located in the store?"

Almost immediately I saw myself standing next to a rack of dark dresses near a cash register. I couldn't tell where it was, so I zoomed back out in the image until I saw the escalators and verified that the "me" in the image was in the front right corner on the first floor of the store.

After work, I went straight to the store and walked directly to the location of the dresses I had seen. I figured it was a *hint,* and that once I was in the general vicinity of the image, I would look around for the dress. It was probably just a way to get me to try that store first. But there, beside the register, was exactly the same rack of dark dresses I had seen. I browsed through the collection and there it was, a classic A-line navy blue dress in my size, sale priced too! I tried it on and it fit beautifully. I couldn't stop smiling. If intuition only served to help me spend less time shopping, it would be worth all the practice. And even if I wasn't right every time, it certainly made shopping a lot more fun.

The greatest gift intuition brought, however, was a deeper understanding of my family. And it came through having greater awareness and sensitivity. For example, I might suddenly know when to ask Tommy if everything was okay. I would "get" messages like, "Julia needs reassurance," or "Let Tommy work through this rough spot on his own." I was more clear about when to leave the kids alone and when to offer help. Intuitively, I seemed to know which open-ended questions to ask in order to help them process a problem they were having. I became better at not jumping in with judgments or advice. I practiced listening to them with more focused attention. The trust I was learning about at work also carried over. I reminded myself that they were on a life journey too, and that when times were tough for them, I trusted that they could work through their problems. I'd be there to help, or to steer them toward the help they needed. And just as I practiced *self*-acceptance, so too, I practiced accepting Tommy, Julia, and Dan.

Most importantly, I reminded myself it was all a practice. I often fell short, being impatient, getting too involved in their issues, or letting my anger take over. But I had this new place to come back to. I had a set of practices and lots of intentions around how I wanted to be as a mother and wife.

I even occasionally had nice moments doing energy work with Tommy and Julia. They didn't want to talk about energy work with me, but it helped them each heal minor running injuries. And as a mother, I deeply appreciated the opportunity to offer loving kindness, along with healing energy, to my teenagers.

"Sometimes *rest* is the way to live."

Calvin

CHAPTER 58

Resting

Sometimes the intuitive messages I received for a client later turned out to be for me as well. It happened after a session with Kriszta.

Her Eastern European heritage was reflected in her unusual name and striking looks. A petite thirty-year-old, with short blonde hair and wide-set green eyes, Kriszta had been recently diagnosed with stage-four colon cancer and was undergoing chemotherapy. Our energy sessions helped her body cope with the harsh side effects of chemo.

She arrived one week with concerns about her finances and feeling pressured to return to work. Her mother had quit her teaching job and moved to Virginia to assist with her care. Kriszta felt bad about needing help from her mother, as well as friends, neighbors, doctors, and nurses. As a mental health social worker, she preferred being in the helping role, and she hated how weak her treatments made her feel. She detested laziness, she said. Kriszta enjoyed her challenging job and was anxious to return to it.

Her intention that day was to receive healing energy and clarity so that she'd know whether to go back to work. She got up on the massage table and laid down. As usual, I put my hands in the space about one foot above her body to both connect with, and sense, her energy field. That day, the moment I put my hands in her field and closed my eyes, a large orange tabby cat appeared in my mind's eye. He had a message. I couldn't help it, I giggled.

"What's so funny?" Kriszta asked.

"I'm sorry. It's just, well," I hesitated unsure of what she would think. Heck, I didn't know what I thought. What was this?

The image stayed, so I continued, "I keep seeing a cat. I've never had a cat show up before. And he seems to have a message for you."

"A cat?" she asked, laughing.

"Yes, very big one, kind of orange with stripes? Do you know this cat?"

"Yes," she said dismissively. "Sounds like my cat, Calvin. Ugh, I am so annoyed with Calvin. I always wondered what he did while I was at work. It turns out that he just lays around all day long. He is so lazy!"

"Well, do you want to hear his message anyway?" I asked.

She hesitated and then with reluctance slowly said, "Okay, let's hear it."

I shifted my attention back to Calvin the cat. "He says," I paused making sure I was getting this message clearly. *"Sometimes rest is the way to live."*

She sighed, "I guess that means he doesn't want me to go back to work. He wants me to be lazy like him."

"No, I think he is literally saying that sometimes rest is the way to live. Just being in a place of rest is okay. Also, he says he'll be with you as the times are right for rest," I said.

We let it go and I did the energy work. Afterwards I talked to her a little about what I had noticed when others were healing from surgery, cancer treatments, or an accident. It appeared to me that much of a person's life energy seemed to be directed internally to the healing. In turn, there was little energy left for chores, grocery shopping, or work. I had seen some people battling disease who refused to give in, and they used all their energy trying to keep up with their regular routines, only to find that they lacked the energy needed for healing and got sicker or took longer to recover. I told her that feeling like you have no energy can be a message from the body suggesting that it needs rest.

When Kriszta came the following week for her appointment she said, "I've decided not to return to work for now."

"And how does that decision feel to you?"

"It seems right. When I paid attention to my body and rested whenever that seemed like a good idea, I felt much better. I even felt well enough to have some friends over to visit."

"How's Calvin?"

"Well you'll like this. I put Calvin's quote by my bed and instead of fussing at him for being lazy, I've told him that he is now my 'devoted companion in rest.' He always comes to curl up beside me when I'm resting."

Soon after this, I received a note card from Kriszta with a big tabby colored cartoon cat on front. I glued a speech bubble to the drawing that said, "Sometimes *rest* is the way to live," and put it on my desk at work. It made me smile and the quote led to helpful discussions with some of my clients who were "rest deprived."

The longer this cat quote sat on my desk, the more I realized how unusual this sentence was. I pondered the notion for myself. I could still remember my father saying, "Work hard, play hard." I couldn't remember hearing the word "rest" mentioned in our house, ever. Go to bed—yes. Take a nap—yes. But *rest?*

Calvin hadn't said, "Sometimes *sleep* is the way to live." I generally thought I should be working, cleaning, taking care of the kids, exercising, or learning something new. And if I was too tired for these "shoulds," that I "should" sleep or take a nap. But Calvin was offering Kriszta—and me—a different possibility. He suggested rest, as in, being still and not *doing* anything. Could I let myself rest, even though I wasn't sick?

I decided to bring the quote home, and I put it on the refrigerator to remind me to consider this notion. I began a practice of occasionally putting everything down for whatever moments I could do so. I would give myself permission to be without a list and without doing anything in particular. It was a practice of sitting or walking and being present and at rest.

When the holidays came, and I found myself getting caught up in all that I had to do, I reminded myself—*Stop and rest.* So I'd stop and just notice—the sounds, smells, or feel of whatever was around me. I'd never thought about rest as a time to just "be." But that's what I experienced. In these moments of non-doing and non-striving, I felt more peaceful. I even noticed that my resting moments had an effect on others. If I went into this place of rest and more ease, my family seemed to experience less stress as well. That year, I moved through the festivities and family visits feeling less overwhelmed than I ever had, doing less and getting more rest.

The bigger surprise was what happened next with my husband.

After the holidays he remarked, "I'm not enjoying work at all."

Since Dan generally loved his job and even had workaholic tendencies, I paid attention to his comment. Dan hardly ever complained.

"Is there anything you can do about it?" I asked.

"Not really, I've just got some very difficult clients and situations to deal with," was his rather discouraged reply.

The weekend came and with it a huge snow storm, unusual for Richmond. For two days, while snowed in, we cooked homemade soups, enjoyed a fire in the fireplace, went sledding down our steep street, and took walks in the snow. Our kids, both in high school, were content hanging out with friends and enjoying the snow. We all slept more than usual. It was quiet. On Monday, still snowed in, we each worked a bit but mostly enjoyed the day together.

Later that week on Friday at dinner he said, "I feel better about work now."

"Oh really? What do you think caused the shift?" I asked expecting to hear how he had dealt with these difficult people and their legal issues.

But instead he said, "I think it's that cat quote that you have up on the refrigerator."

"Really?" I was shocked that he had paid any attention to it.

He said, "I think those days of resting, staring at the fire, and not working—just being—were what I needed to help me feel better about life. The cat was right, sometimes rest is the way to live."

My workaholic husband admitting to the benefit of rest—now there was a miracle.

"People like us, who believe in physics know
that the distinction between past, present and
future is only a stubbornly persistent illusion.

Albert Einstein

CHAPTER 59

—⚏—

Conversing

Although I enjoyed playing with my intuition at home,
occasionally did energy work on my husband or kids, and
integrated what I learned from clients, there were aspects of the
work I tried to keep separate.

It turned out that the practice of being open, staying curious,
and trusting in the mystery had led me to a surprising new skill.

Sometimes I could see and talk to people who were dead.

Luckily it didn't happen often, and I never felt afraid or
anxious. The dead arrived quietly and gently, as if from another
dimension. But their visits did make me pay attention, because
in my experience, they always came for a reason.

My first conversation with a person no longer of our reality, occurred near the end of my first year of private practice.

Cece, a woman I had gotten to know through Joan and Nancy's Wednesday dream group, was diagnosed with stage-four colon cancer and began seeing me for energy work several months into her treatments. Her surgery, chemotherapy, and radiation had taken a toll on her body. The energy work had relieved the pain, allowing her some peace and comfort.

Cece was a distinguished looking fifty-year-old woman with chiseled features and bright hazel eyes. She had traveled the world visiting every continent. Around Richmond, she was the well-known art critic for the local newspaper and a social activist dedicated to civil rights and integration. With her life long interest in African American History and connection to Goochland County, where she grew up, Cece became fascinated by the history of free blacks.

During my sessions, I oftentimes intuited specific questions to ask the client. The week before, I asked Cece if she had any unfinished business she might need to attend to. She told me that just before she was diagnosed, she had finished writing the biography of a free black woman who had lived in Goochland County between 1770 and 1850. Her sudden diagnosis and the ensuing treatments had prevented her from sending it out to agents or publishers. I suggested that she bring the manuscript in to see if we could intuit what, if anything, she was to do with it.

Sadly, that week, she received news that her cancer had spread and was untreatable. She handed the manuscript to me at the beginning of this session, but we didn't discuss it because of her more immediate concerns. Instead, she got up on the massage table and laid down. I lit a candle as usual, and we held the intention that the energy work would offer physical comfort and peace in this moment. I put my hands in the air over her body to connect with her field and to offer the intention. Then I went to her feet and began gently offering her energy, moving next to her leg, my hands on her ankle and knee and then knee and hip.

Gradually, I began to notice a woman who seemed to be standing across the table from me. She was a few inches shorter than me with soft curly brown hair, a solid healthy body and a dark complexion.

"Who are you?" I asked silently to this woman as she stood grounded in another dimension.

"Milly Pierce," she said.

"Oh my gosh, are you the one Cece wrote the book about?"

"Yes," came her clear answer.

I must be imagining this, I thought as I decided to ignore her. Cece was not feeling good, and I needed to focus on her physical well-being. Plus, it had taken a huge leap of faith for Cece to be doing an alternative healing modality like energy work. I didn't think dealing with a "spirit" would interest her at the moment.

As I carried on with my energy work, the woman's presence continued getting stronger and stronger. She would not leave and she would not be dismissed. In an effort to force my imagination to clear, I said, silently and with indignation, "I have no way of knowing that you are Milly Pierce."

A few moments passed and then she said to me, "John Bates. Ask Cece about John Bates."

Clearly this woman would not go quietly, so I decided to say something to Cece. "There seems to be someone around you, Cece," I said tentatively. "Do you want to know about it?"

I assumed she would make light of this and wave me off. Instead, she opened her eyes and looked at me, intrigued, "Yeah. Sure."

"Well," I hesitated, "she says she's Milly Pierce."

Cece smiled knowingly and replied, "I'm not surprised. I thought I sensed her around other times." She seemed relieved as if this confirmed her own experiences. "You know every time I would come to a dead end in my research, I would be led to some new remarkable source of information. My book has 303 footnotes if that gives you any idea how much help I was getting."

"Wow," I said. Then it made me wonder. Does everyone have experiences with dead people, but they just don't talk about it? I still felt unsure that Milly was anything other than imagination. In order to test her existence, I did as she suggested.

"Milly says to ask you about John Bates."

Cece relayed several associations with John Bates from the details of her research, including a John Bates who worked at the Goochland courthouse and a John Bates she knew now. "The Bates were a prominent, white, land-owning family in Goochland County in the 1700 and 1800s," she concluded.

Okay, so maybe this was Milly Pierce looking at me.

"Well Cece," I paused considering what we should do. "You wrote a book about a free black woman who lived two hundred years ago. I'm sure any record of her life was kept by white men. She's standing here ready to talk to you. Is there anything you want to ask her? Anything you couldn't find in your research?"

Cece remained still on the table with me standing at her side. In order to communicate with someone from another dimension, I had to hold a lot of energy and keep a very high level of focused attention. Cece would ask a question and Milly would transmit an answer; sometimes in words, but other answers came as a whole idea or a set of pictures. Some information came as a feeling into my body. Each time, I would translate into words—to the best of my ability—an answer for Cece. The intensity of the process felt a little bit like the physical energy of running a marathon and the mental energy of taking a timed exam.

A long interview ensued. We learned about what led to Milly's status as a free black, the difficulties she faced, and why she was never able to marry her husband legally because she was a free black and he was a slave. We heard the story of how she disowned one of her sons when he went into shipping on the James River because some of the "goods" he transported were slaves. She shared why she had lost touch with her daughters, who had moved west for freedom, and whom she loved and missed. Free blacks, she said, were not allowed to learn to read or write, so mail wasn't an option and safe travel was nearly impossible. Cece had a chance to ask Milly why she had slaves. As a land-owning free black, Milly explained, she was unable to manage her large farm without help. She couldn't hire white farmhands; they wouldn't work for free blacks. Other free blacks were in her same predicament. They, too, needed help with their farms. She had no choice but to hire people who were technically considered slaves.

"Freedom is not as fixed a notion as folks think," Milly said. "Things weren't the way they probably seem when you look at those pages you've been studying." She had tried to give her slaves all the rights allowed them, without getting into trouble with the law.

After about an hour of this conversation, Cece was satisfied with the information and we were about to close when I realized I had a question. "Milly, why did you tell me to ask Cece who John Bates was? Who was he to you?"

"My father," she answered.

"Ohhh," said Cece, a puzzle piece from her research falling into place.

We thanked Milly for her information and I did a closing, bringing the energy back down to a more normal level. Cece got up from the table and was quite energized.

We talked for a few minutes and she said, "Well now that you've met Milly, you'll have to read the book!"

"I plan to begin it tonight!" I replied as we said our good-byes.

I was completely exhausted and my nerves felt jangled. I'd had brief encounters with the dead before but never anything like this. How much of our conversation sprung from my own imagination? Was it nothing more than a projection? I was amazed that Cece never doubted the experience or the messages. I kept shaking my head, trying to clear it. Did that really just happen?

This was my last appointment of the day, and I went straight home and fixed dinner, trying to reconnect with everyday reality. Eating dinner with my family and hearing about everyone's day helped ground me. Afterwards, my husband and I decided to go for a walk to enjoy the summer evening. We were quietly strolling around the nearby lake when he innocently asked, "How was your day?"

I thought about my agreement with Dan to share what I was learning and experiencing with energy work. Was this the time to tell him I see dead people sometimes? I figured this was as good a time as any.

"Well, I had a really big session this afternoon," I began.

"Oh yeah. Can you tell me about it?"

Without mentioning any names, I proceeded to tell him about Cece, her book and Milly. He was listening intently as we slowly walked along the path beside the lake. As I came to the end of the story, he stopped short, turned to me, put his hands on his hips and said, "You know the question, 'How was your day honey?'"

"Yeah?"

"Well, being married to you, it takes on a whole new meaning!"

We laughed and went on to talk about the kids and the usual round of household topics as we walked home.

That night, as we got ready to read in bed, I pulled Cece's manuscript out of my backpack and laid it on my lap. Dan adjusted some pillows behind him and settled in with his latest Grisham novel. He turned to me, rubbing his chin and pondering something. "Do you think Milly was someone who was in heaven and came back to talk? Or do you think she was stuck here somehow, like a ghost?"

"I've been wondering about that too. Even when I was talking to her, I was surprised how unaware she seemed of how much time had passed. She still had a lot of her own personality and actually was adamant that Cece publish the book. My gut feeling is that she is a ghost or someone who is stuck or has decided to stay in what feels like an in-between place to me. But the bottom line is, I really don't know."

"Interesting," he said. He turned his attention back to his book, and I opened Cece's manuscript. There, on the cover page, the title of the book answered Dan's question:

Living in Limbo

Milly Pierce: A Free Woman of Colour and Her Family

"What I see in Nature is a grand design that we
can comprehend only imperfectly, and that must
fill a thinking person with a feeling of humility."

Albert Einstein

CHAPTER 60

—⚏—

Helping

The dead people who showed up in my office were as interesting
and as diverse as the clients they came to visit. Not all of them
were ghosts like Milly.

One day my client Mary Beth came in for her weekly energy
session. She was a nurse practitioner who had become a friend
when we were both teacher trainers in the field of sex education. Later, when she joined the dream group that Barbara and
I led, I came to know her even better. Mary Beth's breast cancer
had reoccurred, and she had decided on the most potent chemotherapy available, despite the severe side effects.

As I began running energy to clear the effects of the chemo,
I started noticing a "presence" and, as it came into view, I saw
a stooped old woman who seemed to be busy working on Mary

Beth. Visually, she was barely noticeable, so I ignored her but appreciated the extra help she seemed to be offering. I assumed, as I did with most clients, that Mary Beth didn't believe in such "presences."

We worked in silence for a time and then as I often do, I asked, "How are you doing?"

"Well Aunt Emma is here working on me."

"Is that who this is? Rather short and kind of bent over with a bad back?"

"Oh yes, that's Aunt Emma."

"Aunt Emma sure seems to know what she's doing."

"Yeah, that would be her. She always was a 'can do' person. And she would want to help me. My shoulders are much better and my whole body feels lighter."

"Great, we'll just continue having her help out."

"Sounds good," she said.

We went back into silence at that point. Once we had acknowledged her presence, Aunt Emma began showing me exactly where to place my hands and helping me with the energy flow. She chose a strong high vibration that was hard for me to hold for too long but seemed to be very helpful for Mary Beth. Near the end of the session, it seemed like Aunt Emma had a direct message.

"Tell Mary Beth that it is not her time to cross over. That is not what the cancer is about." I worried that I was imagining this or that it was simply wishful thinking. But she kept insisting that I say it, so I did. Mary Beth took the message to heart. It was very reassuring and turned out to be true.

Aunt Emma's presence was quite different than Milly's had been. Milly seemed to be in an in-between place. My impression was that she had come to help get the book published, but she was not concerned with Cece. On the other hand, Emma knew Mary Beth in this lifetime. She was more like a benevolent helper, bringing love and healing.

One time I met a person who had died and was both *helpful* and *needed help.* My client Kathy called me distraught. Her father had died suddenly over the weekend, during emergency surgery. "Could you possibly fit me in?" she asked. I'd just had a cancellation and she came in the next morning.

A bright, attractive woman in her mid thirties, Kathy had three school-aged children. She had come for energy work on a regular basis for a couple of years, moving through all kinds of spiritual and body issues including releasing old fears that had held her back.

When she entered my office that day, she collapsed into the chair and began recounting her father's quick decline, emergency surgery, and sudden death. She described a terrible sense of loss. While she talked, I kept noticing an unfamiliar energy behind her right shoulder that I couldn't quite make out. At the end of her long story, she stopped abruptly and said, "Peggy, I think he is hanging around me. Is that possible?"

"Yes, it's possible," I said. "What makes you think that?"

She proceeded to describe a number of mysterious instances in the past twenty-four hours, especially while she was home alone. Several lights had turned on and off, seemingly of their own accord. A framed piece of her son's artwork somehow came up off a large hook and fell to the floor. A short time after she had hung it back up, she found it completely askew. "I just feel like someone is around, Peggy. It's making me crazy."

A former tax attorney, Kathy was very levelheaded. I knew she wasn't making this up or going crazy. Kathy's father had been a brilliant scientist who had helped design the first satellites. He had never believed in God or the afterlife. So what was happening here?

"Sometimes when people who have died are around, it's possible to communicate with them during the energy work. We can invite him and see what he wants. Would you like to try that?" I asked.

"Yes," she said. "I want to find out if he is trying to get my attention."

"Okay, to begin I just need his name."

"Harry."

Kathy laid down on the massage table, and as usual, I began connecting with her field and setting an intention.

Almost as soon as I began sensing in, Kathy piped up, "He's here isn't he?"

"Yes, I believe so." The energy that was beside her was now coming into form. He was standing across from me.

She began to cry.

"If you have anything you want to say, he can probably hear you," I offered.

She told him how much she loved him and what she appreciated about him.

After a time she asked, "Have you been messing with my lights and Kevin's picture?" she asked.

Although Kathy could sense his presence, she couldn't hear his messages, so I tried to communicate for him. "He seems to be saying yes," I said.

"Why did you fiddle with the picture Kevin made for me at school?" There was lots of art by the kids around the house.

"He's saying something about the fact that he never appreciated the warm and loving home you created and what a good mother you are," I said.

As the only child of two smart, hard-working scientists, Kathy said she had felt judged for much of her life, especially in the last ten years, as she had chosen to stay home with her kids. But now her father was sending love and appreciation. She was touched that he'd come to tell her this, and she grieved his loss.

At the end of the session, it occurred to me that I had never asked Kathy, "Can you describe the picture he knocked off the wall?" wondering why he picked that one.

"Yes, Kevin made it in kindergarten. It's a drawing of me and it says:

> "About My Mom
> My mother is beautiful.
> She loves me even more than our dog Barney."

After Kathy left, as I was preparing for my next client, I sensed that Harry was still in my office. I thought I was imagining this, but then he seemed to come sit in my client chair. I shook my head, rubbed my eyes, and paced my office, but I couldn't get this sense of his presence to go away.

"Are you still here, Harry?" I finally asked.

"Yes," he said, "I want to talk."

"I have another client right now, but you can come back at noon."

"Okay," he said and then was gone.

I thought I was clearly losing my mind. Had I really asked a ghost to come back later? But sure enough, just after my next client left, there was Harry sitting across from me. He started right in.

"Where am I?" he asked. He didn't understand what had happened. He couldn't figure out where he was. I looked at this agnostic, a man who was certain there was no life after death, and I told him straight out.

"You died during surgery. You are dead."

"Oh," he said, considering this possibility, "How did I die?"

"You died of physical causes. Your heart stopped."

He was very interested and wanted to know specifically what had happened. I told him they were planning an autopsy and that Kathy could tell him the results.

"Where am I now then?" he asked.

"You seem to be in-between worlds."

"What do I do? I don't like it here."

"You have choices it seems." Using my intuition I tried to get guidance about what to tell him. "I think you can hang around, travel, see people, or go to the funeral tomorrow. Or you can cross over or work toward crossing over."

"Can I smoke?"

"Sure," I answered, as if *I* knew!

"Did I die from smoking?"

"I don't know. Maybe they will find out during the autopsy."

I became concerned that if he continued to hang around Kathy and her family it would make her healing very difficult, especially if she thought he was stuck in some way. I explained this to him, and he definitely didn't want to upset her any further.

"I can try to help you move to a better place if you want," I offered.

After a time, he decided that he was ready to move on. I used a process I had learned for helping people at the time of death. As we began this process, a deep appreciation or sense of honoring of his life and who he was came in around him. A light came over his presence, and he gradually shifted into the brightness.

I said a prayer for him and took a few moments to get centered before I saw my next client. She was a highly intuitive woman who practiced a type of energy work called Healing Touch. She walked into my office, greeted me warmly, then scrunched up her nose and looked around as if searching for something.

"I smell cigarette smoke. Did you just see someone who smokes?"

"There are only two ways to live your life.
One is as though nothing is a miracle,
the other is as though everything is.
I choose the latter."

Albert Einstein

CHAPTER 61

—⫘—

Guiding

My teacher Mary Branch had always encouraged us to clearly articulate how we were receiving intuition. We described physical sensations like heat and cool, density and flow. We reported colors or images visible with our third eye. Some students heard a vibrational tone that informed them about the energy they were running. There were many ways to articulate the way we felt energy and received intuition. We interpreted our sensations and used them to direct our process.

My teacher Helen, on the other hand, had referred to "guides" every time she taught. This made me feel uncomfortable at first. It reminded me of being told in grade school that each of us had a guardian angel. This seemed like a very childish notion.

But Helen told us that her guides came and directed her teaching. Since I consistently learned new things from Helen, I accepted that her intuition arrived to her in the form of what she called "spirit guides" whom *she thought* she could see and hear. For me, it was more comfortable and acceptable to refer to information I received as intuition, so that is how *I thought of it*.

Strangely though, as my energy became stronger and clearer, I began noticing that there were times that I seemed to be getting intuitive messages from a specific location. Instead of receiving information about where to put my hands or which energy to run, it felt like some external conscious "presence" was directing me or even telling me exactly what to do, like Aunt Emma had done when I worked with Mary Beth.

Helen encouraged me to explore what I could about the presence when one showed up. Since I didn't particularly believe that there were actually guides around, I practiced suspending disbelief and simply tried to pay attention to the energetic sensation of another presence in the room.

It wasn't long before I started being able to tell if the presence I felt was masculine or feminine and what quality was being brought to the work. Guidance was being offered and I began to understand it. Helen confirmed what I was being told or shown by each presence or guide. In turn, I received more information about how to offer healing energy. To my surprise, these guides were consistently helpful.

This was very hard for me to accept. The few times outside of class that I'd heard people refer to spirit guides, it seemed inauthentic and ego based. To me it seemed like a form of imagination.

One Christmas, my husband's brother invited a friend to our house for dinner. His friend Michael, a self-professed "angel channeler," proceeded to stir up the whole family by taking each person aside to tell them about the angel or archangel he could supposedly see beside them. He also shared angelic messages. My husband and I were irritated by it all. When Michael came into the kitchen to share his angel-sightings with me, he looked around, squirmed a bit and said, "Um, sorry, I don't see any angel around you." I tried not to respond. We were *all* trying to be nice to him. I suggested that he take a break from his angel work and enjoy the day.

He looked at me, his eyes flitting back and forth, and started backpedaling, "I'm sure it's some big archangel with you that I can't sense. I bet you're an old soul."

I didn't want to be like Michael.

Yet I had to admit, I was now having consistently helpful experiences with these "guides" in my practice. I was only willing to admit this to my close friends and classmates from the Art of Healing.

A friend had given me this intriguing quote by Einstein, which said he chose to live life as if everything was a miracle.

How could Einstein see everything as a miracle? He could explain almost any phenomenon through a mathematical formula or a scientific principle? Yet here he was choosing to view all of life as a miracle? Could *I* choose to live my life through eyes of wonder like Einstein, accepting everything as a miracle? Could I suspend disbelief and allow myself to see this guidance as a mystery, one that could help my clients? When I let myself accept the notion, I found that I liked the possibility that we were being watched over and cared for, that help was available. It felt comforting.

This was yet another form of energy in the natural world for me to ponder. Over time, I began observing closely to see what else I could know about guidance.

Over my years of private practice, I learned that these guides are helpers. Generally benevolent, they came in with a sense of deep caring about the person I was working with. They consistently seemed to know more than me or my client knew about the healing process.

Most of the time, I suddenly sensed their presence or felt a new energy in the space. I never sensed a guide *arriving*. One moment they weren't there; the next moment, they were. They left in a similar fashion, although sometimes the energy seemed to just fade out. But I never saw a guide walking or moving away. To me, seeing a guide was a bit like looking out of a sunlit window, clearly seeing the world beyond, and then suddenly seeing my own reflection or parts of it in the glass. I see the physical world—the window, the trees and grass and street outside—and my image is definitely there, but I can't touch or feel its form. It's just reflected light. So too, I could still see my client, the table, and everything in my office clearly, but I also could see this faint light giving me hints about another presence in the room.

I also had to learn how to work with this guidance. First, after feeling a presence, I might note some identifying features like masculine or feminine, size, age, or an aspect of their appearance. Then I tuned in to see if the guide had come to help. I would oftentimes feel a deep sense of caring for the client. Guides communicated with me wordlessly through a notion, or a whole idea. Some offered me specific ideas about what energy to run or where in the body the healing needed to take place.

Most of the time I worked directly with the guide without ever mentioning it to the client. But there were times when the person noticed that someone was there helping out. A client might say, "It feels like someone is working at my feet," when *my* hands were on her shoulders. In reply I might ask, "What do you think of that?" If they said, "Well that's crazy," or "That's impossible," I would just let it be. But if they said, "I think someone is here helping you," I would open the conversation asking if they could sense anything else about this helper.

It turned out that some people could also feel and identify the quality of the help coming in whether it was healing, strength, compassion, tenderness, etc. Occasionally, the client could identify the guide in some meaningful way.

Dale, a tall thin engineer in his late forties, came to receive assistance to heal chronic shoulder pain from an old injury. Over time, as we set new intentions each week, our conversations shifted to his relationships, and eventually he revealed that he had suffered at the hands of an abusive alcoholic father. One day he came in, sat down, looked at me and began crying. Again. He had cried each session. I sat and waited.

"Walking up the stairs I was just saying to myself—I'm good today. I don't think I'll cry this time. Then I walk in your office and see you and the tears come," he said.

"There are others," I told him, "who cry every time they come see me. Crying can be healing. And we don't allow ourselves to do it enough."

"But I don't feel sad."

"Oftentimes it has nothing to do with being sad. It's about being alive."

But later in the session Dale explained that every time he did energy work with me, he felt a deeply spiritual masculine presence loving him, someone like Jesus. In those moments he felt touched by the loving kindness being offered and tears would come. That day, he felt this loving presence the moment he arrived.

Another time, Marilyn, a lay minister in a local congregation, came to me troubled by what she described as excessive energy. She had just spent a month at an ashram in India where she'd studied meditation, but now she felt overwhelmed and unfocused. During her first session, while I was unblocking her throat chakra, she told me that she thought she was sensing the loving presence of Mother Theresa. After the energy work, she realized that she had been holding back her idea to introduce Centering Prayer, a Christian form of meditation, to her church community. She thought this presence of Mother Theresa might help focus her abundant energy. Months later, she confided that she often prayed to Mother Theresa for comfort and reassurance as she piloted new programs at her church.

For clients like Dale and Marilyn, an encounter with guidance was sacred. I wanted to honor this. I didn't want to explain it away or make it seem ordinary. Nor did I want to talk about it in a way that would over-glorify the experience. Instead I encouraged clients to write about their experience and notice, over time, what healing or learning might come from it.

It was never easy to experience the sacred, then re-enter ordinary routines. But over time in my life, the sacred and the ordinary seemed to be one. Although the appearance of guides could be transcendent; paradoxically, they consistently indicated they'd come to help with daily life—not to draw our attention away from it. To experience the transcendent in this way never diminished the importance of everyday physical reality. It seemed to me, in fact, that the intention of guidance was to help us see life as more precious and more meaningful than we ever imagined.

"But the important thing in God's eyes is not what we have to give, but that we hold nothing back."

John Howard Griffin

CHAPTER 62

—⚋—

Living

During these years of full-time practice, I was constantly learning more about energy healing, human nature, spirituality, intuition, guidance, and intention. But I learned the most about *how to live* from three clients, each of whom came to see me following a diagnosis of stage-four cancer. Gretchen, Kriszta and Cece all fought the disease aggressively with both the latest medical treatments and trying alternative healing modalities. But each reached beyond simply survival; these women were actively trying to be more alive. I was inspired by their aliveness.

Over time, I realized all three had repeatedly shared messages directing *me* to, *Live all the way*. I thought I was already awake and aware and living fully. But I wasn't. Not like they were.

At sixty, Gretchen was full of herself, happy and funny. She didn't give a whit what anyone else thought of her. A tall thin woman who loved hats and wore colorful clothes, she had run a bed and breakfast and been elected to the Board of Supervisors in her rural county before being diagnosed. She also did dream work, was a weaver, and created funny cards out of her photographs. I always greeted her wide smile with my own, whenever I saw her.

Once, in the midst of treatment, she went to a workshop on how to make prayer beads. She decided then and there to make prayer beads for her friends and family. She didn't waste any time or energy wondering if she was *good enough* at beading or if her friends would like what she made. She didn't wonder if they would think the beads were pretty or meaningful. She didn't ask herself if it was worth her time. I don't think she wondered if she could go into business and sell them. I was struck by her complete lack of self-consciousness or second-guessing; it was refreshing.

What Gretchen *did* think about was who the prayer beads were for. As she worked, she told me, she carefully chose just the right stone or symbolic charm for the person she had in mind. She held hopes and prayers for them with the intention that these good wishes would go into the beads. One day, she came in for a session and handed me her gift, a long beautiful set of prayer beads that were made with turquoise and rose quartz that I could also wear as a necklace. A heart-shaped piece of clear quartz hung from the center. I loved it.

Gretchen's prayer beads came from a free-flowing unfettered expression of her love, her creativity, and her generosity. Being surprised by her beading led me to wonder. What was sabotaging my creative endeavors? Could my generosity and creativity be unbound like hers?

Like Gretchen, Kriszta, the spunky thirty-year-old who had learned about rest from her cat Calvin, had little concern for what people thought of her. I might have included myself in this category, too, given my careers in sex education and now energy work. But Kriszta taught me that I was still holding back.

Seven months after her diagnosis, she had surgery to clear an intestinal blockage. I helped her prepare for the surgery energetically, then shared a list of intentions I had written for myself before I had outpatient surgery earlier in the year. Kriszta began working on her intentions right away, adapting some of mine and writing her own.

I had met Kriszta's mother, Barb, and she had offered to call me after the surgery. "You won't believe what Kriszta did," Barb said, when we finally talked.

"What?" I asked.

"Well, the surgical nurse told me that Kriszta entered the operating room and quietly walked around handing every person in the room a copy of her intentions for surgery and recovery."

"She did?" I was shocked she had thought of this. I had suggested that Kriszta share it with her close friends and family so that everyone would be praying with the same intentions. But it hadn't occurred to me to include the doctors, nurses, and staff.

"Yes, and the nurse said that everyone got very quiet. It had even brought tears to their eyes."

I bet it had. There were eleven prayers on the sheet, several of which blessed the doctors, nurses, and other technicians and their work.

Barb went on, "She said the operating room felt almost like a church to her with everyone sending love and prayers to Kriszta during the surgery. At the end she said they all talked about how it was the most sacred surgery they had ever done."

Kriszta's recovery was nothing short of miraculous. She healed faster and needed less pain medication than any patient the nurses could remember.

When Kriszta came in the next week for an appointment, I told her about being surprised to hear she had given her intentions to the staff.

"I never would have had the nerve," I admitted.

"Why not?" she asked completely curious. "I had nothing to lose and everything to gain."

She was right. What held me back, I wondered?

About two months later, the insurance company sent a form letter turning Kriszta down for coverage for a treatment that looked promising. The insurance representative she'd reached by phone had merely reiterated the reasons stated in the form letter. She was heading down to the insurance company headquarters after our appointment.

"I want them to see me. I'm not just some set of lab results or statistics." She said, unafraid. "I want to live. I deserve this chance." Kriszta was fiesty and free and she loved life. I admired her boldness.

Once again, I thought, *I'd never do that*. And then I wondered, *why not*? It felt like something external would prevent me from taking action, like knowing how the health insurance company worked. But in truth it was concern over how I would be perceived. It was time for me to notice when judging thoughts were holding me back.

Months later, as the cancer started ravaging her body, she fought on. Only a few weeks before Kriszta died, she and a friend bought tickets to see Bruce Springsteen in concert. His music had been her favorite ever since she was a little girl. This was the first time she would see The Boss in concert. By then, the cancer was growing in her liver, bones, and brain. On the day of the concert, she willed herself to be well. Afterwards, she said, "I danced in the aisles. I had the best time of my life!" She christened it her Glory Day after her favorite Springsteen song.

Why didn't I dance in the aisles? And what kept me from creating art for the sheer pleasure of creating and sharing it? Could I notice when I was holding back on life? Could I see when I was choosing not to do something because of what others might think of me? What good was that?

What if there was no fear in the way? How would I live then? I wanted to live all the way like Gretchen and Kriszta.

Cece taught me about *receiving* all the way. During one appointment she told me that her sister-in-law Meme had single-handedly kept her out of the hospital that week. Noticing that Cece was having a particularly rough day, Meme offered to stay overnight. Instead of sleeping in the guest room, she had gathered bedding and pillows and slept on the floor beside Cece's bed, close enough to help at a moments notice. Cece hadn't said "no thanks" or "that's okay." She hadn't been embarrassed that she needed so much help. She hadn't asked, "How can I ever repay you?"

Instead, Cece graciously accepted this kind offer. She knew it would probably keep her out of the hospital if Meme could get her through the night. When Cece told me about it, she expressed a deep appreciation. She was amazed that Meme cared for her that much. Cece could be a rather stoic person; Meme was open and warm. She was touched that another human being could be so loving and generous, and she reveled in how good it felt to receive what Meme offered.

This experience softened Cece, and as she continued to be a grateful receiver of loving actions, she became more loving herself. She demonstrated how to take any act of generosity into her heart and accept it with gratitude. Could I learn to receive all the love and support that is offered to me without dismissing it or turning it away?

Living all the way apparently also meant being open to *receiving* all that was coming my way.

Gretchen, Kriszta and Cece's directives to me to *live all the way*, hadn't felt like a push to create a bucket list and frantically try to do every last thing on it. Instead, I had seen how their vitality had fostered awareness of what was most important, which helped each of them live fully until the end.

I wondered what *living all the way* would look like for my own life. For now, I only knew that sometimes I'd allowed fears to direct my life and suppress my creativity and my voice. I was ready to move past these fears. I wrote an intention:

> *Please help me move beyond any and all*
> *unhelpful fears and negative judgments that might hold me back,*
> *so that I may live all the way.*

"May you know the eternal longing
that lives at the heart of time."

John O'Donohue

CHAPTER 63

—⁂—

Cece

How ironic that the three women who taught me how to live,
would also be the ones to teach me how to die with grace.

Cece was my first client who did not get well. Soon after
she shared her Milly Pierce book with me, she decided to accept
hospice care. I wondered why I had felt so clear about doing
energy work with Cece when, in the end, it didn't heal her
body. Was I supposed to get close to Cece, love her, only to lose
her? I was heartbroken, and I asked her whether she wanted to
continue doing energy work.

"Absolutely," she said.

"But it doesn't seem to be healing your cancer."

"I know. But it makes me feel better, and I like being able
to talk freely."

I was glad I could continue to see her. Over the next several months, I discovered that my role as a healer was not to cure Cece's cancer but to support her as she healed other parts of her life. She talked about her dreams and their messages. We talked about death. As she let go of more and more of her past, she found forgiveness and healed some relationships with family members. She continued to receive the love and kindness coming her way from family and close friends.

In her final months, I came to see dying as a sacred time. Cece showed me that we are meant to receive the same tender attention and care leaving this life as we receive when we arrive. I felt honored to share this part of her life with her.

Cece said she'd stopped remembering her dreams, a possible side effect of her intensive drug regimen. "I miss my dreams," she had told me. But as she neared the end of her life, *I* dreamed about *Cece* three nights in a row. I wanted to tell her about them so I called her family and asked if I could come visit. They said it wasn't a good time. But when I told them it was regarding some dreams I wanted to share, Cece told them to let me come over.

When I arrived she was in bed and very weak. She could hardly talk any more but she was very curious about the dreams. She asked the family to leave us alone for a while. I pulled up a chair beside her bed and began:

"In the first dream we were having a party for you," I explained. "Unfortunately, that's all I remembered that night. Luckily, the dream came back the next night. I went over to your house and it was overflowing with guests waiting to celebrate your crossing over. You were in your bedroom with an attendant, a family member, who was going to let us know when you had crossed over. The house was filled with people who had known you from all different times and parts of your life. They were passing around small round plates of cheese and apples.

"In the dream I said, 'This seems like a communion service.' I didn't know anyone at the party so I asked the woman next to me, 'How do you know Cece?'

" 'Oh I knew her when she had the puppy,' she replied.

" 'I never knew she had a puppy,' I said.

"The dream ended as everyone was still happily waiting for your crossing.

"In the third dream, you and I worked together at the newspaper. You had just written a very controversial story, which I helped publish. We had to sneak into the building alone at night and run it through the printing presses ourselves. Once I checked the presses and saw that the story was in print, we went down a long hall and waited in a dark room. I knew some authority was going to come and try to imprison you. I also knew that you could never be imprisoned because you were dying and death would be the ultimate freedom. We didn't know what would happen. I heard their footsteps in the hall. I went over and gave you a big hug and said, 'Please remember, no matter what, how much I love you and especially how much I loved your story.' That's how the dream ended."

I let out a big sigh.

She gave me a strong, long, hand hug. We sat holding hands for a long time. Then she said, "Thank you so much for telling me the dreams. I miss remembering my own. I really like the idea of the party and a communion."

These dreams were hard to share with Cece because they confronted her impending death so directly. But my third dream gave me a lovely way to say goodbye and to tell her that I loved her.

Afterwards, I was looking in the folder where I kept my notes on our sessions, and I came across the very last dream that Cece had remembered, typed up, and shared with me two months earlier. It said,

"I turn and leave, alone. It's night. I get on my bike (motorcycle) and I am riding along a well lit (with lamps) but deserted road. I feel a bit alone, but okay. There's a nice breeze. I feel determined and have a good feeling. I ride as if I know that I'm doing the right and necessary thing, and I am headed home."

When she died, like in *my* dream, there actually was a communing and celebration of life by all those who knew her. At the party I met a woman who had known Cece when she had a puppy.

"Oh Cece loved that puppy, and it was just heart breaking," she said. "The puppy developed a serious and quick spreading cancer. In kindness Cece let her be put to sleep so she wouldn't suffer."

I prayed that *I* could now let go of Cece, grateful that she was no longer suffering. And I hoped that in death, as in her last dream, she was "doing the right and necessary thing and she was headed home." I imagined her riding a motorcycle on the lighted path, entering a vast opening into the unknown.

A week later, her sister-in-law Meme gave me the collage from Cece's treasured art collection that she had bequeathed to me. It was an abstract multimedia piece with images of ladders and windows and light filtering here and there. It was entitled, "The Portal."

> "Stories are medicine. They have such power;
> they do not require that we
> do, be, act, anything—we need only listen."

Clarissa Pinkola Estés

CHAPTER 64

—⁂—

Gretchen

When I met Gretchen she'd fought a hard battle with cancer and was weighing whether to enter hospice care or to try an aggressive new chemotherapy. Her mother had spent almost ten years bedridden and suffering in pain; Gretchen's greatest fear was reliving her ordeal. Because she was strong, Gretchen opted to try the chemotherapy.

One miraculous improvement after another came to Gretchen as we worked together over the next eighteen months. She spent many hours researching diet and alternative healing modalities, and the combination of treatments had been beneficial. But now, a year and a half later, Gretchen was very sick. She had traveled to Ireland for an experimental light treatment, and a month later, when she suffered a stroke, the tests indicated that the cancer was in her brain. The cough she'd developed probably meant the tumors in her lung were growing again, as well.

I came to see her at her home. Her intention during this session was to receive clarity and energy for healing. She hoped to get clear about whether to sign up for hospice. She wondered out loud, "Am I to keep trying so hard to live—or am I to finally give up?"

As I began doing the energy work, I kept being distracted by a notion. Finally, I spoke up.

I whispered in her ear. "Gretchen, I know that you aren't feeling well, but I keep getting that I should tell you a story. Is that okay?"

She shook her head yes.

It was strange. I knew I was to tell her about my client Phyllie, but I didn't know which part of her story might be meaningful for Gretchen. I pulled up a stool and sat near her head, so she wouldn't have to strain to hear me.

"My client Phyllie came in to see me two months ago in November. She was my writing teacher's eighty-five-year-old mother. She had advanced macular degeneration but was otherwise very healthy. Even though she was almost completely blind, she 'looked' around and told me how much she loved my office and how happy she was to 'see' me. Phyllie was very lively and had a great sense of humor so we had a lot of fun during her session.

"Almost as soon as she got off the table she asked me directly, 'Do you think my time to cross over is soon?'

"I considered the question for a minute and remembered this bright light that we had both experienced around her and I replied, 'Phyllie you seem very healthy and full of life to me.'

"She said, 'I wonder why Spirit is having me hang around so long?'

"She told me that it was hard being blind, unable to read, watch TV, or help her daughter in the house they shared. She didn't feel like she was accomplishing anything. She had been a spiritual seeker for years and had a daily meditation practice, but she missed reading and learning.

"Then she said to me, 'You know every day I tell Spirit that, whenever it's time, I'm ready to go.'

"This took me by surprise. I had always thought that a person either chose to live or was suicidal and wanted to die. This was a new idea. She was holding the intention to both live *and* be ready to die. She wasn't resisting either life or death.

"I felt compassion for her. Living through long, and for her, empty days sounded very hard. I remembered that she had studied a form of energy work that was helpful for distance healing. I wondered if she might be willing to send healing energy to some of my clients, once I asked their permission. Phillie was delighted at the prospect.

"But it was not to be. I got a call three days later, saying that she had died while sitting in bed doing her early morning meditation. She had lived with her daughter Phyllis for the past five years and had only moved from California to Virginia for the last ten of her eighty-five years. From the way Phyllie had described her life, I only expected a handful of people at the memorial service in Phyllis' backyard. Instead, over one hundred of us gathered around a small tree planted in her honor.

"The service began with readings by the family. Then others were invited to speak, if they chose. We heard stories of Phillie offering her sage advice, or remembering people in her prayers with inexplicably miraculous results. We heard about her Sunday morning walks to Patty's house, where she rubbed her feet and helped relieve her chronic pain. She'd helped form a macular degeneration support group, naming it, 'The Immaculate Degenerates.' And once, she put an ad in the local newspaper offering free prayers. She was in her eighties and blind when most of these stories took place. It was the most beautiful service I had ever attended, a true honoring of her life."

I stopped. I felt foolish because surely Gretchen was too sick to listen to all this. I thought she might have even slept through it. Instead she opened her eyes and looked at me, tears streaming down her face and said, "Thank you, that was just what I needed to hear."

It was only later that I put the pieces together. Gretchen had been afraid that giving up her fight to live would mean that all the research, diets, chemo, and alternative treatments had been a waste of time. All her work would be in vain; she would die anyway. But those years had sparkled with family time, dream group meetings, and travel. She and her husband were best of friends and they'd enjoyed being together. She'd made prayer beads for loved ones.

Gretchen went into hospice the next day. She insisted on bright purple sheets for her hospital bed. In those last two weeks, she slept most of the time. Her last words to her husband and daughters were, "I feel so good" and "I love you." When she died, the intention she had set after our session that day was at her bedside. It read,

"When the time is right, may I die peacefully with ease and grace."

And so she did.

I like to think that Phyllie was there to welcome her.

> "Love is the willingness to create the space
> in which something is allowed to change."

Harry Palmer

CHAPTER 65

—∭—

Kriszta

Kriszta's cancer was aggressive, but like Gretchen, she'd experienced a number of miraculous healings and had already lived longer and more comfortably than her doctors had predicted. Eight months into our sessions, I intuited to ask what she thought happened when a person died. I hated getting this kind of intuition. Kriszta was young and focused on her fight against the cancer. I admired her vitality. Why did I need to ask her about death? I didn't know. But I trusted my intuition and asked her.

She gave me a rather matter-of-fact technical answer about what happens to the cells of our physical body when we die. To her, death was a biological event only. I told her that I used to believe that too. In my twenties and thirties nature was my church, and I prayed to the creativity and beauty of it all. I, too, thought my death would be like that of any animal in the natural world. But since then my experiences had revealed another possibility. I felt that I was supposed to tell her what had changed my mind. And so I did.

She listened respectfully straight-faced, obviously not shifting her viewpoint one iota. She seemed uninterested. I finished by saying, "You might want to notice your life experiences coming up." As soon as these words came out of my mouth, I wondered where in the world that suggestion had come from. Sometimes my intuition spoke before I could think. We began the energy work.

It was a difficult session. She had gotten scans back showing the tumor on her liver was growing again. For forty minutes, I went through the motions of clearing and chelation, holding her intention for well being and healing. The session felt strange, though. I couldn't feel the energy or see it. The entire session was hands-on prayer. I trusted that something was happening, I just didn't know what it was. I felt nervous when we ended because I had nothing to write down and no real feedback for her. When she got off the table, she sat in the chair and looked at me so directly that it spooked me.

"What did you notice?" I asked hoping that it hadn't been a total loss.

She just kept staring at me and through me. "Is everything okay?" I asked.

Finally she said, "I just had a strange experience."

"Oh yeah, what was that?" still nervous since I couldn't tell that anything happened.

"I had the experience of being outside my body."

"Mmm," I said, waiting to see if she would say more.

"No you don't understand. I was me looking down at my body. I was me outside my body."

"Interesting. How did you feel?"

"I felt great, very peaceful. I was still completely *me,* but I was outside of my body. How could that be?"

"See if you can stay with the experience. You might want to write about it."

After that, I noticed some small shifts. Once during a music therapy session for relaxation, she had felt the presence of her deceased aunt and grandmother. When I asked what that was like, she said they were very comforting and supportive. She liked the idea that these two women were there for her.

During her last month, I helped convince Kriszta to get hospice services by explaining she'd be helping her mother, who needed support with Kriszta's care. I promised her that she could discontinue hospice care whenever she felt well enough. I took the opportunity to tell her about the intention that Gretchen had written when she began receiving hospice care.

A week before she died, I went to see Kriszta at her home. After the session I felt sad, knowing that she was near the end. That night, I had a vivid dream where Kriszta came to me looking absolutely beautiful and healthy. She said, "Don't worry. I'm well. Look at me." She radiated light, joy, and well-being. I still felt sad about Kriszta when I woke up, but I also felt certain her spirit was well.

The day before she died, I did some gentle energy work with her while she slept. Her mother told me she hadn't spoken all day. After the energy work, Kriszta suddenly opened her eyes and said, "The tumor on the back of my head has shrunk. Feel it." She took my hand and showed me. "Isn't that great?" she asked.

I wondered if this comment was a form of denial. I had recently read *A Year To Live* by Stephen Levine. In his work, he noticed that sometimes, even when people know they're dying, some keep talking about life. The issue, he decided, wasn't denial. Instead, he wondered if we reach a place where we know with certainty that life and death are seamless. Is it this knowing, that the life of the spirit continues, that sometimes speaks at the end? I thought maybe this was true for Kriszta.

Kriszta *lived all the way* until it was her time to go.

After she passed, her mother shared with me the intention that Kriszta had written and had put on the night table by her bed. It read,

> "If I am meant to cross over,
> May I let go when I am ready.
> May I do so peacefully with ease
> and without pain or struggle.
> May Aunt Betsy, Aunt Eva,
> Grandma Farago, and Jenny
> Be with me.
> And may they show me the way
> Peacefully into the light."

"At that moment life itself is such a gift that there are no expectations put upon it—all of life is precious—even the hard parts."

John Howard Griffin

CHAPTER 66

—⦿—

More

Shortly after Kriszta's death, I went for an energy session with a healer who suggested I put up shields and boundaries so that I wouldn't feel so much grief when I lost a client. I stared at her blankly, knowing full well that I would not erect boundaries to spare myself the grief that arises naturally from love and loss. I wouldn't give up one minute of meaningful intimacy or offering of loving-kindness to shield myself from sadness. Everything this healer was suggesting contradicted what I'd learned from Cece, Gretchen, and Kriszta. I'd rather live embracing both joy and anguish, love and loss, life and death.

How could I hope to meet the end of my life with this same *grace* I'd found in Cece, Gretchen, and Kriszta?

The answer seemed to be to *live all the way*. Wasn't that what I had witnessed in each of them? Didn't they live each day with as much consciousness and awareness as their dying bodies allowed? Through them, I saw that it was possible to love whatever moments were left available to them: A husband's steady presence, delight in a new set of purple sheets, the sound of the baby birds singing outside the window, the fragrance of the pink rose a friend set by the bed. They were grateful for these things and comforted by even the gentlest healing energy I offered them. Even as the stomach stopped digesting food, the liver stopped sorting toxins, and the lungs didn't oxygenate blood well enough for complex thoughts, they had each kept love alive. In the very end, Gretchen, Cece, and Kriszta each expressed two essential qualities: gratitude and love. These expressions of the heart seemed present until the beating of the physical heart ceased. Maybe to die with grace meant to *love all the way.*

"Truth is what stands the test of experience."

Albert Einstein

EPILOGUE

Had I really asked myself, "Is that all there is?" and answered "yes"? At the age of forty, had I actually believed that was true?

Instead I'd found that healing and forgiveness were possible. I'd embraced a vision, deciphered the hidden messages in my dreams, confronted the blank page and filled it, and discovered that my intuition wasn't a curse to fear but a natural human gift. Through the Unitarian Church, the Chrysalis Group, and dream work, I developed a strong, deeply personal, spiritual life. I learned about energy healing, and studied, practiced, and became a healer.

Life was *full* of more.

After spending much of my life believing that I might not be lovable, I found that my life was rich with family, friends, students, and clients all sending love my way. Love that I could learn to *receive* unconditionally.

There was more to *me,* more to each one of us, than I could ever have imagined. And I still had the sense that more possibilities were waiting to reveal themselves.

My experiences told me repeatedly that there was more to life than our physical lifetime. My encounters with Milly, Aunt Emma, and Harry were hints that life continued after the body ceased. My Vision, my guidance, all led me to wonder about realms beyond our physical reality.

So many moments in my life were, in essence, repeating the same message.

There is more. There is more. There is more.
Look for the more. Be more. Live more. Love more.

And so my journey continues.

Acknowledgements

"If God speaks to us other than through official channels (like the Bible), then I think he/she speaks to us largely by what happens to us."

Frederick Buechner

When I began putting my stories in writing, I began to see the patterns that shape every life: How one thing followed another, how small kindnesses at the right moment had tipped the balance, how guidance was present—always, and how meaning was inherent in all of it, even the hard stuff. But stories don't grow into books without people who believe in them. And in my case, there were many.

For my wonderful friends who have sustained me through the arduous process of uncovering the truth, searching for what was essential, and articulating the ineffable, thank you for your heartfelt support and wise counsel—Barbara Outland, Kay Davidson, Jane Hopkins, Joan Garrabrant, Carol Jacobs, Jane Leipis, Donna D'Angelo, Rick McHenry, and Kristina Aschenbach. Thanks to author Phyllis Theroux, my writing teacher, who has loved my stories and always believed I had a book in me. And for my exceptional writing group, Millie

Cain, Sherrie Najarian, Lee Knapp, and Constance Costas— all talented writers, curious readers and helpful editors. And for my dear friends of old who walked beside me as these stories unfolded, making all the difference in my times of need —Shannon LeJeune, Mary Meurisse Richardson, and Elly Driggers. I thank you.

For Dan, Tommy, Kay, Jane, and Barbara, my early readers as I began to weave my stories into a book, thank you for somehow knowing, before I could ever know, that my stories would become this book. I am deeply grateful for your kind encouragement and helpful suggestions.

For Constance Costas, editor extraordinaire, thank you for loving my book enough to add your skillful content editing and your amazing gift of creativity. To Julie Hulett, for generously sharing her expertise as a copy editor.

To The Monroe Institute staff and fellow program participants for providing a safe place to explore the natural human capacity to shift states of consciousness, expand intuition, and seek guidance in its many forms. Thank you for helping me trust and understand my experiences even further as I wrote the book. A special thanks to Karen Malik, senior facilitator at the Monroe Institute, for her compassionate mentoring.

And finally, and most importantly, for my family—For my son, Tommy, singer/songwriter/guitarist for Jukebox the Ghost—for sharing his creative journey with me, and modeling the courage it takes to live the creative life. For my daughter, Dr. Julia, family physician, soon to be Geriatrician, for her healing presence and for our many wonderful talks about paths to healing—both allopathic and alternative. And to my son-in-law, Andrew Breton, a quick-thinking, creative writer, with whom I've delighted in sharing my path to publication.

And most especially, I am grateful for my husband and best friend, Dan, who offered sage advice and seemingly endless daily support for the writing of this book. For his capacity to see past all my doubts, always knowing this book was meant to be.

About the Author

An intuitive energy healer in private practice, Peggy C. Siegel has taught numerous classes on dream work, intuition and personal spirituality. A former adjunct faculty member at Virginia Commonwealth University, she holds a Master's in education and has published two books and a curriculum on sexuality. Peggy and her husband Dan have two grown children and live in Richmond, Virginia.

For more information about Peggy Siegel's workshops and private practice, please visit www.peggysiegel.net.